# Pro Apache Beehive

KUNAL MITTAL AND SRINIVAS KANCHANAVALLY

Apress®

**Pro Apache Beehive**

**Copyright © 2005 by Kunal Mittal and Srinivas Kanchanavally**

Softcover re-print of the Hardcover 1st edition 2005
All rights reserved. No part of this work may be reproduced or transmitted in any form or by any means, electronic or mechanical, including photocopying, recording, or by any information storage or retrieval system, without the prior written permission of the copyright owner and the publisher.

ISBN (pbk): 1-4302-1189-X

Printed and bound in the United States of America 9 8 7 6 5 4 3 2 1

Trademarked names may appear in this book. Rather than use a trademark symbol with every occurrence of a trademarked name, we use the names only in an editorial fashion and to the benefit of the trademark owner, with no intention of infringement of the trademark.

Lead Editor: Steve Anglin
Technical Reviewer: Dilip Thomas
Editorial Board: Steve Anglin, Dan Appleman, Ewan Buckingham, Gary Cornell, Tony Davis, Jason Gilmore, Jonathan Hassell, Chris Mills, Dominic Shakeshaft, Jim Sumser
Associate Publisher: Grace Wong
Project Manager: Kylie Johnston
Copy Edit Manager: Nicole LeClerc
Copy Editor: Kim Wimpsett
Assistant Production Director: Kari Brooks-Copony
Production Editor: Linda Marousek
Compositor: Susan Glinert Stevens
Proofreader: Sue Boshers
Indexer: Carol A. Burbo
Artist: Wordstop Technologies (P) Ltd, Chennai, India
Interior Designer: Van Winkle Design Group
Cover Designer: Kurt Krames
Manufacturing Manager: Tom Debolski

Distributed to the book trade worldwide by Springer-Verlag New York, Inc., 233 Spring Street, 6th Floor, New York, NY 10013. Phone 1-800-SPRINGER, fax 201-348-4505, e-mail orders-ny@springer-sbm.com, or visit http://www.springeronline.com.

For information on translations, please contact Apress directly at 2560 Ninth Street, Suite 219, Berkeley, CA 94710. Phone 510-549-5930, fax 510-549-5939, e-mail info@apress.com, or visit http://www.apress.com.

The information in this book is distributed on an "as is" basis, without warranty. Although every precaution has been taken in the preparation of this work, neither the author(s) nor Apress shall have any liability to any person or entity with respect to any loss or damage caused or alleged to be caused directly or indirectly by the information contained in this work.

The source code for this book is available to readers at http://www.apress.com in the Downloads section.

*I would like to dedicate this book to my wife, Neeta, and to my dogs, Dusty and Snowie. They have been extremely patient during the authoring process and all the missed weekend activities that I had to put on the back burner as I was writing this book. Neeta has been extremely patient and has helped me by sharing my other responsibilities so that I could focus on the book.*

*I would also like to thank my coauthor, Srini, who has worked several long hours coming up with all the examples you see in this book. Every single line of code was written by him.*
*—Kunal Mittal*

*I dedicate this book to my wife, Harini, for all her love, support, encouragement, and sacrifice.*

*To my parents, family, and friends: thank you all, you make life wonderful.*
*—Srinivas Kanchanavally*

# Contents at a Glance

# Contents

# Foreword

Tools are the lifeblood of progress. Vision, discovery, and serendipity typically help identify the goal. However, to get to the goal in an efficient, scalable, and repeatable manner, we need to have appropriate tools.

When applied to software development, it is easy to see that we as an industry can hope to achieve our goals of radical improvements in developer productivity, interoperability, maintainability, and reuse only if we create the appropriate development and deployment tools. The Apache Beehive framework and the XMLBeans toolset play a key role in the march toward better enterprise software. Their importance is magnified because of their credentials—Apache in the open-source juggernaut and XML in the Web Services and Service-Oriented Architecture (SOA) avalanche.

This book by Kunal Mittal and Srinivas Kanchanavally provides a simple and practical guide for using these two tools. It contains easy-to-read, interesting tutorials and use cases that you can immediately leverage in software development projects.

Dr. Rajiv Gupta

*Entrepreneur, technologist, and Web Services pioneer with E-Speak at HP*

# About the Authors

**KUNAL MITTAL** is a consultant specializing in Java technology, the J2EE platform, Web Services, and SOA technologies. He has coauthored and contributed to several books on these topics. Kunal works as an applications architect for the Domestic TV division of Sony Pictures Entertainment. In his spare time, he does consulting gigs for start-ups in the SOA space and for large companies looking to implement an SOA initiative. You can contact Kunal through his Web site at `http://www.soaconsultant.com` or via e-mail at `kunal@kunalmittal.com`.

**SRINIVAS KANCHANAVALLY** is a Software Architect with CoreObjects Software Inc. in Los Angeles, California. He has an in-depth understanding of Java and J2EE. He also has vast experience designing large-scale J2EE application architectures. Srini has worked with Java, J2EE, Struts, WebLogic, and WebLogic Portal on client projects. And he has several years of experience working with various open-source frameworks and tools such as JBoss/Tomcat, MySQL, JUnit, and HTTPUnit.

# About the Technical Reviewer

**DILIP THOMAS** is an open-source enthusiast who keeps a close watch on LAMP technologies, open standards, and the full range of Apache Jakarta projects. He is a coauthor of *PHP MySQL Website Programming: Problem–Design–Solution* (Apress, 2003) and a technical reviewer/editor on several open-source/open-standard book projects. Dilip is an editorial director at Software & Support Verlag GmbH.

Dilip resides in Bangalore with his beautiful wife, Indu, and several hundred books and journals. You can reach him via e-mail at `dilip.thomas@gmail.com`.

# Acknowledgments

I had a vision for this book. My coauthor, Srini, and editor, Steve Anglin, trusted me and gave me an opportunity to write this book.

Srini and I would like to thank Steve Anglin, Kylie Johnston, Kim Wimpsett, Linda Marousek, and all the other folks at Apress who we don't even know but who have dedicated a lot of time and energy to get this book out.

We'd also like to thank Dilip Thomas for providing technical insights into the book. His detailed technical review and suggestions have been tremendously valuable.

—Kunal Mittal

# Introduction

Welcome to *Pro Apache Beehive*. SOA and Web Services are finally coming to the forefront of the IT industry. Most companies, large and small, are talking about these technologies and planning a course to adopt them. And J2EE development is still on the front lines for large, mission-critical applications.

The Apache Beehive project introduces several new technologies that simplify J2EE development as well as make your applications more service oriented. Beehive provides a layer of technologies that build on the annotations that were introduced in Java 1.5. (Think of annotations as deployment descriptors but in your code instead.)

NetUI, JSR 181, Web Services, and Controls in Apache Beehive allow you to quickly build robust, scalable, service-oriented J2EE applications. Combined with the power of XMLBeans, which is a Java-XML binding technology, this project is gaining a lot of momentum.

In this book, we'll show you how to build applications using these technologies. Be prepared to get down and dirty with some code.

## How This Book Is Structured

This book consists of eight chapters and three appendixes:

In Chapter 1, we explore the challenges of enterprise software development. We talk about the role of Java, J2EE, and SOA in addressing the challenges that CIOs face when delivering software. We then introduce BEA WebLogic Platform and talk about the birth of the Apache Beehive project.

In Chapter 2, we introduce Web Services and SOA. We then talk about how the Apache Beehive project and XMLBeans support and simplify SOA-based development.

In Chapter 3, we introduce annotations. We talk about the basic annotations introduced with Java 1.5. We then show you the annotations introduced with BEA WebLogic Workshop and compare them to the annotations in the Apache Beehive technologies.

In Chapter 4, we introduce the NetUI and Page Flow technologies that are part of Apache Beehive. We talk about the overall architecture of Page Flows and briefly cover the NetUI tag libraries.

In Chapter 5, we take a deep dive into the NetUI and Page Flow technologies that are part of Apache Beehive. We examine the important concepts of Page Flows and show examples of all the NetUI tags.

In Chapter 6, we cover Apache Beehive Controls. We talk about the overall architecture of a Control and show several examples of the different types of Controls you can build.

In Chapter 7, we explain the Web Services capabilities of Apache Beehive. We also explain the JSR 181 standard and show examples of how Apache Beehive supports and leverages this standard.

In Chapter 8, we cover the XMLBeans Java-XML binding technology. We show several examples of how you can simplify working with XML using this technology.

In Appendix A, we show you how to download the different pieces of software that you'll need to install in order to follow along with the examples in the book.

In Appendix B, we show you how to download and set up the Eclipse IDE and Pollinate plug-in. We also show you how to use these to develop and deploy Apache Beehive code.

In Appendix C, we show you how to get involved in these open-source projects and how to contribute to their continuous development.

# Prerequisites

Please read Appendix A for details on the several software packages you'll need to download and install in order to write, compile, deploy, and test the code you'll write using Apache Beehive and XMLBeans in this book.

A basic familiarity with Java and J2EE is expected. Familiarity with Web Services is a plus.

# Downloading the Code

The scripts in this book are available in ZIP format in the Downloads section of the Apress Web site (`http://www.apress.com`).

# Contacting the Authors

You can reach Kunal Mittal via his Web site at `http://www.soaconsultant.com` or via e-mail at `kunal@kunalmittal.com`, and you can reach Srinivas Kanchanavally at `k_cnu01@yahoo.com`.

CHAPTER 1

# What's Apache Beehive?

Welcome! You've obviously picked up this book because you've heard about Apache Beehive and want to learn more. More than likely, you're working on some sort of J2EE Web application. You might even be an expert on BEA WebLogic Server and the technologies introduced by WebLogic Workshop. If not, never mind—this book is not about BEA WebLogic, and it's not about BEA WebLogic Workshop. It's about a set of technologies that are part of the Apache Beehive project. Specifically, it's about Service-Oriented Architecture (SOA)–based development. It's about using a technology such as Struts and using XML, Web Services, and J2EE technologies to simplify SOA development.

This book is targeted at developers and architects who are interested in exploring several new technologies that simplify SOA and Web application development.

In this chapter, you'll briefly learn about the WebLogic Workshop IDE and how it's integrated into WebLogic Platform. With the release of WebLogic Workshop, BEA introduced several underlying technologies. Recently these technologies were released to the Apache Open Source Foundation. This book will cover all these technologies in detail and show you how to use them with or without WebLogic Server. In fact, the primary platform for this book is Apache Tomcat.

The book takes a hands-on approach to explaining the Apache Beehive technologies. In other words, be prepared to get down and dirty with the code. We'll introduce several concepts and show you some code but then leave you with exercises or challenges. We'll provide complete solutions, but we definitely don't recommend that you jump directly to them. We'll point out some tips and tricks, best practices, and so on, but at the end of the day, Apache Beehive is still a nascent technology—so no one is really a master.

You'll begin by learning about the challenges of enterprise application development and about how WebLogic Workshop addresses some of those challenges. We'll then introduce the Apache Beehive project and XMLBeans. This will set the stage for learning all about SOA in Chapter 2.

## Enterprise Application Development: The Challenges

The rise in IT spending that took place in the late 90s has definitely declined. Forrester Research (`http://www.forrester.com/`) shows that IT spending increased about 20 percent in 2000. Since then, it has fallen constantly every year. In 2003, Forrester Research did predict a slight rise, but the analysts don't predict it to rise to the 2000 level until about 2005. So, these figures seem to complicate the lives of CIOs. CIOs have the toughest challenges today when choosing technology, products, and services while also ensuring productivity and security and providing new value-added business features. In the following sections, we'll describe some of the key challenges that CIOs need to address, often with smaller budgets and more stringent software needs.

## Delivering to the Customer

Time to market and productivity issues are key. End users are expecting software sooner rather than later. Applications must be built correctly the first time, and they must continue to evolve as the business requirements change and as management leads the business through new evolution. The ever-changing needs of the business, the customers, the partners, the vendors, and everyone else involved in this value chain must be quickly and accurately represented in the applications that support these entities.

Therefore, enterprises today need business applications that accommodate increasing functionality with constantly changing scope. A service-oriented approach promises to address this problem through the implementation of granular services that can be shared and reused across the enterprise. These services can be easily maintained, delivering greater agility and a higher quality of service at lower costs.

Most CIOs are focusing on choosing widely adopted standards for software development. This enables software development teams to concentrate on satisfying the business requirements quickly and with more predictable results. IT teams don't have or can't afford the luxury to experiment with technologies. Programming models must evolve to support customers, each requiring a different user interface. This will range from browser-based HTML, Java applet clients, CGI-based Web pages, and dynamic ASP- or JSP-based sites to WAP- or WML-based wireless devices such as PDAs.

If you think satisfying the business requirements is all CIOs need to do, you'll definitely be surprised. Users now not only want to see their data in a variety of formats but also want this data to come from distinct, disparate, distributed data sources. This means you need to integrate with other applications, not only within your own enterprise but many times across enterprise boundaries. New business models and a more demanding business world demand that executives have all sorts of information at their fingertips. You need to ensure security, transactional integrity, auditing, logging, and monitoring across these systems. In addition, you can't forget about the integration of business processes. The data and the core business services provided by one system need to be available to other systems to avoid redundancy in building and maintaining the same functionality twice.

In addition, given evolving business requirements, it's important that IT organizations have the ability to make quick changes in technology decisions. Organizations need to be able to mix and match products and technologies to provide the optimum configuration to solve the business needs. This flexibility is required right from the hardware and operating system level to the application deployment platforms and the tools used for application development.

These challenges clearly help motivate the need for standards in the programming model and consistency between programming teams.

## Getting the Best Performance

One of the other key requirements for applications today is that they should support high volumes of users and yet provide low response times. Typically, a user doesn't want to wait for more than a few seconds to see data. Systems also need to be available 24×7 and be highly fault tolerant. Imagine that there's a power failure at the Amazon.com server farm or, even worse, the software had a bug and something went wrong, and you were in the process of placing an order when something went wrong. You have no clue whether your order was processed. The next day, you place your order again successfully. However, the first order actually had been processed. So, you end up with two books and two charges on your credit card. Although you'll never know the actual cause of the problem, needless to say that you won't be a happy camper and probably won't shop at that business again.

Imagine for a minute that the application is not a simple Amazon.com shopping cart that you can easily repopulate. Instead, it's some budgeting application or policy management application, and you've spent the last hour filling in dozens of screens' worth of form data. And for some reason, you lose your connection for a few seconds and lose all your data. This could be something such as a browser crash at your end or something more serious on the server side. Now you're really mad.

This brings up the requirements for features such as automatic load balancing, failover, and user data replication across all layers of the architecture. Applications should be able to handle the highest anticipated user volumes, always leaving room for the most unexpected usage patterns, and should be able to switch configurations on the fly.

## Securing Your Applications

Security is more of an issue than ever. It used to be sufficient to restrict the outside world from accessing your data. However, since applications spanning enterprise boundaries now share data, protecting sensitive data is more critical. You're exchanging sensitive data with all your suppliers, customers, and partners. You need to implement the levels of security and data access policies carefully to ensure integrity of the data being shared.

On the flip side, the users don't make this task any easier. They insist on a single sign-on not only across all internal applications but also across these enterprise boundaries. Technologies such as Microsoft Passport are fast gaining popularity. The security mechanisms need to support this functionality while maintaining the highest levels of integrity.

Introduce wireless to this equation. Most executives do or soon will have some sort of wireless connection to the Internet. This could be a cell phone, BlackBerry, or laptop. They will soon start demanding the same reports and data that they can access on their desks from their wireless devices. How do you maintain security configurations in these scenarios?

## Integrating Your Applications

Large enterprises over the years have collected data in several different software systems. The challenge today is how to reuse these systems and be able to extract data from them as needed to serve your evolving business. To do this, IT departments need standards-based access to these back-end systems and need to be able to ensure security, transactional control, resources, and so on. You can use several technologies from Web Services to simple JDBC to address these issues. Standard Enterprise Application Integration (EAI) techniques have evolved to provide standardization on the integration problem.

### Having Freedom of Choice

IT departments need the flexibility to be able to mix and match solutions to form their optimal architecture. They need to be able to choose in small chunks—right from the choice of an application server to the development tools and frameworks they use. They also need the flexibility to move from one configuration to another as business requirements change or better technology becomes available. In addition, they need to be able to choose tools and solutions that can help them deliver their business applications cheaper, faster, and better.

## How Java Fits Into All of This

Now that I've covered some of the various challenges CIOs face, you may be wondering how Java and J2EE address some of these issues. We'll begin with a brief introduction to Java and then talk about J2EE's role.

### The Growth of Java

Java today has become one of the leading languages for enterprise application development. Java is a 100 percent object-oriented language. The syntax looks very much like C++ but without some of the nightmares such as pointers and memory management. This makes it easier for new programmers to come up to speed with the language and also provides relief for experienced object-oriented programmers, who don't have to spend hours debugging a typical C++ core dump. In addition, Java is a reliable software platform. Compile-time and then runtime error checking teach programmers to have more reliable programming habits.

Java runs on all modern operating systems. Java code runs on top of a Java Virtual Machine (JVM). A compiler takes the Java code and compiles it into bytecode. The JVM interprets this bytecode at runtime. Sun and various other vendors ship platform-specific JVMs on which the Java bytecode runs. This allows developers to write code on any platform and deploy on another platform (see Figure 1-1). The JVM provides low-level support for operating system optimizations, shielding application developers from these issues.

Java is a free language. Anyone can download the latest version of the Java 2 Standard Edition Development Kit (JDK) from Sun and start developing and deploying Java applications. When you download the JDK, you get two items:

- *Java API*: This is a rich collection of classes that provides a programming framework for programmers.
- *JVM*: This is what allows the Java code to run on different platforms. The JVM is platform specific.

Figure 1-2 shows how a Java program sits on top of the APIs that eventually run using the JVM.

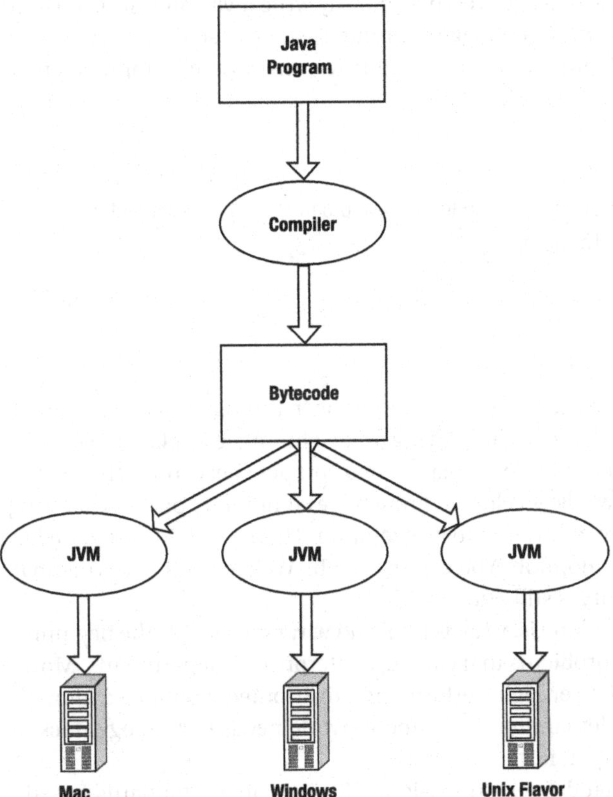


**Figure 1-1.** *Cross-platform Java code*

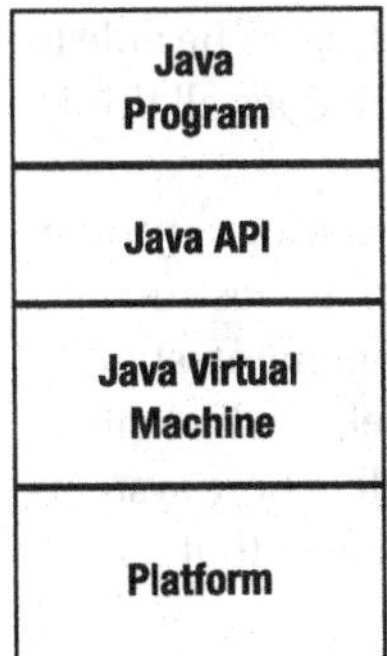


**Figure 1-2.** *Java runtime*

Java is a secure language in various aspects, from the sandbox model for applet security to security for user authentication, encryption of data, and cryptography. With a built-in security model for applets and applications, Java works well in network and multiuser environments. The multithreading capability allows for concurrent activity for enterprise users and is supported from the ground up throughout the Java platform.

Numerous vendors provide tools to help developers quickly write Java applications. These tools range from code libraries and IDEs to debuggers, profilers, and test suites. This allows teams to quickly ramp up Java development, QA, and production environments for their enterprise applications.

---

■ **Further Reading** Sun provides a good introduction to the Java programming environment at `http://java.sun.com/docs/white/langenv/`.

---

## The Role of J2EE

J2EE is about seven years old. In these years, the IT sector has been through intensive turmoil. We've seen the rise and fall of several companies playing in the enterprise application space. Microsoft made a huge push toward its new .NET platform to compete head-on with Sun's J2EE initiative. However, J2EE, like Java, is developed through the community process, allowing all the leading software companies to contribute to its evolution. This gives J2EE a slight edge over .NET in terms of evolution and adoption. You can search the Web for numerous comparisons between J2EE and .NET. The jury is still out.

The question you're most likely asking is, what is J2EE and why do I care? At the beginning of this chapter we described typical problems that can hurt enterprise IT departments. More and more IT teams are required to deliver high-performance, distributed, and transactional applications. The fast-evolving and demanding e-commerce world needs technology stacks that help deliver business value cheaper, faster, and better.

J2EE is a technology platform that delivers this vision. J2EE is an open, standards-based development and deployment platform for building *n*-tier, Web-based, and server-centric enterprise-strength applications. It provides a distribution application model, a reusable component-based architecture, unified security models, and a highly reliable transaction model. J2EE is built on top of the Java 2 Standard Edition Development Kit. Thus, to be able to run a J2EE application, you'll need a JVM and the Java libraries. Like Java, J2EE does all this in a platform- and vendor-independent manner.

Before J2EE, developers spent a majority of their time dealing with system programming details rather than being able to focus on business logic. They had to deal with issues such as transaction programming, threading, security, persistence, resource management, state management, and so on. Certain proprietary frameworks were available to help with some of these, but they made the system not totally portable, extensible, or maintainable. These systems couldn't interact with each other without going through a major integration effort that itself cost millions of dollars.

J2EE has changed this scenario. The J2EE platform includes the technology specifications, a reference implementation, a compatibility test suite, and a BluePrints program that describes the best practices and design patterns for J2EE development.

# Introducing Service-Oriented Architecture (SOA)

Now we'll take a couple pages to introduce you to SOA. Chapter 2 is devoted to SOA, so there we'll really drill into what SOA is. However, the introduction in this chapter is also important because it'll help you put the Apache Beehive technologies in context.

How does SOA really impact technology choices? How do these concepts help address the challenges of the corporate CIO?

No single technology, protocol, or product makes up SOA. Instead, SOA is a set of tools, technologies, frameworks, and best practices that enable the quick and easy implementation of services. In addition, SOA is a methodology for identifying reusable services in your applications and in your organization. SOA is not a product or standard.

SOA is focused on being a technology and process framework that allows enterprises to identify, build, exchange, and maintain their business processes as services rather than large monolithic applications that today are often termed *instant legacy*.

SOA existed well before Web Services. Think back to COBRA and IDL. These are just flavors of SOA. As Gartner (`http://www.gartner.com/`) puts it, "Through 2008, SOA and Web services will be implemented together in more than 75 percent of new SOA or Web services projects (0.7 probability)." This means Gartner is predicting that Web Services will be the primary technology used for SOA-based development.

The technologies that enable SOA are targeted at reducing the complexities involved in software development. They address the issues with distributed software, multiple platforms, and application integration. SOA provides an application architecture where you define processes as services that have a well-defined interface. These services are dynamically invokable over a network.

For CIOs, SOA enables faster time to delivery of business processes and cost reduction because of lower development and maintenance costs. In short, SOA is a potential solution to all the challenges discussed earlier in this chapter. So, where does Apache Beehive fit it?

Apache Beehive is a project that enables faster, better, cheaper J2EE and SOA development based on the technologies initially introduced by BEA in WebLogic Workshop. However, before jumping into Apache Beehive, let's look at how it was born.

# Introducing BEA WebLogic Platform

BEA is among the leading vendors that deliver on the promises that J2EE makes. The company is very active—along with Sun, IBM, HP, and several other vendors—in defining the next generation of J2EE standards. Today, according to every major IT analyst, WebLogic Server is the among the leading J2EE application servers in the market. BEA has more than 2,000 partners and earns more than a billion dollars in annual revenue. Their customer list is impressive and at times spans 100 percent of a particular industry vertical in the Fortune 1000 list.

---

■ **Further Reading** You can read more about BEA customers at `http://www.bea.com/framework.jsp?CNT=index.htm&FP=/content/customers`.

---

BEA WebLogic Platform provides a collection of tools that enable agile enterprise development. We'll introduce these tools in this chapter but go into depth on each of these tools throughout this book. Figure 1-3 shows BEA WebLogic Platform at a high level. You'll be referring to this figure throughout the book as you dissect each of these components and see how other BEA components, which are not shown in this figure, fit in.

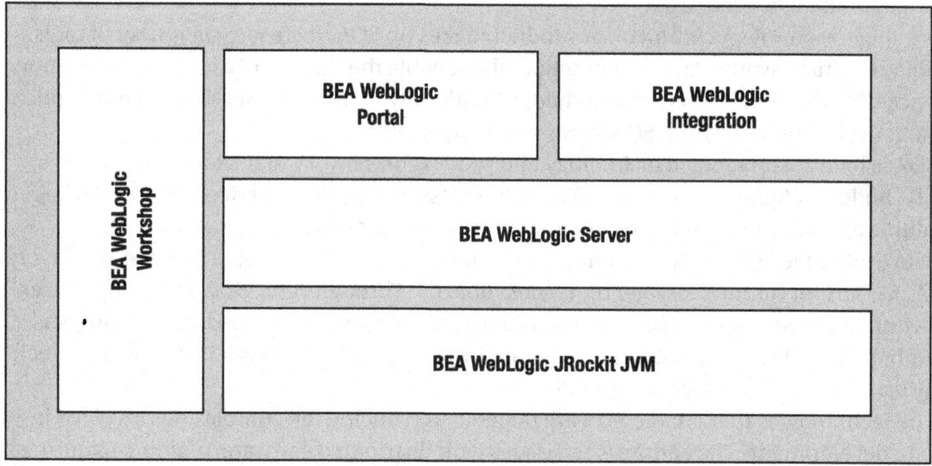


**Figure 1-3.** *BEA WebLogic Platform*

In the following sections, we'll briefly introduce each component.

## BEA WebLogic Server

WebLogic Server implements the J2EE and Web Service standards and is today the leading J2EE application server in the market. It simplifies the development, deployment, integration, and management of enterprise applications.

## BEA WebLogic Workshop

WebLogic Workshop provides a unified and integrated development environment for IT teams. It allows integration with legacy applications, Web Service development, .NET, and various developer tools to quickly and easily develop, debug, and deploy J2EE applications. WebLogic Workshop has been a major driving force behind the convergence of BEA WebLogic Platform.

## BEA WebLogic Integration

BEA released WebLogic Integration in June 2001. WebLogic Integration provides a framework for business integration, application integration, data interchange, and business process management. It's built on top of WebLogic Server and is fully standards compliant. It implements the Java Connector Architecture (JCA), Java Message Service (JMS), and several Web Service standards such as SOAP, WSDL, and UDDI. WebLogic Integration can coordinate transactions across multiple systems (as long as they support the XA protocol), enabling the automation of business processes that flow through multiple systems. WebLogic Integration is probably the most complex product in the BEA suite.

## BEA WebLogic Portal

WebLogic Portal now supports the new portal specifications and provides a rich environment for content management, search, and wireless. It allows Web Services to be exposed as portlets and provides a rich environment to interact with these portlets.

## BEA WebLogic JRockit

WebLogic JRockit is a JVM that's designed specifically for J2EE. It's optimized highly for server-side Java applications to address the performance requirements of J2EE. This is a relatively new offering from BEA.

# What Does BEA WebLogic Platform Provide?

WebLogic Platform 8.1 is the latest release from BEA that encompasses all the components described at a high level in the previous sections. The following are some of the benefits of adopting this platform:

- Single, unified, middle tier that provides the infrastructure on which you can build your business applications. You don't need several products to make up your middle tier.
- Single installation for all the components. You don't need to do any after-installation tweaks or configuration changes. The installation comes complete with a JVM, JDK, individual components, and fully built samples that span each of the components.
- All components built on top of the reliable, scalable, and available WebLogic Server. WebLogic Server forms the core runtime container for all J2EE and Web Service applications.
- All components built using standard J2EE technologies.
- A unified development environment for WebLogic Portal, WebLogic Integration, and Web Services.
- A single management and monitoring infrastructure for the different components.
- Unified JMS messaging throughout the platform.
- Complete support for all Web Service technologies and standards such as SOAP, WSDL, UDDI, and so on.

---

■ **Further Reading** You can read more about Simple Object Access Protocol (SOAP) at `http://www.w3.org/TR/SOAP/`.

---

---

■ **Further Reading** You can read more about Web Services Description Language (WSDL) at `http://www.w3.org/TR/wsdl`.

---

■ **Further Reading** You can read more about Universal Description, Discovery and Integration (UDDI) of Web Services at `http://www.uddi.org/`.

---

# Exploring the History of BEA WebLogic Workshop

WebLogic Workshop was first introduced into BEA WebLogic Platform as a Web Service IDE. It enabled quick and visual development, deployment, and management of Web Services. Since then, BEA has enhanced the tool to be not only a standard Java IDE but also the IDE for the entire WebLogic Platform. For example, if you've used EBCC with WebLogic Portal 7, or the Business Process Editor with WebLogic Integration 7, you'll see that with the 8.1 release of WebLogic Platform, all the functionality from these distinctly different tools has been incorporated in WebLogic Workshop.

When using WebLogic Platform 8.1, you're almost forced to use WebLogic Workshop. This is definitely true if you're doing development using WebLogic Portal or WebLogic Integration. As you can imagine, this is very proprietary, and thus IT teams have been skeptical about using WebLogic Workshop. In today's fast-changing technology world, no one wants to be locked into one vendor or one technology. This is the fundamental issue in the Java versus .NET battle. Also, WebLogic Workshop is just in its infancy and has several usability and performance issues that have made IT teams shy away from it.

BEA quickly addressed these issues head-on. In the early part of 2004, BEA donated several proprietary technologies to the open-source community primarily to increase the adoption of WebLogic Workshop, which is the basic entry point into the WebLogic Platform suite. For typical J2EE applications deployed on WebLogic Server, WebLogic Workshop serves only as a basic IDE; for development in WebLogic Portal, WebLogic Integration, or BEA Liquid Data for WebLogic, WebLogic Workshop forms the only IDE you can really use.

By providing several open-source technologies, such as XMLBeans, Java Page Flows, Controls, and others, BEA hopes that several plug-ins will be created so that more popular development tools can be used to develop J2EE and Web Service applications on WebLogic Workshop.

# Introducing Apache Beehive

On May 25, 2004, BEA and Apache announced the birth of the Beehive project. The project focuses on simplifying J2EE and Web Service programming by using the concept of annotations that's fast becoming part of Java. Service-oriented development is also a major emphasis of this project.

The Apache Beehive project was created to support the Java Page Flow (JPF) technology, Controls, and Web Services based on JSR 181.

Java Page Flows are built on top of Struts. The most fundamental value-add in Java Page Flows is the support for annotations and metadata. Instead of writing the Struts configuration file, metadata is automatically generated that does the same thing. In addition, just like Struts has some tag libraries to help in the front-end development, Java Page Flows use a technology called NetUI. NetUI is a set of tag libraries, quite similar to the Struts tag libraries.

Actually, if you look at the Beehive project, you won't see Java Page Flows. You'll see NetUI, which includes Java Page Flows. This might not seem intuitive, so be careful.

The Apache Beehive project is built on Java 1.5 and can run on most application servers. In this book, we'll show you how to use Beehive with Apache Tomcat and, in some places, with BEA WebLogic Server. In addition, developers don't need to use WebLogic Workshop to develop Beehive components. In fact, the standard IDE is Eclipse. Eclipse recently launched a project called Pollinate that provides a plug-in to Eclipse to support Beehive development. You'll explore this in more detail in this book. Figure 1-4 gives you a glimpse of the Eclipse IDE with the Pollinate plug-in. This figure also gives you a first glimpse at some Apache Beehive code.

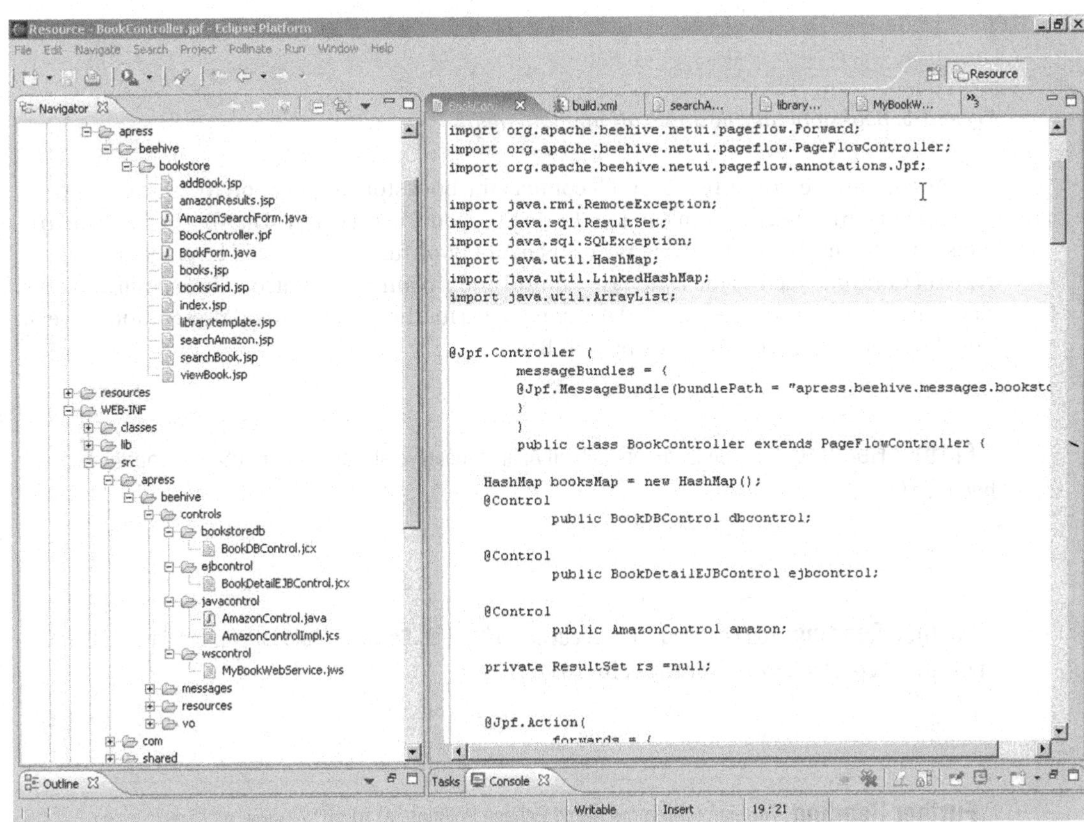


**Figure 1-4.** *Eclipse IDE with Pollinate*

If you look at Figure 1-4 carefully, you'll notice that the code is somehow related to a bookstore. In this book, you'll build a bookstore as the sample application to demonstrate the features of Apache Beehive and XMLBeans. In each chapter you'll add more functionality to this application. Figure 1-5 shows you the main menu for the bookstore application that you'll build.

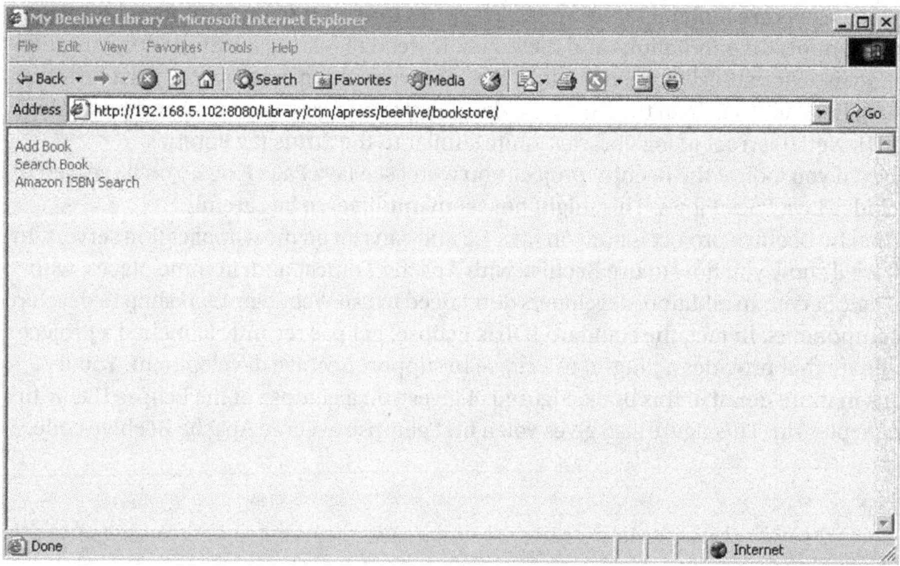


**Figure 1-5.** *Bookstore sample application, main menu*

As you can see in Figure 1-5, you'll connect the bookstore application to Amazon.com for searching the Amazon.com catalog. To do this, you'll use a Control in Apache Beehive to consume the Amazon.com Web Services. The Add Book functionality will leverage several types of Controls, such as the Database Control and a plain Java Control. The overall application will use the Java Page Flow/NetUI technologies for the controller and presentation layers. You'll represent the `book` object using XMLBeans.

---

■ **Further Reading** You can learn more about Apache Beehive at `http://incubator.apache.org/beehive/`.

---

■ **Further Reading** You can read more about JSR 181, Web Services Metadata for the Java Platform, at `http://jcp.org/en/jsr/detail?id=181`.

---

■ **Further Reading** You can read more about Eclipse Pollinate at `http://www.eclipse.org/pollinate/`.

---

# Introducing XMLBeans

XML is pretty much becoming the standard form for data representation. Almost every industry is now building standards that define their data as XML. This enables organizations to exchange data. For example, without standards, it's hard for an airline to exchange passengers' ticketing information with different travel agents. The entire travel industry, for example, now follows XML standards for defining and exchanging data. This can enable airlines, hotels, cruise lines, and travel agents to seamlessly exchange data. This in turn enables more service orientation.

Developers have always had a hard time with this. In an object-oriented world, what good is data formatted in XML? It goes back to the same concept as relational data. Using a relational database is a good way to store data, but in an object-oriented world, you eventually need to convert that relational data into objects. This gave birth to a generation of Object-Relational (OR) mapping tools. XMLBeans is the same thing as XML-object mapping. XMLBeans provide a way to map XML data to objects. XMLBeans fully support XML Schemas and provide an easy API to access XML data as if you were accessing data in a JavaBean. This technology was born at BEA, and in September 2003 BEA released the XMLBeans technology as open source. XMLBeans 1.0 is currently a stable release, and a lot of work is taking place to make it more suitable for large Web Service applications.

---

■ **Further Reading** You can read more about XMLBeans at `http://xmlbeans.apache.org/`.

---

# So, What's Next?

This book is going to dig deeply into the different technologies that are part of the Apache Beehive project. It will also cover Apache XMLBeans in detail. We'll use several small examples to demonstrate the various features of these technologies. In the next chapter, we'll explain the concepts behind SOA. This will provide you with the background to understand how the different technologies that are part of Apache Beehive actually help simplify SOA-based development. If you're already an expert on SOA, you can just read the "So, What's Next?" section in Chapter 2 and jump ahead.

CHAPTER 2

# Introducing Web Services and SOA Fundamentals

In this chapter, we'll introduce you to Web Services and Service-Oriented Architecture (SOA). We won't go into all the details of what these technologies are and what they can do; our goal is to provide enough background so you can understand the value of these technologies. You'll also see how SOA relates to Apache Beehive.

## Introducing Web Services

As a Java programmer, you've undoubtedly heard of Web Services. You might have read several articles on it or even used Web Services in some capacity. The following section is a ten-minute overview of Web Services. Then we'll cover Web Service technologies and define enterprise-class Web Services.

### Web Service Overview

Web Services, simply put, are just another way to access remote code over a network. Before the introduction of Web Services, technologies such as the Common Object Request Broker Architecture (CORBA) and Java's Remote Method Invocation (RMI) were a popular way to provide this functionality.

Specifically, Web Services are a set of specifications built on top of open, cross-platform standards such as TCP/IP, HTML, and XML to provide loosely coupled, highly interoperable, standards-based access to remote services over a network. Figure 2-1 shows the basic flow of a Web Service.

A Web Service consists of a *service provider* that is defined in the Web Services Description Language (WSDL) and published using a Universal Description, Discovery and Integration (UDDI) directory, called a *registry*. A *service requestor* (Web Service client) discovers the Web Service in the UDDI registry. Then the service requestor communicates with the service provider using SOAP over some transport protocol, generally HTTP.

We'll cover the core Web Service specifications in the next section.

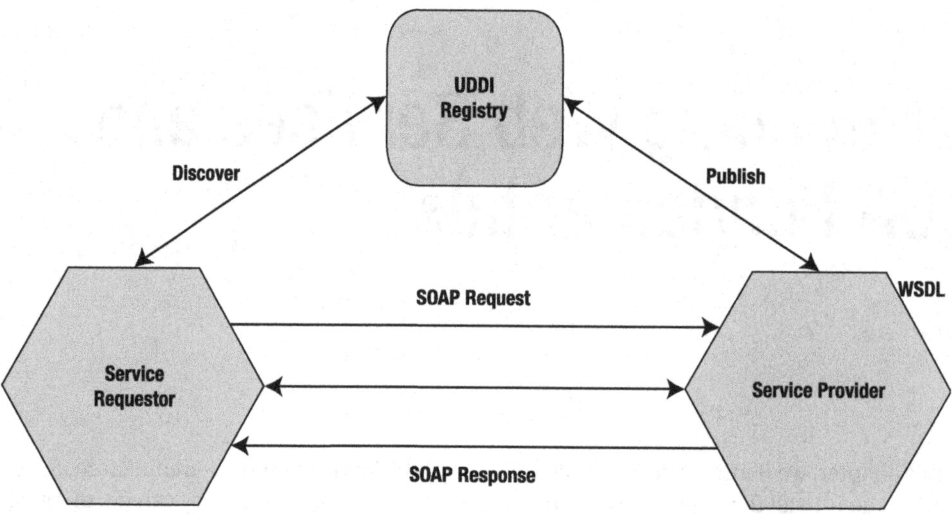


**Figure 2-1.** *Basic Web Service flow*

## Basic Web Service Technologies

In the following sections, you'll learn about three core technologies that you'll use when working with Web Services: SOAP, WSDL, and UDDI. We'll also mention some other, miscellaneous technologies that are involved with Web Services.

### Simple Object Access Protocol (SOAP)

The Simple Object Access Protocol (SOAP) is a W3C standard. According to the SOAP 1.1 specification, SOAP is a lightweight protocol for the exchange of information in a decentralized, distributed environment. SOAP is a definition built on top of XML. It allows service providers and service consumers to exchange data over a network. Today, the exchange of SOAP messages takes place primarily over HTTP; however, nothing in the SOAP specification restricts the exchange to HTTP. SOAP allows objects of any kind, on any platform, and written in any language to interoperate. SOAP has been implemented on more than twenty platforms and in more than fifty programming languages.

---

■ **Further Reading** You can read more about SOAP at `http://www.w3.org/TR/SOAP/`.

---

### Web Services Description Language (WSDL)

The Web Services Description Language (WSDL) is built on top of XML and contains information about the interface, semantics, and execution of a Web Service. It defines the services that are provided and the format and semantics of the data that a Web Service accepts and returns. A WSDL definition contains four critical pieces of data:

- Interface information describing all publicly available functions
- Data type information for all message requests and message responses
- Binding information about the transport protocol to be used
- Address information for locating the specified service

---

**Further Reading** You can read more about WSDL at `http://www.w3.org/TR/wsdl`.

---

### Universal Description, Discovery and Integration (UDDI)

You've used an Internet search engine, right? Imagine a world where every company has tons of services (or more specifically, Web Services). The Universal Description, Discovery and Integration (UDDI) specification defines a search engine for Web Services. You aren't required to expose your Web Services in a UDDI registry; however, by doing so, you allow more users to be able to locate and use your Web Services. UDDI definitions aren't specific to SOAP services. Any sort of Web Services can be described in a UDDI registry.

You've definitely heard about the Amazon.com and Google.com Web Services. We predict a whole new set of business models that can potentially arise when companies start leveraging Web Services from other companies. Let's say you want to buy this book. On the Apress Web site, you search for it. Apress makes a call to the Amazon.com Web Service to get you pricing information and the names and addresses of five bookstores that are closest to your location that carry this book. Then it uses a Google.com or MapQuest.com Web Service to show you these stores on a map.

This is just a basic example; business models like this will evolve as more and more Web Services are published in UDDI registries.

---

**Further Reading** You can read more about UDDI at `http://www.uddi.org/`.

---

### Other Web Service Standards

In addition to these three core standards that define Web Services, numerous other standards help deliver the promise of Web Services. Table 2-1 lists some of them; keep in mind that these URLs were accurate at the time of writing but, like everything on the Web, are subject to change. If you find one that's out-of-date, you can search the Web or the BEA dev2dev site (`http://dev2dev.bea.com/`) to learn more about these proposed standards.

Table 2-1 is by no means exhaustive, but it gives you a good idea of the types of technology support that you can expect to see for Web Services in the near future. These all help move Web Services from hype to reality and lead to the development of truly enterprise-class Web Services.

**Table 2-1.** *Miscellaneous Web Service Standards*

| Web Service Standard | URL |
|---|---|
| SOAP 1.2 Attachment Feature | `http://www.w3.org/TR/2004/NOTE-soap12-af-20040608/` |
| Web Services Addressing | `http://www.w3.org/Submission/ws-addressing/` |
| Web Services Reliable Messaging | `http://www.oasis-open.org/committees/tc_home.php?wg_abbrev=wsrm` |
| Web Services Policy Framework and Web Services Policy Attachment | `http://schemas.xmlsoap.org/ws/2004/09/policy/` |
| Web Services Coordination | `http://dev2dev.bea.com/technologies/webservices/ws-coordination.jsp` |
| Web Services Transaction | `http://dev2dev.bea.com/pub/a/2004/01/ws-transaction.html` |
| Web Services Security | `http://www.oasis-open.org/committees/tc_home.php?wg_abbrev=wss` |
| Web Service Choreography Interface | `http://www.w3.org/TR/wsci/` |

## Enterprise-Class Web Services

Web Services promote simplicity in design and development and offer universal applicability to almost all business problems. But what impact do Web Services have in an enterprise, and what will be the rate of adoption of this technology stack? Understanding the difference between simply deploying a Web Service and deploying a truly enterprise-class Web Service–based architecture will help you understand the true impact of Web Services.

In the following sections, we'll explain what exactly enterprise-class Web Services are. This is important because vendors—including BEA, IBM, Sun, Oracle, Microsoft, Tibco, and webMethods—all define enterprise-class Web Services and SOA differently. Not surprisingly, these definitions are tailored to match their product offerings.

For example, webMethods defines an enterprise Web Service as "the coupling of Web Services functionality with the integration and business process management of webMethods Integration platform" (defined in the webMethods whitepaper "Enterprise Web Services in the Financial Services Industry"). Clearly, this definition supports the webMethods suite of products.

### Web Services vs. Enterprise-Class Web Services

Today, Web Services exist totally on the surface of their true potential. Deploying a simple stock-ticker, currency-converter, or weather-brief Web Service doesn't encompass the full power and potential of Web Services. Broadly, an enterprise-class Web Services can be defined as a Web Service that demonstrates loose coupling, interoperability, and asynchronous interactions.

According to various research publications, application integration is one of the top three priorities of a Fortune 1000 CIO. Initially, in the early stages of Web Service adoption, it was clear that Web Services would be used in the traditional Enterprise Application Integration (EAI) world to help legacy applications integrate and coexist. Even though simple Web Services such as a stock ticker demonstrate loose coupling, interoperability, and asynchronous interactions, they do not show the potential for Web Services in the EAI world.

An effective enterprise-class Web Service architecture demonstrates the integration of applications and provides a programming model that reduces the complexity of developing loosely coupled, coarse-grained, asynchronous, and interoperable services and applications. It goes beyond a traditional stock-ticker Web Service and addresses the needs of the EAI market.

The future of Web Services will be the definitive platform for integrating enterprise applications, but realizing this future requires more than simple, RPC-style Web Services. While meeting the requirements defined previously, Web Services must also be reliable, available, and scalable to meet the rigorous demands of the changing business. Because of tight IT budgets and fixed resources, these enterprise-class Web Services need to be easy to develop in greatly shortened time frames. It's also important to note that the number of skilled enterprise J2EE developers is about 25–30 percent that of traditional developers (VB, C++, COBOL and so on). This ratio is slowly increasing, but this shows the need for Web Services to be easy to develop, deploy, and orchestrate.

### Defining Enterprise-Class Web Services

So, with the background information from the previous section, you can define an enterprise-class Web Service as the following:

- A Web Service demonstrates loose coupling, interoperability, and asynchronous interactions.
- A Web Service is easy to develop, deploy, and orchestrate.
- A Web Service is highly scalable, available, and reliable.
- A Web Service has configurable usage policies that govern the SLAs, error handling, and security requirements.
- A Web Service has policies that are dynamically configurable. Different versions of the Web Service can operate using different policies.

You now know the fundamentals of a Web Service, so in the next section we'll introduce and define SOA.

## Introducing SOA

SOA and service-oriented programming are the new buzzwords in IT. Further, SOA and Web Services are almost thought of as the same thing. We could easily spend this entire chapter clearing up this myth, but that isn't our purpose here. SOA isn't the same as Web Services; however, the Web Service technology is the most promising technology for enabling a true SOA. Figure 2-2 shows you how SOA is actually in the middle of the technology star and can be implemented using any technology.

---

■ **Note** SOA and Web Services aren't the same thing. We aren't emphasizing this distinction in this chapter primarily because, although not the same, Web Services are the best technology for SOA today. In other words, the two are very closely linked.

---

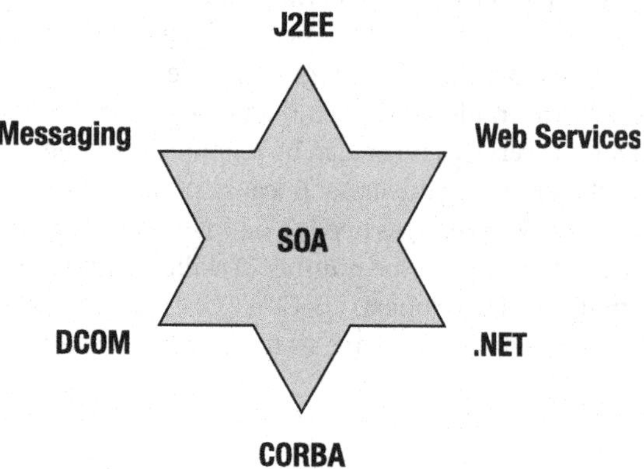


**Figure 2-2.** *SOA using different technologies*

Before we get into the definition of SOA, we'll first define a service.

## What's a Service?

A *service* is a discrete piece of code that solves a business problem, is technology agnostic, is network addressable, and has a published interface. But this is a loaded and still incomplete definition. It's really hard to describe a service in one sentence. So, we'll provide a more complete definition of a service; specifically, a service has all of the following characteristics:

*Solves problem*: A service is a piece of code that solves a business problem. By this definition, every piece of code in your application is a potential service—accessing a database, printing a report, generating data for a report, and so on. However, not all pieces of your code will satisfy the other pieces of this definition.

---

■ **Further Reading** For more information about services, read "Service-Oriented Modeling and Architecture: How to Identify, Specify, and Realize Services for Your SOA" at `http://www-128.ibm.com/developerworks/webservices/library/ws-soa-design1/`.

---

*Is technology agnostic*: A service is a piece of code that's technology agnostic. This means that the service can be written in any programming language and then invoked by code from another programming language.

*Is transport independent*: A service is also transport independent. This means the service can be invoked using any communication protocol (HTTP, TCP/IP, RMI, and so on). The point of interaction between a consumer and a service is a SOAP message, not a technology touch point. Today, however, the primary transport protocol for services is HTTP.

*Is network addressable*: A service is network addressable. This means that a service can be invoked over a network—intranet or extranet. Think of this for a minute. By this definition, any EJB in your system is a service, and any COM/CORBA object is a service. However, it's important to understand that you need to have *all* of the pieces described in this definition to be a service. For example, if you're network addressable but not technology agnostic, you're not a service. This rules out CORBA or EJBs from being services.

*Has a published interface*: A service has a published interface. This means the service has a clear set of inputs and outputs. These are typically in the form of SOAP messages but don't have to be.

*Is transparent to its location*: A service is transparent to its location. This means the client shouldn't need to know when, where, or how the service is built. All the client needs to do is invoke the service based on the published interface.

In this definition, we've left out the fact that a service is generally discoverable. This is a valid requirement for a service, but it isn't mandated.

All Web Services are services, but not all services are Web Services. This relationship goes back to our statement that the Web Service technology is only one of the technologies that can be used to build your SOA. In addition, another key point to remember is that just because you have a Web Service doesn't mean you have an SOA. Figure 2-3 shows the relationship between SOA and Web Services.

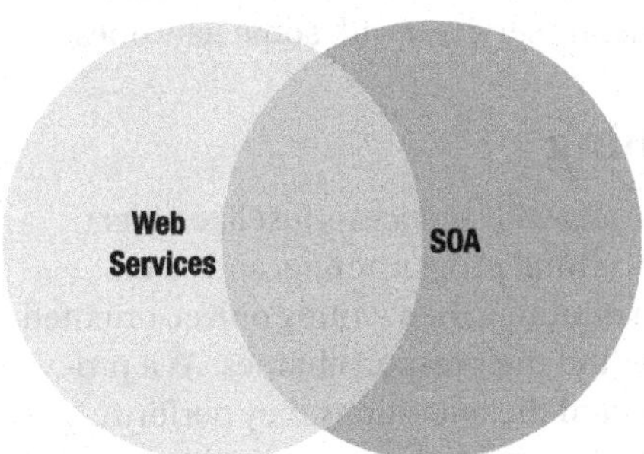


**Figure 2-3.** *Relationship between SOA and Web Services*

---

**■ Note** To reiterate, all Web Services are services, but not all services are Web Services.

---

## Defining SOA

Several ways to define SOA exist. A great article, "A Defining Moment for SOA," presents an aggregation of 50 definitions of SOA. As SOA enthusiasts, we definitely recommend you read this article: `http://searchwebservices.techtarget.com/originalContent/0,289142,sid26_gci1017004,00.html`.

You can think of SOA as a process and a methodology. It's a set of tools, technologies, frameworks, and best practices that enable the quick and easy implementation of services. In addition, the process of developing SOA uses a methodology for identifying reusable services in your applications and organization. SOA is an enabler for loosely coupled applications that are service oriented.

SOA isn't a single product or a standard.

---

■ **Further Reading** Visit Kunal Mittal's site at `http://www.soaconsultant.com/html/soup.shtml` to learn about a new methodology for SOA-based development, the Service-Oriented Unified Process (SOUP).

---

SOA is a collection of services. Each service is a step in a business process. A *business process*, then, can be defined as a collection of ordered services. In SOA environments, the business drives the services, and the services drive the architecture, or SOA. The key factor is that the services are loosely coupled. This is obvious if you revisit the definition of a service. Since a service is a discrete piece of code with a defined set of inputs and outputs, you can swap out a service in a business process quite seamlessly. This is the meaning of *loosely coupled*. This also automatically leads to business agility, as you can add/remove/change services in a business process quickly to meet the changing demands of the business. A new business process isn't a new software project; rather, it's the assembly to preexisting services, with some new ones.

## Defining Service-Oriented Programming

*Service-oriented programming* is, simply put, programming with services—just like object-oriented programming, rules-based programming, procedural programming, and so on.

Let's talk about object-oriented programming for a minute. When writing object-oriented code, a developer is interested in identifying the classes and their responsibilities. As a programmer, you define the objects, the data they contain, and the operations they perform.

Service-oriented programming is no different. A developer building services needs to do the following:

1. Identify the operations/functions that should be exposed as services.
2. Build the service.
3. Expose the interface to the service.
4. Publish the service so that it's network addressable.

On the flip side of the coin, a developer that's consuming a service needs to do the following:

1. Discover which service they want to consume.
2. Understand the operations and interface.
3. Implement the binding to the service to invoke its operations.
4. Execute the service.

When building services, you might still be using object-oriented programming or other traditional programming paradigms. The difference is that when you start thinking about services, you're no longer building large and complex object models. Instead, you're designing business-aligned components at a coarser-grained level rather than objects at a fine-grained level.

## Exploring the Role of XML in SOA

XML is a key technology enabler for SOA-based applications. Just like Web Services, XML isn't required for SOA, but it's one of the best technologies today to enable service orientation.

The main reason behind this is that XML allows you to build data dictionaries that are well defined and that can be validated. When you work with Web Services, you'll primarily exchange SOAP messages that are built on top of XML. One of the first steps in working with Web Services is validating the input and output messages. The Web Service provider validates the input they receive, and the consumer validates the response they get back from the Web Service. This is a key feature of XML, thus making it an ideal technology for Web Services and SOA.

We've now given you enough of a background on SOA and Web Services to talk about how Apache Beehive enables SOA and SOA-based programming.

---

■ **Further Reading** For more information about SOA, refer to "SOA Learning Guide" at `http://searchwebservices.techtarget.com/generic/0,295582,sid26_gci1068517,00.html?Offer=Wswnsoalg` and BEA's SOA Resource Center at `http://www.bea.com/framework.jsp?CNT=index.htm&FP=/content/solutions/soa/`.

---

■ **Further Reading** For more information about SOA and Web Services, refer to the WebServices.org site at `http://www.webservices.org/`.

---

# How Does Apache Beehive Enable SOA?

Two key pieces of the Apache Beehive technologies focus on SOA. These are Controls and Web Services.

Figure 2-4 shows you how Controls and Web Services fit into the typical Web Service flow shown in Figure 2-1 earlier in this chapter. The following sections will describe the two technologies.

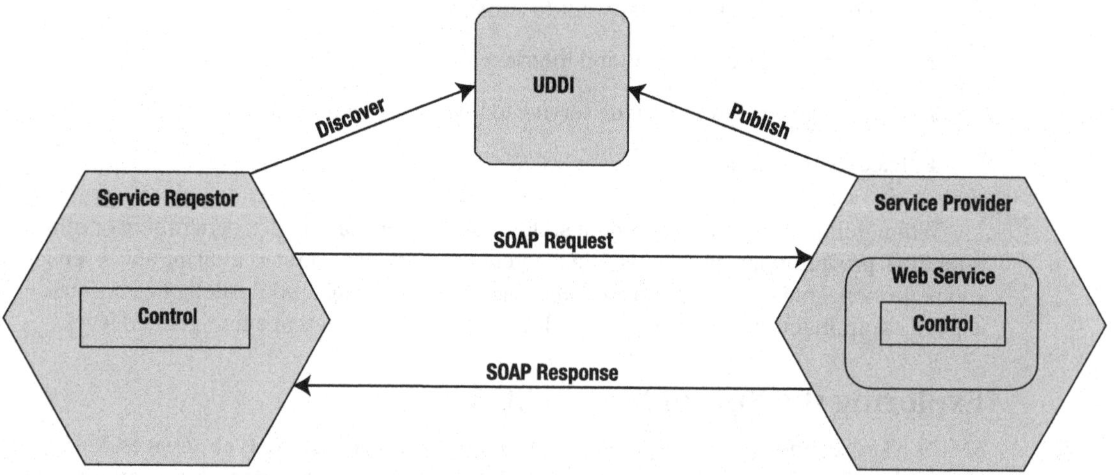


**Figure 2-4.** *How does Beehive fit into SOA?*

## How Do Controls Relate to SOA?

Controls are a new concept in Apache Beehive and play a big role in SOA-based development. A Control is nothing more than a Java object that encapsulates some business logic or controls the access to some resource such as a database or external application. A Control has a well-defined interface. Think of a Control as a service enabler. A Control is not a service but can easily be exposed as a service, thus enabling service orientation, or SOA.

## How Do Apache Beehive Web Services Relate to SOA?

Well, as discussed in the chapter, the Web Service technology is one of the most promising technologies today for enabling SOA. Apache Beehive simplifies the development of Web Services and the consumption of Web Services. It uses a standard SOAP implementation and leverages the three main standards for Web Services: SOAP, WSDL, and UDDI.

## How Do XMLBeans Relate to SOA?

XML is a big part of SOA. Just like with Web Services, you aren't required to use XML in SOA applications; however, today XML is the most likely technology that you would use for data exchange in SOA applications.

The XMLBeans project is an open-source project that simplifies how developers work with XML. It's an XML-Java binding technology, much like what a Object-Relational (OR) mapping tool does for databases. XMLBeans are good for communicating between Web Services, which are the key elements of SOA applications today. We'll discuss this further in Chapter 8.

# So, What's Next?

Apache Beehive is based heavily on a concept called *annotations*. Before you can dive into the different Beehive technologies and start writing code, you need to spend a few minutes learning about annotations. So, Chapter 3 will introduce this concept, show you how annotations work in the latest version of Java, and explain how Apache Beehive leverages the concept of annotations. You'll also see some of the Java annotations, the BEA WebLogic Workshop annotations, and then the Apache Beehive annotations.

CHAPTER 3

# Introducing Annotations

Java 1.5, or the "Tiger" release, is probably the most significant revision to Java since its original inception. It includes several new features, such as generics and annotations. The concept of annotations isn't new to Java. The first incarnation of annotations was in Javadocs comments and keyword modifiers. But this was fairly limited and did not allow developers to define their own annotations. Tags such as `author`, `param`, `return`, and `deprecated` are all examples of annotations. Even the `transient` attribute that prevents an instance variable from being serialized is somewhat an example of an annotation.

With Java 1.5, Sun has taken annotations to a new level. In this chapter, we'll briefly talk about what are annotations and how they're used in Java 1.5.

Now, with Java embracing annotations even more, why should the J2EE community stay behind? Even before Java 1.5, BEA released the Java Page Flow technologies, which were based on their own proprietary annotation language. In addition, the Apache Beehive project completely embraces this concept. The majority of this chapter will explore the different annotations used by Apache Beehive and other J2EE development, such as EJBs.

If you're someone who has extensively used WebLogic Workshop and now needs to migrate all your Workshop code to Beehive, you'll find this chapter particularly interesting. You'll realize that the small differences in the annotations are probably your starting point in this code migration.

## What's an Annotation?

So, what's an annotation? An *annotation* is metadata that's translated into something meaningful at compile time or runtime. *Metadata* is really some data about some other piece of data. It allows you to provide the ability for the compiler (in this case, the annotations processor) to make certain decisions for you. These decisions typically result in generating some code behind the scenes.

---

**Further Reading** You can find a really good article on annotations at `http://www-106.ibm.com/developerworks/java/library/j-annotate1/`.

---

Annotations can be read by source code, by compiled code, or at runtime using reflection. Annotations have a few key advantages:

- They save the programmer from having to write boilerplate code to do the same, repetitive tasks.
- They save the programmer from having to manage certain information in external files, such as deployment descriptors.
- Annotations can also be used for compile-time checking such as producing warnings and errors for different failure scenarios.

With Java 1.5, finally, annotations are a typed part of the language, and the version even comes with some prebuilt annotations, one of which can be used to mark a class as deprecated. You now get a syntax for declaring annotation types, a class file representation for annotations, APIs to access the annotations, and an annotation processing tool to process the annotations.

Let's take a quick look at some basic annotations in Java 1.5.

## Basic Java 1.5 Annotations

Java 1.5 uses annotations extensively. Java 1.5 comes with seven prebuilt annotations.

### java.lang.Override

The `java.lang.Override` syntax is as follows:

```
@Target(value=METHOD)
@Retention(value=SOURCE)
public @interface Override
```

This annotation overrides a class or a method that's declared in a superclass. The value of this annotation is to enforce compile-time checking. For example, if the superclass or method is declared as final, the compiler will throw an error. Conversely, assume that you misspell the method you're trying to override. The compiler would normally treat this like any new method. Using the annotation would tell the compiler to throw an error message, as now it can check a superclass to make sure the method is actually being overridden. Typically, no error would have been thrown, thus making it difficult to debug this issue. Another example would be if you forgot to specify that your class extends from another class. You can't really override a method that isn't being inherited from a superclass. The following is a specific example:

```
 @Override
public String toString() {
        return super.toString() + " my custom implementation " ;
  }
```

### java.lang.Deprecated

The java.lang.Deprecated syntax is as follows:

```
@Documented
@Retention(value=RUNTIME)
public @interface Deprecated
```

This isn't specifically new and behaves similarly to the Javadocs tag @deprecated. For example:

```
@Deprecated public String myMethod() {
    return "Hello world!";
}
```

A *deprecated* method is one that has been replaced by some other method. Developers shouldn't use a deprecated method, as there is no guarantee that a later version of the class will still contain that method.

### java.lang.annotation.Documented

The java.lang.annotation.Documented syntax is as follows:

```
@Documented
@Retention(value=RUNTIME)
@Target(value=ANNOTATION_TYPE)
public @interface Documented
```

This annotation shows that you want Javadocs created for this element.

### java.lang.SuppressWarning

The java.lang.SuppressWarning syntax is as follows:

```
@Target(value={TYPE,FIELD,METHOD,PARAMETER,CONSTRUCTOR,LOCAL_VARIABLE})
@Retention(value=SOURCE)
public @interface SuppressWarnings
```

You can use this to suppress any warnings in the code. Why would you want this? Well, it really addresses the "type-safe" collections issue. With generics in Java 1.5, you can create collections that are not type-safe. The compiler will throw an appropriate warning, so you can use this annotation to suppress these warnings.

However, we recommend using this annotation with extreme caution.

### java.lang.annotation.Inherited

The java.lang.annotation.Inherited syntax is as follows:

```
@Documented
@Retention(value=RUNTIME)
@Target(value=ANNOTATION_TYPE)
public @interface Inherited
```

This is similar to the "override" annotation. It basically defines that this class is inherited. If no superclass has an annotation for this type, then an error will be thrown.

## java.lang.annotation.Retention

The `java.lang.annotation.Retention` syntax is as follows:

```
@Documented
@Retention(value=RUNTIME)
@Target(value=ANNOTATION_TYPE)
public @interface Retention
```

Retention takes a single value of the type `RetentionPolicy`. There are three possible values for `RetentionPolicy`:

- `SOURCE`: Annotations are specific to the source code; they don't become part of the class files and hence should be discarded by the compiler.
- `CLASS`: This is the default behavior. The annotations are part of the class files and are checked at compile time but are ignored by the Virtual Machine at runtime.
- `RUNTIME`: Annotations are executed at both compile time and runtime.

## java.lang.annotation.Target

The `java.lang.annotation.Target` syntax is as follows:

```
@Documented
@Retention(value=RUNTIME)
@Target(value=ANNOTATION_TYPE)
public @interface Target
```

`@Target` indicates the type of element for which this annotation is applicable. These are as follows:

- `TYPE` (class, interface, or enum declaration)
- `FIELD` (includes enum constants)
- `METHOD`
- `PARAMETER`
- `CONSTRUCTOR`
- `LOCAL_VARIABLE`
- `ANNOTATION_TYPE`
- `PACKAGE`

## JSR 175

JSR 175 (A Metadata Facility for the Java Programming Language) is a JSR aimed at standardizing the metadata annotations concept across Java. This JSR was motivated by the innovations in the JavaBean and EJB specifications. For example, JavaBeans introduced the concept of having a `getFieldName` and `setFieldName` method for each instance variable. This has become a noted standard, and reflection is used extensively to enable this. The EJB specification introduced the concept of having deployment descriptors and a notation to describe methods as `home` and `remote`. These sorts of concepts led to the realization that an annotation model, as introduced earlier in this chapter, would add tremendous value to Java programmers.

JSR 175 provides the following:

- It provides the ability for a programmer to provide information as metadata for classes, interfaces, methods, and variables.
- The metadata will be interpreted by development tools, such as IDEs, compilers, and the JVM.
- The syntax of the metadata isn't enforced, and several possibilities are presented. The most popular and widely adopted seems to be the Javadocs notion, such as `@metadataannotation`.
- It provides an API that allows developers to define their own metadata annotations.
- It provides a mechanism to access the metadata at compile time, deploy time, and runtime.

---

■ **Further Reading** For more information on JSR 175, visit the JCP site at `http://www.jcp.org/en/jsr/detail?id=175`.

---

## JSR 181

JSR 181 (Web Services Metadata for the Java Platform) is similar to JSR 171 but specific to Web Services. This JSR aims to address the following specific common needs of Web Service programming:

- Enables programmers to write and deploy Web Services that comply with all SOAP and WSDL standards.
- Provides the ability to deploy the Web Services that are built using JSR 181 to any J2EE-compliant server.
- Separates public interfaces and the implementation details. This is important, as in many cases the public interfaces are exposed to the consumers before the implementation details are worked out.
- Supports asynchronous Web Service communication.

---

■ **Further Reading** For more information on JSR 181, visit the JCP site at `http://www.jcp.org/en/jsr/detail?id=181`.

---

You'll look more closely at JSR 181 when we cover the Apache Beehive implementation in Chapter 7.

# Using Annotations in WebLogic Workshop

BEA has definitely been a pioneer at introducing this annotations programming model and has played a big role in its adoption and standardization. Let's first look at the annotations introduced by BEA in WebLogic Workshop. These annotations predated JSR 175 and JSR 181, and even Java 1.5. They basically extended the Javadocs notations. It's no doubt these JSRs have been influenced by these annotations, as well as have learned from some shortcomings in BEA's incarnation of annotations.

To demonstrate the annotations in WebLogic Workshop, we'll pull code from various samples that ship with the product.

---

■ **Note** Code from this chapter will not be included on the Web site.The code here is just to explain the concept of annotations. You should be able to find all the code shown in this chapter in the `samples` directory of your WebLogic installation.

---

## Java Page Flows

The Java Page Flow technology introduced in WebLogic Workshop 8.1 has several annotations. We won't get into the details of these too much but instead just provide a quick look at them. In the next section, when you learn about the annotations for the Page Flows in Apache Beehive, you'll be able to appreciate the changes and move toward a more simplified and standard annotations model.

Glance through the code in Listing 3-1.

**Listing 3-1.** *A Java Page Flow Controller in WebLogic Workshop*

```
import com.bea.netuix.servlets.controls.portlet.backing.PortletBackingContext;
import com.bea.netuix.servlets.controls.window.WindowCapabilities;
import com.bea.wlw.netui.pageflow.PageFlowController;
import com.bea.wlw.netui.pageflow.Forward;

/**
 * This is the default controller for a blank Web application.
 *
 * @jpf:controller
```

```
 * @jpf:view-properties view-properties::
 * <!-- This data is autogenerated.
*   Hand-editing this section is not recommended. -->
 * <view-properties>
 * <pageflow-object id="pageflow:/Controller.jpf"/>
 * <pageflow-object id="action:begin.do">
 *   <property name="x" value="60"/>
 *   <property name="y" value="80"/>
 * </pageflow-object>
 * <pageflow-object id="page:index.jsp">
 *   <property name="x" value="220"/>
 *   <property name="y" value="80"/>
 * </pageflow-object>
 * <pageflow-object id="page:error.jsp">
 *   <property name="x" value="220"/>
 *   <property name="y" value="160"/>
 * </pageflow-object>
 * <pageflow-object id="forward:path#index#index.jsp#@action:begin.do@">
 *   <property name="elbowsY" value="72,72,72,72"/>
 *   <property name="elbowsX" value="96,140,140,184"/>
 *   <property name="toPort" value="West_1"/>
 *   <property name="fromPort" value="East_1"/>
 *   <property name="label" value="index"/>
 * </pageflow-object>
 * </view-properties>
 * ::
 */
public class Controller extends PageFlowController {
    /**
     * @jpf:action
     * @jpf:forward name="index" path="index.jsp"
     */
    protected Forward begin()   {
        return new Forward("index");
    }
}
```

The controller code is basically a Java source code file with the extension `.jpf` to denote that it's a Java Page Flow. It follows the same structure as any Java source code file. The only difference is that in a typical file the comments don't mean anything to the compiler. In this case, the comments are specifying different annotations. For example, this annotation tells the compiler that this class is a Java Page Flow controller:

```
@jpf:controller
```

The next set of annotations is as follows:

```
@jpg:view-properties
```

These are used only by the editor, in this case WebLogic Workshop. This draws a graphical representation of the Page Flow and how it connects various actions and JSPs (see Figure 3-1).

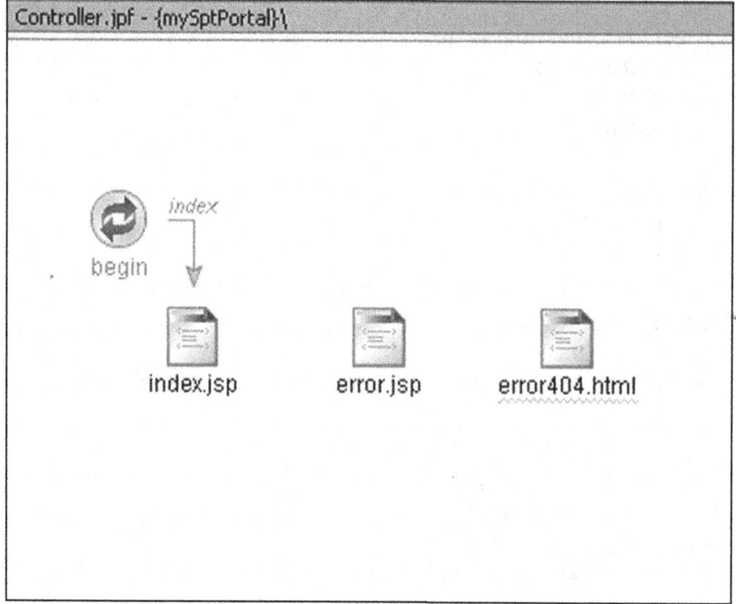


**Figure 3-1.** *Simple Page Flow view in WebLogic Workshop*

The controller code shown in Figure 3-1 is pretty basic in what it represents. Just to give you a feel for what it can look like, see Figure 3-2, which shows a more elaborate Page Flow view.

Let's continue dissecting the annotations. The next and last set you see in this basic example is as follows:

```
/**
 * @jpf:action
 * @jpf:forward name="index" path="index.jsp"
 */
```

These annotations define that the method is an action. The forward defines the next step in the Page Flow. In this case, the `begin` method (similar to the `main` method of a Java class) sends the users to the `index.jsp` page.

We won't go any deeper with this. We recommend you open a JPF file from one of the BEA sample directories and take a look at some more annotations.

The one take-away from this section is that the annotations in WebLogic Workshop are very different in format from the Java 1.5 annotations you saw in the previous section. You'll notice more differences as we talk about annotations in the "Controls" and "Web Services" sections.

At the end of the chapter, we'll go full circle and show you how the annotations in Apache Beehive take the concepts from WebLogic Workshop but follow the annotations format of Java 1.5.

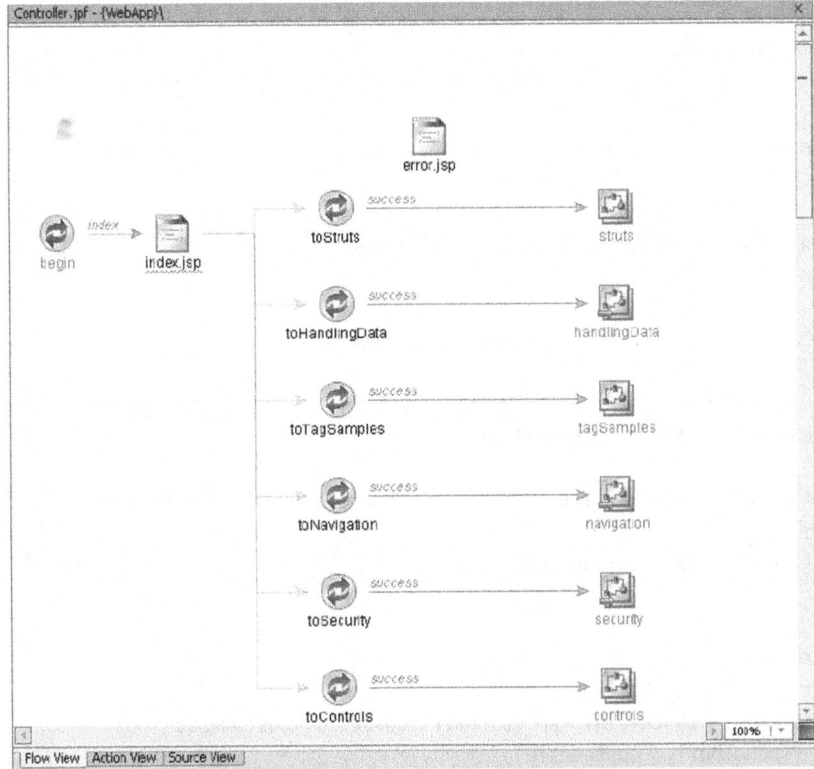


**Figure 3-2.** *Detailed example of a Page Flow view in WebLogic Workshop*

## Controls

Controls are another new technology introduced by BEA WebLogic Workshop. They're quite a revolutionary concept. They form a façade for developers to access business logic and external resources such as a database or a legacy system. They provide a common interface to all resources and allow you to work with them as you would with any Plain Old Java Object (POJO). WebLogic ships with several out-of-box Controls and provides a programming model for custom Control development.

A Control is basically an annotated Java class. Let's look at a simple Control. Listing 3-2 shows a simple Java Control created in WebLogic Workshop.

**Listing 3-2.** *A Simple Java Control*

```
package verifyFunds;

import com.bea.control.*;
import java.sql.SQLException;

/**
 * A Database Control to support the VerifyFunds sample Control. Provides access
 * to a database for purchase order requests.
 *
 * @jc:connection data-source-jndi-name="cgSampleDataSource"
 */
public interface ItemsDatabase
    extends DatabaseControl, com.bea.control.ControlExtension
{
    /**
     * Select item price based on item number.
     *
     * @jc:sql statement="SELECT price FROM items WHERE itemnumber = {itemNumber}"
     */
    double selectItemPrice(int itemNumber);

    /**
     * Insert purchase and customer information into a.
     * table that correlates the two.
     * @jc:sql statement="INSERT INTO po_customers (orderid, customerid)
     *    VALUES ({poNumber}, {customerID})"
     */
    void insertItemCustomer(int poNumber, int customerID);

    /**
     * Insert purchase order and item information into
     * a table that correlates the two.
     * @jc:sql statement="INSERT INTO po_items
*  (orderid, itemnumber, quantity) VALUES ({poNumber}, {itemNumber}, {quantity})"
     */
    void insertPOItem(int poNumber, int itemNumber, int quantity);

    /**
     * Select the number of items available based on item number.
     *
     * @jc:sql statement="SELECT quantityAvailable FROM items
     * WHERE itemNumber = {itemNumber}"
     */
    int checkInventory(int itemNumber);
```

```
    /**
     * Update the item inventory.
     *
     * @jc:sql statement="UPDATE items SET quantityAvailable
     * = {newQuantityAvailable} WHERE itemnumber={itemNumber}"
     */
    int updateInventory(int itemNumber, int newQuantityAvailable);
}
```

Let's examine the first annotation in this code:

```
@jc:connection data-source-jndi-name="cgSampleDataSource"
```

This annotation's `jc` defines this class to be a Java Control. The fact that this code has a connection annotation and a data source defines that this is a Database Control. The following is another example of a Control annotation:

```
@jc:ejb home-jndi-name="ejb20-containerManaged-AccountHome"
```

This defines an EJB Control and provides the `jndi` name to the `home` interface of the EJB. The following is another example of an annotation in the code shown in Listing 3-2:

```
@jc:sql statement="SELECT price FROM items WHERE itemnumber = {itemNumber}"
```

In this case, you're defining a SQL statement that this Database Control would execute. The `{itemNumber}` tag denotes that this will be a parameter to the `sql` statement.

Fortunately, Controls in WebLogic Workshop don't need the complex view properties for their graphical representation. Figure 3-3 shows the Database Control you just looked at in Listing 3-2.

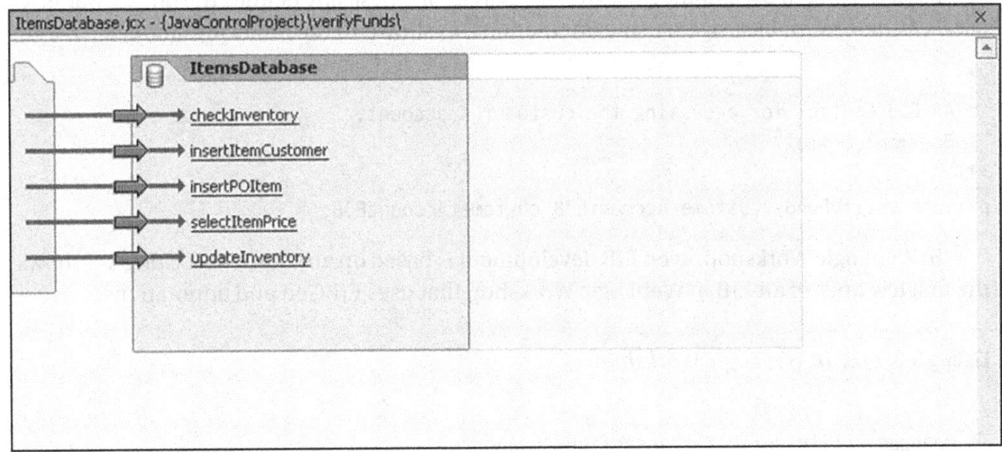


**Figure 3-3.** *Database Control in WebLogic Workshop*

Once again, let's see a more complex example where a Control uses another Control (see Figure 3-4).

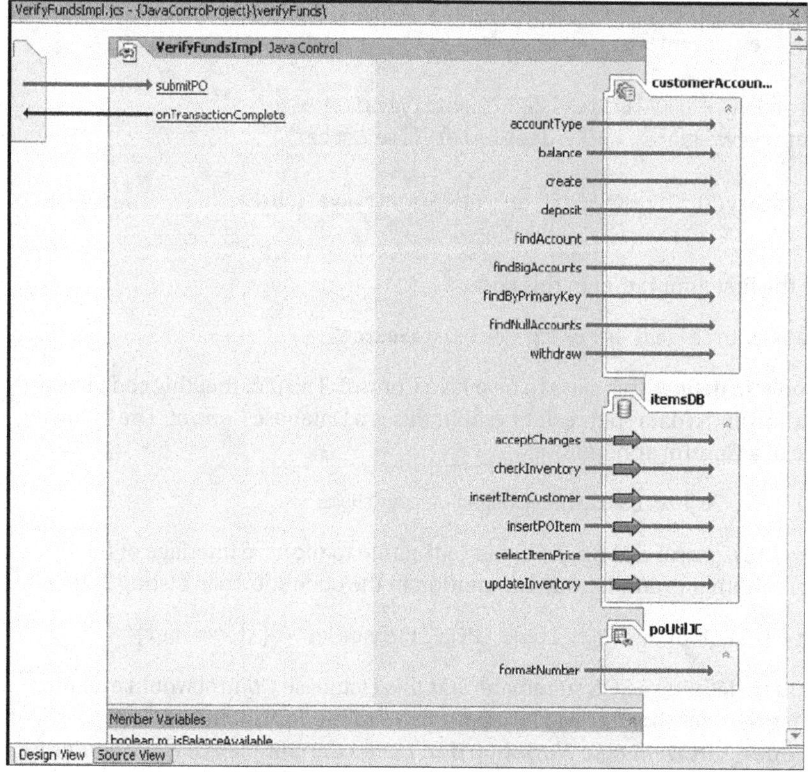


**Figure 3-4.** *Multiple Controls in WebLogic Workshop*

For a Control to use another Control, the parent one basically defines the ones it wants to use as instance variables, again using annotations, as shown in the following snippet:

```
/**
 * An EJB Control for accessing the customer's account.
 * @common:control
 */
private verifyFunds.CustomerAccountEJB customerAccountEJB;
```

In WebLogic Workshop, even EJB development is based on annotations. Listing 3-3 shows the first few lines of an EJB in WebLogic Workshop that uses EJBGen and annotations.

**Listing 3-3.** *EJBs in WebLogic Workshop*

```
/**
 * @ejbgen:entity default-transaction="Supports"
 *   ejb-name = "BMPItem"
 *   persistence-type="bmp"
 *   prim-key-class="java.lang.Integer"
 *
 * @ejbgen:jndi-name
```

```
 *   local  = "ejb.BMPItemLocalHome"
 *
 * @ejbgen:file-generation local-class = "True"
* local-class-name = "BMPItem"
* local-home = "True"
* local-home-name = "BMPItemHome"
* remote-class = "False"
*  remote-home = "False"
*  remote-home-name = "BMPItemRemoteHome"
* remote-class-name = "BMPItemRemote"
*  value-class = "False"
* value-class-name = "BMPItemValue"
*  pk-class = "True"
 *
 * @ejbgen:resource-ref jndi-name="cgSampleDataSource"
* sharing-scope="Shareable"
*  auth="Container"
* type="javax.sql.DataSource"
* name="jdbc/cgSampleDataSource"
 */
public class BMPItemBean
  extends GenericEntityBean
  implements EntityBean
{
```

In Listing 3-3, the @ejbgen annotation defines an entity bean. You do get a graphical representation of the EJB, just like you do with Java Page Flows and Java Controls.

## Web Services

Web Services are the last set of WebLogic Workshop annotations we'll discuss. Web Services in WebLogic Workshop are written as .jws files. Listing 3-4 shows the code for a simple banking Web Service.

**Listing 3-4.** *Web Service Code in WebLogic Workshop*

```
package creditReport;

/**
 * Bank.jws is a very simple service for use by the CreditReport.jws sample
 * service. Bank simulates a "long-running" procedure by using a timer
 * to delay its asynchronous response.
 *
 * Note that Bank.jws and IRS.jws are identical except for method names
 * and the default duration of the timer timeout.
 * @common:target-namespace namespace="http://workshop.bea.com/Bank"
 */
```

```
public class Bank implements com.bea.jws.WebService
{
    /**
     * @jc:timer timeout="10 seconds"
     * @common:control
     */
    private com.bea.control.TimerControl timer;

    /*
     * Store the customer ID number that is passed in so we can use it in the
     * asynchronous response.
     */
    private String ssn;

    public Callback callback;

    public interface Callback
    {
        /**
         * <p>onDeliverAnalysis is a callback delivered to the client when
         * processing is complete.</p>
         *
         * @jws:conversation phase="finish"
         */
        public void onDeliverAnalysis(String result);
    }

    /**
     * Starts the asynchronous analysis operation.  When analysis is complete
     * the onDeliverAnalysis callback will be called. If cancelAnalysis is
     * invoked before the results are delivered, results will never be delivered
     * @common:operation
     * @jws:conversation phase="start"
     */
    public void startCustomerAnalysis(String ssn)

    {
        /* store the customer ID for later use */
        this.ssn = ssn;

        /*
         * start the timer, which simulates starting the
         * long-running analysis procedure
         */
        timer.start();
    }
```

```
    /*
     * Handler for onTimeout events from the "timer" Timer Control.
     * onTimeout simulates the long-running procedure reaching completion,
     * so a result is sent to the client via the onDeliverAnalysis callback.
     */
    private void timer_onTimeout(long timeout)
    {
        /*
         * Use a completely arbitrary scheme to decide who's approved and
         * who's not.  Some people think real banks work this way.
         */
        if ((ssn.length() > 2) && (ssn.charAt(2) <= '5'))
        {
            callback.onDeliverAnalysis("Approved");
        }
        else
        {
            callback.onDeliverAnalysis("Denied");
        }
    }

    /**
     * <p>Cancels the analysis.  The onDeliverAnalysis callback
     * will not be called and the conversation is finished.</p>
     *
     * @common:operation
     * @jws:conversation phase="finish"
     */
    public void cancelAnalysis()
    {
        timer.stop();
    }
}
```

As an exercise, you might want to list all the annotations you see in this code sample. Note that you define the class to be a Web Service, define the operations of the Web Service, and then use a Java Control for some timer functionality. Refer to Figure 3-5 for a graphical view of this Web Service. Use that to correlate to the annotations in the code.

So, now that you've seen some basic annotations in WebLogic Workshop, let's quickly look at the annotations in Apache Beehive. Pay close attention to the differences.

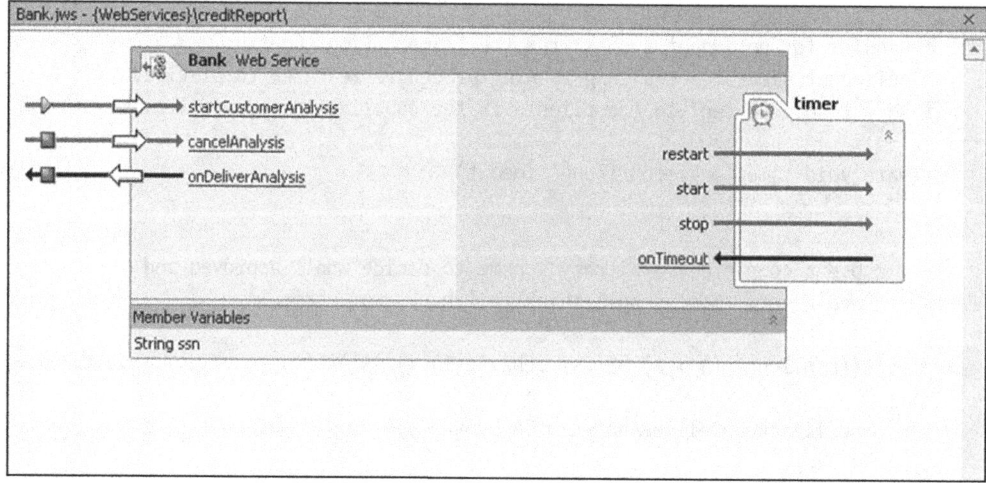


**Figure 3-5.** *Web Services in WebLogic Workshop*

# Introducing Apache Beehive Annotations

In the following sections, you'll look at the different annotations in Apache Beehive. Please remember that you have still not learned to use these technologies. Thus, it will be futile to try to understand the details of all these annotations at this point. The purpose here is to get a sense of the annotations programming model. Don't worry if you don't understand what each annotation means or does. You'll know all there is to know by the time you get through this book.

## Page Flows/NetUI

A Page Flow is nothing but a simple Java class. The following annotations define it to be a Page Flow:

```
@Jpf.Controller
public class Controller extends PageFlowController {
```

In the WebLogic Workshop Page Flow, you achieved this same behavior with the following annotation:

```
/**
* @jpf:controller
*/
public class Controller extends PageFlowController {
```

In an Apache Beehive Page Flow, you can define forwards as follows:

```
@Jpf.Action(
  forwards = {
    @Jpf.Forward( name="...", path="..." ),
    @Jpf.Forward( name="...", path="..." ),
 }
)
```

By contrast, in a WebLogic Workshop Page Flow, the forwards would look like the following:

```
/**
 * @jpf:action
 * @jpf:forward name="..." path="..."
 * @jpf:forward name="..." path="..."
 */
```

## Controls

Controls in Apache Beehive are the same as Controls in WebLogic Workshop. Let's look at the subtle differences in the annotations.

In Apache Beehive, you could define a simple Control using the following code:

```
package hellocontrol;

import org.apache.beehive.controls.api.bean.ControlInterface;

@ControlInterface
public interface Hello
{
    public String hello();
}
```

As an exercise, we recommend you generate a simple HelloWorld Control in WebLogic Workshop and compare the annotations. You can use the previous sections of this chapter as a reference to map the annotations in your new HelloWorld Control.

## Web Services

Before jumping into learning how to write Beehive code, let's spend a couple quick minutes looking at the annotations in a Beehive Web Service. The following code snippet shows a simple HelloWorld Web Service:

```
@WebService
public class HelloWorld
{
    @WebMethod
    public String sayHelloWorld()
    {
        return "Hello world!";
    }
}
```

Now take a quick peek at a HelloWorld Web Service in WebLogic Workshop:

```
/**
 * @common:target-namespace namespace="http://workshop.bea.com/HelloWorld"
 */
public class HelloWorld implements com.bea.jws.WebService {
    /**
     * @common:operation
     */
    public String sayHelloWorld()   {
        return "Hello, World!";
    }
}
```

This should again give you a flavor of the subtle differences between the annotations in WebLogic Workshop and Apache Beehive. The only real difference between the two implementations is the annotations. If you're a seasoned Page Flow developer in WebLogic Workshop, you probably should spend a few more minutes examining the differences.

# So, What's Next?

You now know what annotations are. You examined the concept of annotations from a high level, and you then skimmed over the annotations that are part of Apache Beehive. As you learn more about the Apache Beehive technologies, you'll keep revisiting the concept of annotations and diving deeper into the specific annotations that you'll need to use as an Apache Beehive programmer. You need to do this because Apache Beehive uses a lot of different annotations.

Next, let's start writing some code using Apache Beehive. You'll start by using the Page Flow and NetUI technologies. Chapter 4 will provide a quick introduction to these technologies, and in Chapter 5 we will dive into the details.

CHAPTER 4

# Dissecting Java Page Flows

BEA originally launched the Java Page Flow technology with WebLogic Workshop. BEA also introduced a related technology, NetUI, which is a set of tag libraries that provide a binding between Java Page Flows (the controller layer) and Java Server Pages (the presentation layer). NetUI in Apache Beehive is a combination of the NetUI tag libraries and Java Page Flows. (In fact, we could have called this chapter "Dissecting NetUI.")

---

**Note** In this book, we'll refer to these two components as separate pieces. So, whenever we say *Page Flows*, we simply mean Java Page Flows. Whenever we say *NetUI*, we mean the NetUI tag libraries.

---

In this chapter, you'll look at the basic architecture of Java Page Flows and NetUI tags. You'll see the original Page Flows in WebLogic Workshop and then look at the Beehive version. You'll learn about the overall architecture, the classes, and the APIs you'll need to use to leverage Java Page Flows and NetUI.

The intent of this chapter is to introduce you to these technologies. You'll actually dig deeper into them in Chapter 5. Even if you've already worked with Page Flows in WebLogic Workshop, we recommend at least skimming through this chapter to get a basic overview of the differences between the two versions (WebLogic Workshop Page Flows and Beehive Page Flows). Even if you're an expert on the WebLogic Workshop version, or even if you're an expert on Beehive itself, you'll find this chapter useful as a ready-to-use reference/refresher.

## Introducing Java Page Flows

In the typical Model-View-Controller (MVC) design pattern, Java Page Flows form the controller layer. They're assisted by the NetUI tag libraries in the presentation layer. Java Page Flows are built on top of Struts—which, as you know, is one of the most widely adopted MVC frameworks available today. So, why not just use Struts?

Java Page Flows leverage the core functionality of Struts but remove a lot of the grunt work you have to do with Struts. By *grunt work*, we mean managing the deployment configuration files (such as the `struts-config.xml` file). The original version of Page Flows from BEA introduced a declarative programming language that was automatically generated and maintained by

WebLogic Workshop. The Apache Beehive version of Page Flows uses JSR 175 for its metadata definition. (You saw the details of this in Chapter 3.)

As mentioned, Page Flows leverage all the features of Struts, such as the validation framework. You'll see this in more detail in Chapter 5. You can actually have a single Web application that has a combination of Struts and Page Flows.

So, let's actually look at a Page Flow.

## Page Flows in WebLogic Workshop

This book is not about WebLogic Workshop, so we won't go into the details of how you start building Page Flows in WebLogic Workshop. Let's just assume that you built a simple HelloWorld Page Flow using WebLogic Workshop (see Listing 4-1).

---

■ **Note** See the BEA Web site (`http://www.bea.com`) for information on how to download and install BEA WebLogic Workshop 8.1. See the documentation on the BEA developer site (`http://edocs.bea.com`) to learn how to work with BEA Page Flows.

---

**Listing 4-1.** *`helloworld.jpf` in WebLogic Workshop*

```
package helloworld;
import com.bea.wlw.netui.pageflow.Forward;
import com.bea.wlw.netui.pageflow.PageFlowController;

/**
 * @jpf:controller
 * @jpf:view-properties view-properties::
 * <!-- This data is autogenerated.
* Hand-editing this section is not recommended. -->
 * <view-properties>
 * <pageflow-object id="pageflow:/helloworld/HelloWorldController.jpf"/>
 * <pageflow-object id="action:begin.do">
 *   <property value="80" name="x"/>
 *   <property value="100" name="y"/>
 * </pageflow-object>
 * <pageflow-object id="forward:path#success#helloworld.jsp#@action:begin.do@">
 *   <property value="44,20,20,60" name="elbowsX"/>
 *   <property value="92,92,-4,-4" name="elbowsY"/>
 *   <property value="West_1" name="fromPort"/>
 *   <property value="North_1" name="toPort"/>
 *   <property value="success" name="label"/>
 * </pageflow-object>
 * <pageflow-object id="page:helloworld.jsp">
 *   <property value="60" name="x"/>
 *   <property value="40" name="y"/>
```

```
 * </pageflow-object>
 * </view-properties>
 * ::
 */
public class HelloWorldController extends PageFlowController
{


    // Uncomment this declaration to access Global.app.
    //
    //     protected global.Global globalApp;
    //

    // For an example of Page Flow exception handling,
    // see the example "catch" and "exception-handler"
    // annotations in {project}/WEB-INF/src/global/Global.app

    /**
     * This method represents the point of entry into the Page Flow
     * @jpf:action
     * @jpf:forward name="success" path="helloworld.jsp"
     */
    protected Forward begin()
    {
        return new Forward("success");
    }
}
```

Notice that this code snippet is mostly full of Java comments. As described in Chapter 3, these are the different annotations that support the execution of the actual Page Flow.

All Page Flows have a `begin` method. This is similar to the `main` method in a Java class. In this example, the `begin` method does only one thing: it directs you to the `helloworld.jsp` page. Listing 4-2 shows this JSP.

**Listing 4-2.** *`helloworld.jsp` in WebLogic Workshop*

```
<%@ page language="java" contentType="text/html;charset=UTF-8"%>
<%@ taglib uri="netui-tags-databinding.tld" prefix="netui-data"%>
<%@ taglib uri="netui-tags-html.tld" prefix="netui"%>
<%@ taglib uri="netui-tags-template.tld" prefix="netui-template"%>
<netui:html>
    <head>
        <title>
            WebLogic Workshop - Hello World
        </title>
    </head>
```

```
    <body>
        <p>
           Hello World !!
        </p>
    </body>
</netui:html>
```

This JSP is simple enough. You can easily compile and deploy this Page Flow from within WebLogic Workshop and see its execution.

---

■ **Note** BEA WebLogic 9.*x* (`http://e-docs.bea.com`) will be based on the Apache Beehive version of Page Flows rather than the proprietary version of Page Flows you'll find in BEA WebLogic 8.1.

---

Now, let's see the same Page Flow in Apache Beehive.

## Page Flows in Apache Beehive

The HelloWorld example in Beehive looks a little different from the WebLogic Workshop version. Let's first look at the controller in Listing 4-3.

**Listing 4-3.** *`helloworld.jpf` in Apache Beehive*

```
import org.apache.beehive.netui.pageflow.PageFlowController;
import org.apache.beehive.netui.pageflow.annotations.Jpf;
import org.apache.beehive.netui.pageflow.Forward;

@Jpf.Controller (

        simpleActions= {

                @Jpf.SimpleAction (name="cancel", path="begin.do")
                }
)

public class HelloWorldController extends PageFlowController

{
```

```
@Jpf.Action (
        forwards= {
                @Jpf.Forward (name="success", path="helloworld.jsp")
                }
        )
 public Forward begin()

 {
        return new Forward("success"); }
```

You'll immediately notice that this version of the Java Page Flow is a lot shorter and crisper. All the Javadocs annotations at the beginning of the class code are no longer needed in the Apache Beehive version. Listing 4-4 shows the JSP that goes with this controller.

**Listing 4-4.** *`helloworld.jsp` in Apache Beehive*

```
<%@ page language="java" contentType="text/html;charset=UTF-8"%>
<%@ taglib uri="http://beehive.apache.org/netui/tags-html-1.0" prefix="netui"%>
<netui:html>
  <head>
    <title>beehive - hello world</title>
    <netui:base/>
  </head>
  <netui:body>
    <p>
      Hello World !!
      <br>
     </p>
  </netui:body>
</netui:html>
```

The "How to Run the Sample Code" sidebar will show you how to set up and run this example in your own environment.

## HOW TO RUN THE SAMPLE CODE

Use the following steps to set up and run the HelloWorld example in your own environment.

### Make a Project Folder

First, make sure you've read Appendix A. Then, on your C: drive, create a directory named `beehive-projects`. In the `beehive-projects` directory, create a directory named `helloworld`. Before proceeding, confirm that the following directory structure exists:

```
C: \
  beehive-projects
    helloworld
```

*Continued*

### Copy Runtime JARs to the Project Folder

Copy the folder `BEEHIVE_HOME/samples/netui-blank/resources` into your project folder, `C:\beehive_projects\helloworld`. `BEEHIVE_HOME` is the top-level folder of your Beehive installation, as explained in Appendix A.

Copy the folder `BEEHIVE_HOME/samples/netui-blank/WEB-INF` into your project folder, `C:\beehive-projects\helloworld`.

Now, assemble the runtime resources for your Page Flow application. The runtime JARs include the Page Flow runtime, the `NetUI` tag library, and so on. You can load these resources into your project's `WEB-INF/lib` folder using the following Ant command at the command prompt:

```
ant -f %BEEHIVE_HOME%\ant\buildWebapp.xml
    -Dwebapp.dir=C:\beehive-projects\helloworld deploy.beehive.webapp.runtime
```

This command will copy all JAR files to the `WEB-INF/lib` directory. Next, create the controller file, the central file for any Page Flow. Then, in the directory `C:/beehive-projects/helloworld`, create a file named `HelloWorldController.jpf`. In a text editor (or your IDE of choice), open the file `HelloWorldController.jpf`. In the directory `C:/beehive-projects/helloworld`, create a file named `helloworld.jsp`.

### Compile and Deploy the Page Flow

You're now ready to compile the Page Flow and deploy it to Tomcat. Start the Tomcat server. Using the command shell opened in the previous step, at the command prompt, enter the following:

```
ant -f  %BEEHIVE_HOME%\ant\buildWebapp.xml
   -Dwebapp.dir=C:\beehive-projects\helloworld
   -Dcontext.path=helloworld  build.webapp  deploy
```

To undeploy the application, use the following Ant command:

```
ant  -f %BEEHIVE_HOME%\ant\buildWebapp.xml
   -Dwebapp.dir=C:\beehive-projects\helloworld
   -Dcontext.path=helloworld  undeploy
```

Let's now look at a more detailed example. In this example, you'll extend the HelloWorld controller to actually have some basic "login" functionality.

Figure 4-1 shows the basic functionality you'll implement in the HelloWorld controller.

For this example, you'll implement three actions—`begin`, `processLogin`, and `showLogin`—that go to three different JSPs. There's a login form where the user can fill in their username and password. When the user submits the form, they will be directed to `success.jsp`. Listing 4-5 shows the controller code for this simple Page Flow.

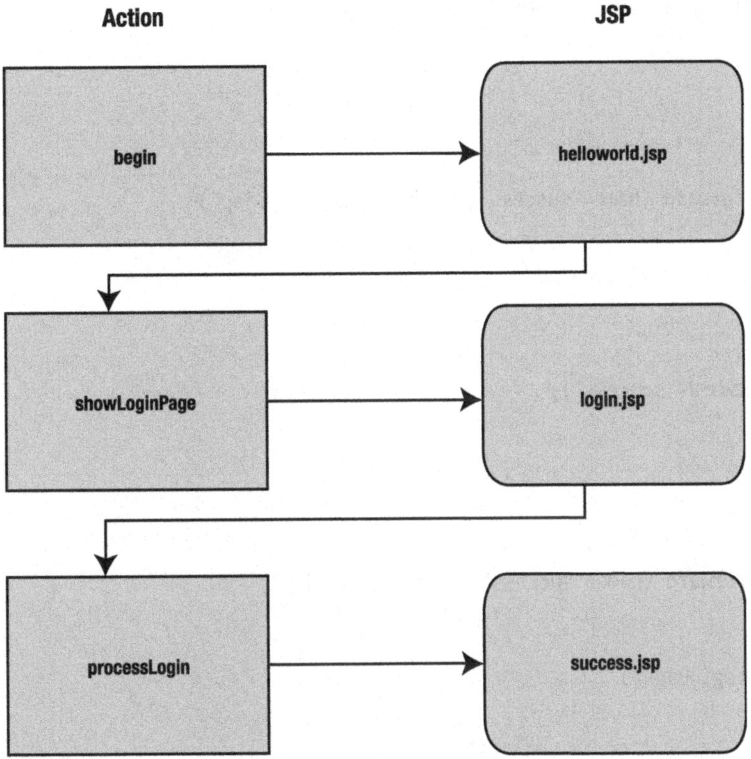


**Figure 4-1.** *Basic login process in the HelloWorld controller*

**Listing 4-5.** *`helloworld.jpf` Extended for Login Functionality*

```
import org.apache.beehive.netui.pageflow.PageFlowController;
import org.apache.beehive.netui.pageflow.annotations.Jpf;
import org.apache.beehive.netui.pageflow.Forward;

import helloworld.forms.LoginForm;


@Jpf.Controller (

        simpleActions= {

                @Jpf.SimpleAction (name="cancel", path="begin.do")
                }
)
```

```
public class HelloWorldController extends PageFlowController

{

@Jpf.Action (
        forwards= {
                @Jpf.Forward (name="success", path="helloworld.jsp")
                }
        )
 public Forward begin()

 {
        return new Forward("success");
 }


@Jpf.Action (
        forwards= {
                @Jpf.Forward (name="success", path="login.jsp")
                }
        )
  public Forward showLoginPage()

 {
        return new Forward("success"); }

 @Jpf.Action(
        forwards = {
            @Jpf.Forward(name = "success", path = "success.jsp")
        }
    )
    public Forward processLogin(LoginForm form)
    {
        System.out.println("User Name: " + form.getUsername());
        System.out.println("Password: " + form.getPassword());
        return new Forward("success");
    }


}
```

To make this work, add just one line of code to `helloworld.jsp`:

```
<netui:anchor action="showLoginPage">Login</netui:anchor>
```

This translates to a link that the user can click in `helloworld.jsp`. This will trigger the `showLoginPage` action and take the user to `login.jsp`. Listing 4-6 shows `login.jsp`.

**Listing 4-6.** *login.jsp*

```
<%@ page language="java" contentType="text/html;charset=UTF-8"%>
<%@ taglib uri="http://beehive.apache.org/netui/tags-html-1.0" prefix="netui"%>
<netui:html>
  <head>
    <title>Login</title>
    <netui:base/>
  </head>
  <netui:body>
    <p>
     <p>
           <netui:form action="processLogin">
           <p>User Name:
                 <netui:textBox dataSource="actionForm.username"/>
              <p>Password:
              <netui:textBox dataSource="actionForm.password"
                            password="true" size="20"  />
             <dataSource="actionForm.name"/>
             <p><netui:button type="submit">Submit</netui:button>
             <netui:button  action="cancel">Cancel</netui:button>
           </netui:form>
         </p>

    </p>
  </netui:body>
</netui:html>
```

The login JSP introduces the concept of a form. This is a basic form that looks a lot like a JavaBean or a Struts form class. It has basic getters and setters for the fields you've displayed in the JSP. NetUI and Page Flows provide automatic binding between the form variables and the JSP fields. (You'll learn more about this in Chapter 5.) Listing 4-7 shows the `LoginForm` class.

**Listing 4-7.** *LoginForm.java*

```
package helloworld.forms;

import org.apache.beehive.netui.pageflow.FormData;

public class LoginForm extends FormData
{

    private String username;
    private String password;
```

```
    public void setUsername(String name)
    {
        this.username = name;
    }

    public String getUsername()
    {
        return this.username;
    }

    public void setPassword(String password)
    {
        this.password= password;
    }

    public String getPassword()
    {
        return this.password;
    }
}
```

The example you've just seen is very basic. However, it will help you identify the different pieces of the Page Flow architecture.

# Introducing Page Flow Architecture

In the following sections, we'll talk about the basic architecture and components that make up Java Page Flows and the NetUI tags.

## Page Flow Components

The different components of a Page Flow are as follows:

- Controllers
- Form classes

### Controllers

The `Jpf.Controller` annotation is the meat of a Page Flow. It's just a file that contains Java code and annotations. The extension of this file is `.jpf`. As you saw in the previous example, a controller consists of several actions. This is unlike Struts—where one action is one class. You can think of a controller as a collection of action classes. The different annotations of a Page Flow are as follows:

- Jpf.Catch[]: Exceptions that the controller catches. We always recommend catching at least the Exception class to handle any unexpected/unhandled exceptions.
- Jpf.Forward[]: The different forwards. Each action has one or many forwards.
- global forwards: Any global forwards. For example, when an exception is caught, you might need a global forward. We always recommend having at least one of these go to some error page when an exception is thrown, as described in the Jpf.Catch item.
- boolean loginRequired: Does this controller require the user to be logged in to execute the actions defined in this Page Flow?
- Jpf.MessageResource[] messageResources: Which message resources to use for error messages. This is similar to the Struts message resources.
- Jpf.MultipartHandler multipartHandler: Does this controller need to access multipart forms?
- boolean nested: Is this Page Flow a nested Page Flow?
- boolean readOnly: The actions do not modify any member variables.
- String[] rolesAllowed: The roles that can access actions in this Page Flow.
- Jpf.SimpleAction[] simpleActions: The simple actions in this Page Flow.
- boolean singleton: Is this Page Flow a singleton?
- String strutsMerge: The location of the Struts merge file.
- Jpf.ValidatableBean[] validatableBeans: The validation rules for the beans.
- String validatorMerge: The location of the ValidatorPlugIn merge file.

---

■ **Caution** Since Apache Beehive is still in early development, we recommend looking at the Javadocs online for the latest and greatest list of methods and functionality. See http://incubator.apache.org/beehive/apidocs/classref_pageflows/index.html.

---

The PageFlowController class provides more than just actions. Figure 4-2 shows the basic relations between the FlowController parent class and the PageFlowController class. (Note that the figure shows only some of the methods in the classes; see the Javadocs for a complete listing of all the methods available in these classes.)

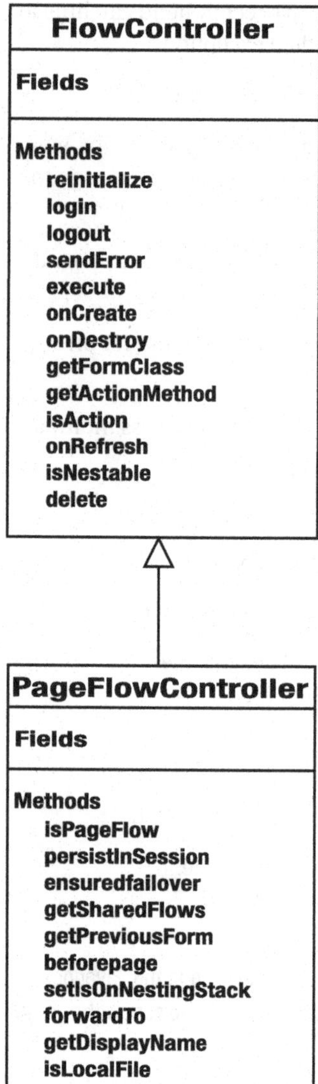


**Figure 4-2.** *Class diagram of* `FlowController` *and* `PageFlowController`

Let's look at a few of the methods that you might use more regularly than others:

- `afterAction`: This method is a callback that occurs after any user action method is invoked.
- `beforeAction`: This method executes before any action executes. It's sort of a `preProcess` method for an action.
- `onCreate`: This executes when the Page Flow is created; you can use it to initialize any instance variables for the Page Flow.

- `onDestroy`: This executes when the Page Flow is destroyed; you can use it to clean up any variables.
- `onRefresh`: This is specifically important in a portal environment when no action needs to be executed and you'd rather just render a previously displayed JSP.
- `isNestable`: This determines whether this Page Flow can be nested.
- `isSingleton`: This determines whether this Page Flow is a singleton.

---

■ **Tip** As you start working with Page Flows, refer to the `PageFlowUtils` class. It provides a bunch of helper methods that you'll find useful.

---

## Action and Forward Classes

Integral parts of using a Page Flow controller are the action classes and the forward classes. Let's quickly take a look at what they offer.

### Action

The following are the annotations that are available for an action class:

- `Jpf.Catch[]`: The different exceptions caught by this action.
- `Jpf.Forward[]`: The different forwards defined by this action.
- `boolean loginRequired`: Does this action require that the user be logged in?
- `boolean readOnly`: A guarantee that this action does not change any Page Flow variables.
- `String[] rolesAllowed`: The roles that can access this action.
- `String useFormBean`: The form bean that this action class uses.
- `Jpf.ValidatableProperty[] validatableProperties`: The properties of the form bean that need to be validated.
- `Jpf.Forward validationErrorForward`: The forward to use when there is any validation error.

### Forward

The following are the annotations offered by the forward classes:

- `Jpf.ActionOutput[] actionOutputs`: List of action outputs.
- `boolean externalRedirect`: Redirect to some external action
- `Jpf.NavigateTo navigateTo`: The page or action to navigate to
- `String outputFormBean`: Output form bean

- `Class outputFormBeanType`: Output form bean type
- `String path`: The path to forward too, usually a JSP
- `boolean redirect`: Redirect or not
- `boolean restoreQueryString`: Whether the original query string will be restored on a rerun of a previous action
- `String returnAction`: The action to be executed on the original Page Flow

---

■ **Tip** We recommend you look at the different methods on the `Forward` object. They will prove to be useful as you start building complex Page Flow applications.

---

## NetUI Components

NetUI is a set of tag libraries that you will use as part of your JSPs. These tag libraries are JSP 2.0 complaint. Three tag libraries make up NetUI:

- `NetUI`
- `NetUI-data`
- `NetUI-template`

---

■ **Caution** The `NetUI-data` and `NetUI-template` tag libraries depend on the `NetUI` tag libraries. All the base classes for the three tag libraries are provided as part of the `NetUI` (HTML) tag library.

---

The basic functionality in these tag libraries is to simplify JSP development and provide automatic data binding between the view and controller layers. These tags come with JavaScript support, so you can work with them like you would the standard HTML tags (input, select, and so on).

---

■ **Note** You will see examples of how to use each of the tags in the next chapter.

---

### NetUI

The `NetUI` name is a little misleading. Think of this tag library as `NetUI-html`. That makes it clearer, doesn't it? This tag library contains the tags similar to the `struts-html` tag library. Table 4-1, which comes straight from the Javadocs, shows the tags in this library. As you'll see, this library contains the standard tags that you might use with vanilla HTML development.

**Note** The reason I've simply cut and paste the information from the Javadocs is because, at the time of writing this book, Apache Beehive is still in the beta stage. Therefore, some of these methods might change. Visit the Beehive documentation page for the latest Javadocs at `http://incubator.apache.org/beehive/reference/taglib/index.html`.

**Table 4-1.** *NetUI Tag Library*

| Tag | Description |
| --- | --- |
| `<netui:anchor>` | Generates an anchor that can link to another document or invoke an action method in the controller file |
| `<netui:attribute>` | Adds an attribute to the parent tag rendered in the browser |
| `<netui:base>` | Provides the base for every URL on the page |
| `<netui:bindingUpdateErrors>` | Renders the set of error messages found during the process of resolving data binding expressions (`{pageFlow.firstname}`, `{request.firstname}`, and so on) |
| `<netui:body>` | Renders an HTML `<body>` tag with the attributes specified |
| `<netui:button>` | Renders an HTML button with the specified attributes |
| `<netui:checkBox>` | Generates a single HTML checkbox |
| `<netui:checkBoxGroup>` | Handles data binding for a collection of checkboxes |
| `<netui:checkBoxOption>` | Renders a single HTML checkbox within a group of checkboxes |
| `<netui:content>` | Displays text or the result of an expression |
| `<netui:error>` | Renders an error message with a given error key value if that key can be found in the `ActionErrors` registered in the `PageContext` at `org.apache.struts.action.Action.ERROR_KEY` |
| `<netui:errors>` | Renders the set of error messages found in the `ActionErrors` registered in the `PageContext` at `org.apache.struts.action.Action.ERROR_KEY` |
| `<netui:exceptions>` | Renders exception messages and stack traces inline on the JSP |
| `<netui:fileUpload>` | Renders an HTML input tag with which users can browse, select, and upload files from their local machines |
| `<netui:form>` | Renders an HTML form that can be submitted to a Java method in the controller file for processing |
| `<netui:formatDate>` | Renders a formatter used to format dates |
| `<netui:formatNumber>` | Renders a formatter used to format numbers |
| `<netui:formatString>` | Renders a formatter used to format strings |

**Table 4-1.** *NetUI Tag Library (Continued)*

| Tag | Description |
| --- | --- |
| <netui:hidden> | Generates an HTML hidden tag with a given value |
| <netui:html> | Renders an <html> tag |
| <netui:image> | Renders an HTML <image> tag with the specified attributes |
| <netui:imageAnchor> | Generates a hyperlink with a clickable image |
| <netui:imageButton> | Renders an <input type="image"> tag with the specified attributes |
| <netui:label> | Associates text with an input element in a form |
| <netui:parameter> | Writes a name-value pair to the URL or the parent tag |
| <netui:parameterMap> | Writes a group of name-value pairs to the URL or the parent tag |
| <netui:radioButtonGroup> | Renders a collection of radio button options and handles the data binding of their values |
| <netui:radioButtonOption> | Generates a single radio button option in a group of options |
| <netui:rewriteName> | Allows a name, typically either an id or name attribute, to participate in URL rewriting |
| <netui:rewriteURL> | Allows a tag name, typically either an id or name attribute, to participate in URL rewriting |
| <netui:scriptContainer> | Acts as a container that will bundle JavaScript created by other <netui...> tags and outputs it within a single <script> tag |
| <netui:scriptHeader> | Writes the <script> that JavaScript will include in the HTML <head> tag |
| <netui:select> | Renders an HTML <select> tag containing a set of selectable options |
| <netui:selectOption> | Renders a single <option> tag |
| <netui:span> | Generates styled text based on a String literal or data binding expression |
| <netui:textArea> | Renders an HTML <input> tag of type "text" |
| <netui:textBox> | Renders an HTML <input type="text"> tag |
| <netui:tree><br><netui:treeContent><br><netui:treeHtmlAttribute><br><netui:treeItem><br><netui:treeLabel><br><netui:treePropertyOverride> | Renders a navigable tree of TreeElement tags |

## NetUI-data

The NetUI-data tag library is used to bind data from forms and the controller to the JSP. It allows you to quickly display lists of data (such as search results). See Table 4-2, which shows the Javadocs information about this tag library.

**Table 4-2.** *NetUI-data Tag Library*

| Tag | Description |
|---|---|
| <netui-data:anchorColumn> | |
| <netui-data:callMethod> | Calls methods on any Java classes |
| <netui-data:callPageFlow> | Calls methods on the controller file (which is a JPF file) in the same directory as the JSP |
| <netui-data:caption> | |
| <netui-data:cellRepeater> | Renders individual cells of an HTML table |
| <netui-data:columns> | |
| <netui-data:configurePager> | |
| <netui-data:dataGrid> | |
| <netui-data:declareBundle> | Declares a java.util.ResourceBundle as a source for displaying internationalized messages |
| <netui-data:declarePageInput> | Declares variables that are passed from the controller file to the JSP |
| <netui-data:footer> | |
| <netui-data:getData> | Evaluates an expression and places the result in the javax.servlet.jsp.PageContext object, where the data is available to JSP scriptlets |
| <netui-data:imageColumn> | |
| <netui-data:literalColumn> | |
| <netui-data:message> | Provides a message schema, which can be parameterized to construct customizable messages |
| <netui-data:messageArg> | Provides a parameter value to a message schema |
| <netui-data:methodParameter> | Provides an argument to a method-calling tag |
| <netui-data:pad> | Sets the number of items rendered by a tag |
| <netui-data:renderPager> | |
| <netui-data:repeater> | Iterates over a data set to render it as HTML |
| <netui-data:repeaterFooter> | Renders the footer of a Repeater tag |
| <netui-data:repeaterHeader> | Renders the header of a Repeater tag |
| <netui-data:repeaterItem> | Renders an individual item in the data set as it's iterated over by the Repeater tag |
| <netui-data:serializeXML> | Serializes an XMLBean into the output of a JSP in order to move data to the browser for data binding |

### NetUI-template

The `NetUI-template` tag library is used to create subsections (or templates) from your JSPs. See Table 4-3, which displays the Javadocs information about this tag library.

**Table 4-3.** *`NetUI-template` Tag Library*

| Tag | Description |
|---|---|
| `<netui-template:attribute>` | Defines a property placeholder within a template |
| `<netui-template:divPanel>` | Creates an HTML `<div>` tag that may contain additional tags |
| `<netui-template:includeSection>` | Defines a content placeholder within a template |
| `<netui-template:section>` | Sets HTML content inside placeholders defined by an `IncludeSection` tag |
| `<netui-template:setAttribute>` | Sets a property value in a template page |
| `<netui-template:template>` | Points a content page at its template page |

You've just seen a brief overview of Page Flows and NetUI. Now let's see how all this plays together.

## Reviewing Page Flow Architecture

The best way to explain the overall architecture of Page Flows and NetUI is to map these to the standard MVC model, as shown in Figure 4-3.

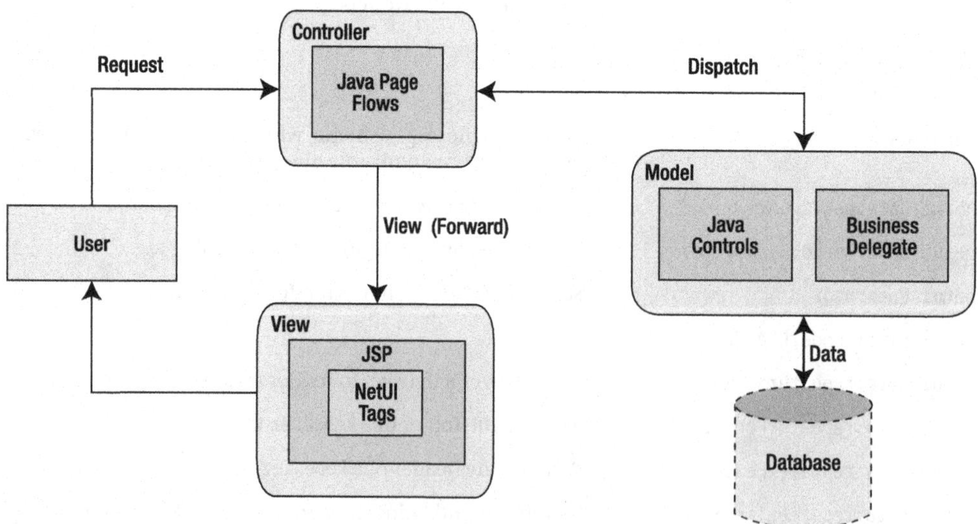


**Figure 4-3.** *MVC architecture of Page Flows and NetUI*

Think of the controller bucket as being the Page Flow controllers. If you're familiar with Struts, this bucket is filled by Struts actions. The *view* is a collection of JSPs and some tag libraries, in this case the NetUI tag libraries. In Struts, it would be the Struts tag libraries. The model layer is not really predetermined by Page Flows. As part of the Apache Beehive project, there is a technology called *Controls*. This is a model layer technology, which we'll discuss in Chapter 6.

However, for purposes of Java Page Flows, the model layer could be anything. You could obviously use Controls. Or, you could have a set of Java classes that serve as business delegates, which then interact with your EJBs, DAOs, and other classes.

Throughout the chapter, I've alluded to the real advantages of Page Flows over Struts:

- *Ease of use*: The main development savings between Struts and Page Flows is the JSR 175 metadata support. While developing Page Flows, you don't need to manually maintain the `struts-config` files.
- *Data binding*: With Page Flows and NetUI, you get automatic data binding between the form variables and the form fields in the JSP.
- *Exception handling*: This goes back to the annotations. You can define how all your exceptions get handled using the annotations. As a best practice, we recommend always catching the `Exception` class at the Page Flow level. This allows you to handle any otherwise uncaught exceptions.
- *Nested Page Flows*: The whole concept of nested Page Flows is new. We'll explain this in Chapter 5.
- *State management*: Page Flows automatically maintain state. This feature is even more important if you're working with portals.
- *Portal use*: Page Flows were originally developed for portal development. Thus, a lot of the features are targeted toward portal projects.
- *Service orientation*: The integration of Page Flows with Java Controls leads to a more service-oriented approach for application development.

# So, What's Next?

In this chapter, you saw the basic components that make up Java Page Flows and NetUI. You also looked at a quick example and then drilled down into the overall architecture of these technologies. Now, let's really see some examples that show you how to work with these technologies and explore all the features. We recommend jumping to Appendix B to learn how to set up the Eclipse Pollinate IDE to build Page Flows and then turning to Chapter 5.

CHAPTER 5

# Using NetUI and Page Flows

In the previous chapter, you learned the basics of NetUI and Page Flows. In this chapter, we'll show how to build a Page Flow controller and how to use the various NetUI tags. In the process, we'll also show how to build a simple bookstore application using these technologies.

## Creating the Sample Bookstore Application

The sample application you'll create in this book is a bookstore application. In this chapter, you'll build some basic functionality for the application, which isn't database-driven. You'll hard-code the list of books that the application will use. In later chapters, as you learn more about Web Services and Controls, you'll extend this example to use those technologies to connect to the Amazon.com Web Service and to a database using a Database Control.

### Setting Up the Bookstore Application

So, first refer to Appendix B to set up Eclipse and Pollinate. Once you've done that, launch Eclipse, and create a Pollinate Web application. Call it *bookstore*.

Next, from the code that you downloaded from the Apress Web site, copy the code from the `demo` directory in the project's folder:

```
<ECLIPSE HOME>\workspace\BookStore\bookStoreWebApp\demo
```

Typically, the code should compile correctly, without any errors. If there are errors, they might be specific to your installation. For example, you'll need to set the Pollinate plug-ins to use JDK 1.5.

To do this, make sure you're pointing to a JDK 1.5 directory, not a JRE 1.5 directory. You can do this in the Preferences dialog box, as shown in Figure 5-1; open it by selecting the Window ➤ Preferences menu item.

Another common issue is that to run Pollinate you need the `tools.jar` file from your JDK to be in the `bootclasspath`. To do this, you'll need to modify your `eclipse.bat` file to look like this:

```
set JDK_HOME=c:\java\jdk1.5.0
eclipse -vm "C:\Program Files\Java\jre1.5.0\bin\javaw"
-vmargs -Xmx256M -Xbootclasspath/a:%JDK_HOME%\lib\tools.jar
```

Once you have these basic things taken care of, you should be able to simply right-click the project (anywhere in the Eclipse Navigator) and select Run Web App.

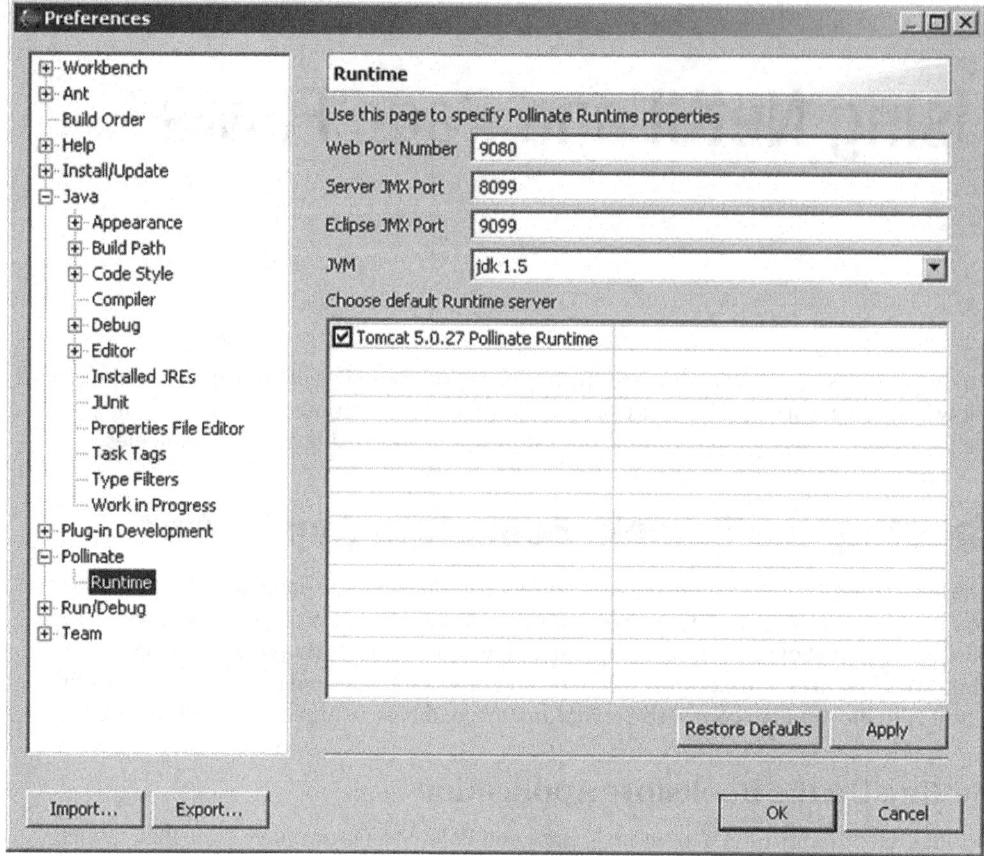


**Figure 5-1.** *Setting up Pollinate to use the correct JDK*

## Running the Sample Bookstore Application

When you run the application, you'll see three basic screens:

- Add Book
- View Book Details
- Search Book

Go through the screens to get a feel for what this sample application does. Granted, it's pretty basic for now.

We'll now explain the code for this application so you can understand the different aspects of the Page Flow and NetUI technologies involved.

## Looking at the Code

The code for this application is quite simple. You have one controller (or Page Flow) and a few JSPs. Let's start by looking at the controller.

## Controller

This controller is as basic as it gets. However, it will help lay the foundation of what a Page Flow controller looks like and how you can work with different methods within this controller. Listing 5-1 shows the complete code. After the listing, we'll explain it piece by piece.

**Listing 5-1.** *The Bookstore Controller*

```
package demo;

import org.apache.beehive.netui.pageflow.PageFlowController;
import org.apache.beehive.netui.pageflow.Forward;
import org.apache.beehive.netui.pageflow.annotations.Jpf;
import java.util.HashMap;

@Jpf.Controller(
 messageResources = {
        @Jpf.MessageResource(name = "Messages")
    }
)
public class Controller extends PageFlowController {

    public HashMap bookTypes = new HashMap();

    protected void onCreate()   {
        bookTypes.put("book","Book");
        bookTypes.put("magazine","Magazine");
        bookTypes.put("journal","Journal");
        bookTypes.put("newspaper","News Paper");
        bookTypes.put("electronic","e-books & Docs");
    }


    /**
     * This method represents the point of entry into the Page Flow
     */
     @Jpf.Action(
        forwards = {
            @Jpf.Forward(name="success",path="bookMenu.jsp")
        }
     )
    protected Forward begin()     {
        return new Forward("success");
    }
```

```
    @Jpf.Action(
     forwards = {
         @Jpf.Forward(
             name = "success",
             path = "addBook.jsp")
     }
    )

     protected Forward showAddBookPage()
{
    return new Forward("success",new BookForm());
}

  @Jpf.Action(
    forwards = {
        @Jpf.Forward(
            name = "success",
            path = "searchBook.jsp")
    }
  )

protected Forward showSearchBookPage()    {
    return new Forward("success");
}

  @Jpf.Action(
    forwards = {
        @Jpf.Forward(
            name = "success",
            path = "addBook.jsp")
    },
    validationErrorForward = @Jpf.Forward(name =
            "failure", navigateTo = Jpf.NavigateTo.currentPage)
  )

protected Forward addBook(BookForm form)   {
    return new Forward("success", new BookForm());
}

 @Jpf.Action(
    forwards = {
        @Jpf.Forward(
            name = "success",
            path = "searchResults.jsp")
    }
 )
```

```
    protected Forward searchBooks()
    {
        return new Forward("success");
    }
      @Jpf.Action(
        forwards = {
            @Jpf.Forward(
                name = "success",
                path = "viewBook.jsp")
        }
      )

    protected Forward viewBook()    {
        return new Forward("success",getBook());
    }

      @Jpf.Action(
        forwards = {
            @Jpf.Forward(
                name = "success",
                path = "viewBook.jsp")
        }
      )

    protected Forward submitForm(BookForm form)
    {

        return new Forward("success",getBook());
    }

    private BookForm getBook()
    {
        BookForm bookDetails= new BookForm();
        bookDetails.setName("Pro Apache Beehive");
        bookDetails.setType("Book");
        bookDetails.setAuthor("Kunal, Srini");
        bookDetails.setIsbn 1-59059-515-7");
        bookDetails.setCatalogNo("101");
        bookDetails.setPublication("Apress");
        bookDetails.setPublicationDate("07/05/2005");
        bookDetails.setComments("This book teaches you how to work with
              Apache Beehive and XMLBeans.");
        bookDetails.setInStock(true);

        return bookDetails;
    }
}
```

The logical place to start dissecting this controller is at the top. First, you will see a set of import statements. These should be nothing new to a Java programmer, so let's move on. The next block of code is an annotation:

```
@Jpf.Controller(
 messageResources = {
        @Jpf.MessageResource(name = "Messages")
    }
    )
```

This annotation specifies a resource bundle. In this case, a file called `Messages` must exist in the classpath (under the `WEB-INF/classes`). This displays the error message caused by validation. Moving on, the next block of code you'll encounter is as follows:

```
public HashMap bookTypes = new HashMap();

protected void onCreate()   {
    bookTypes.put("book","Book");
    bookTypes.put("magazine","Magazine");
    bookTypes.put("journal","Journal");
    bookTypes.put("newspaper","News Paper");
    bookTypes.put("electronic","e-books & Docs");
}
```

This defines an instance variable called `bookTypes`. In other words, there's nothing special here. The next method is `onCreate`. As you've probably guessed, this method is called when an instance of this controller is created. Think of this as the constructor to this class. In this example, you're populating the instance variable `bookTypes` in the `onCreate` method. It's important to remember that `onCreate` is not an action. It's a plain old Java method.

Similar to the `onCreate` method, you'll see an `onDestroy` method and an `onRefresh` method. The `onDestroy` method is similar to a destructor. The `onRefresh` method is specifically useful in portal applications. You can use it to do some processing when a page is refreshed or when a portlet is refreshed.

---

■ **Note** If you're using any session variables, or placing things into the session, the `onDestroy` method is a good place to do some cleanup. You shouldn't leave stuff in the session any longer than is absolutely needed. This method is executed when the controller class is destroyed.

---

The next snippet of code is the `begin` action:

```
 @Jpf.Action(
    forwards = {
        @Jpf.Forward(name="success",path="bookMenu.jsp")
    })
protected Forward begin()     {
    return new Forward("success");
}
```

The begin action is similar to the main method in a Java class. It's the first method that's executed by the controller (obviously after the constructor and the onCreate method). In this code snippet, you can see several things. For instance, the annotation is a forward that describes what should happen after this method is executed. In this example, you have only one place that the user can have this method execute, and that's to the bookMenu.jsp file. Any action can have several different forward annotations. These forwards can be to other actions, other controllers, or JSPs.

In this example, the begin method simply calls a forward called success, which sends you to bookMenu.jsp. In bookMenu.jsp, as you'll see in the next section, the user can click a link that calls a specific action in the controller. So, we'll now move on and show a little more of this controller.

The next interesting snippet of code is as follows:

```
protected Forward showAddBookPage()     {
    return new Forward("success",new BookForm());
}
```

On the surface this looks simple enough. The interesting thing is that you're creating a new instance of a form object and passing it to the forward. This makes a form object available to the JSP. It provides automatic data binding capabilities between the controller and the JSP via this form. The only other interesting part of this controller is the following annotation set:

```
@Jpf.Action(
     forwards = {
        @Jpf.Forward(
            name = "success",
            path = "addBook.jsp")
     },
     validationErrorForward = @Jpf.Forward(name = "failure", navigateTo = ➥
               Jpf.NavigateTo.currentPage)
 )
```

In this snippet, you see a simple forward, and you see a new annotation called validationErrorForward. What this is saying is that if there are any validation errors in processing the form, you want to forward to the failure forward. There's an inline definition of what the failure forward looks like, which is also interesting. The failure forward is saying that it should navigate to the current page. This means that on any validation error you'll return the user to the same page, which displays the error messages. The NetUI tags and the JSP take care of displaying the messages, as you'll see when we dissect the JSP in the next section.

Let's take a quick look at the BookForm class next; see Listing 5-2.

**Listing 5-2.** *BookForm Class*

```
package demo;

import org.apache.beehive.netui.pageflow.FormData;
import java.util.HashMap;
import java.util.LinkedHashMap;
import javax.servlet.http.HttpServletRequest;
```

```
import org.apache.struts.action.ActionError;
import org.apache.struts.action.ActionErrors;
import org.apache.struts.action.ActionMapping;

public class BookForm extends FormData {

        private String id=null;
        private String name=null;
        private String type=null;
        private String author=null;
        private String publication=null;
        private String publicationDate=null;
        private String isbn=null;
        private String catalogNo=null;
        private String comments=null;
         private boolean inStock=false;
         private String action=null;


    public BookForm()   {
    }

    public String getId() {
        return this.id;
    }

    public void setId(String id) {
        this.id = id;
    }

    public String getName() {
        return name;
    }

    public void setName(String name) {
        this.name = name;
    }

    public String getType() {
        return type;
    }

    public void setType(String type) {
        this.type = type;
    }
```

```
public String getAuthor() {
    return author;
}

public void setAuthor(String author) {
    this.author = author;
}

public String getPublication() {
    return publication;
}

public void setPublication(String publication) {
    this.publication = publication;
}

public String getPublicationDate() {
    return publicationDate;
}

public void setPublicationDate(String publicationDate) {
    this.publicationDate = publicationDate;
}

public String getIsbn() {
    return isbn;
}

public void setIsbn(String isbn) {
    this.isbn = isbn;
}

public String getCatalogNo() {
    return catalogNo;
}

public void setCatalogNo(String catalogNo) {
    this.catalogNo = catalogNo;
}

public String getAction() {
    return action;
}
```

```
    public void setAction(String action) {
        this.action = action;
    }

    public String getComments() {
        return comments;
    }

    public void setComments(String comments) {
        this.comments = comments;
    }

    public boolean isInStock() {
        return inStock;
    }

    public void setInStock(boolean inStock) {
        this.inStock = inStock;
    }


      public ActionErrors validate(final ActionMapping oMapping,
                      final HttpServletRequest request) {
        final ActionErrors errors = new ActionErrors();
        System.out.println("we are here");
        if (this.getName()==null || this.getName().equalsIgnoreCase("")) {
                errors.add("error.bookDetails.requiredName",
                      new ActionError("errors.required","Name\\Title"));
            }
        if (this.getType()==null || this.getType().equalsIgnoreCase("")) {
                errors.add("error.bookDetails.requiredType",
                      new ActionError("errors.required","Type"));
            }
        if (this.getAuthor()==null || this.getAuthor().equalsIgnoreCase("")) {
                errors.add("error.bookDetails.requiredAuthorName",
                      new ActionError("errors.required","Author"));
            }
        if (this.getPublication()==null ||
                this.getPublication().equalsIgnoreCase("")) {
                errors.add("error.bookDetails.requiredPublicationName",
                      new ActionError("errors.required","Publication"));
            }
        if (this.getIsbn()==null || this.getIsbn().equalsIgnoreCase("")) {
                errors.add("error.bookDetails.requiredISBN",
                      new ActionError("errors.required","ISBN"));
            }
```

```
        if (this.getCatalogNo()==null || this.getCatalogNo().equalsIgnoreCase("")) {
                errors.add("error.bookDetails.requiredCatalog",
                        new ActionError("errors.required","Catalog"));
          }

          return errors;
    }
}
```

The BookForm class looks like a simple JavaBean. The only method of real interest is the validate method. If you've worked with Struts, this should be quite familiar. Basically, you're validating each field that you need some validation rule on. If there's any error, you're adding an error key into the ActionErrors object. The error key is basically a key into the resource bundle that you specified in the controller using annotations.

---

**Note** You can also use Struts-based XML validation by defining the validation rules in an XML file.

---

You can bind each NetUI tag to any variable in the form (although you do need to worry about the "type" of data to which you bind). For example, you can't bind a checkbox to a Float variable. Table 5-1 shows the data types required for the binding to work.

**Table 5-1.** *NetUI: Form Data Binding*

| NetUI Tag | Java Data Type |
|---|---|
| <netui:checkBox> | Boolean or java.lang.Boolean |
| <netui:checkBoxGroup>, <netui:radioButtonGroup> | String[] |
| <netui:hidden>, <netui:text>, <netui:textArea> | String |

Now let's look at a couple of JSPs.

## bookMenu.jsp

Listing 5-3 shows the first JSP that's invoked by the Page Flow; this happens in the begin method.

**Listing 5-3.** *bookMenu.jsp*

```
<%@ page language="java" contentType="text/html;charset=UTF-8"%>
<%@ taglib uri="http://beehive.apache.org/netui/tags-html-1.0" prefix="netui" %>
<%@ taglib uri="http://beehive.apache.org/netui/tags-template-1.0"
      prefix="netui-template"%>
```

```
<table border="0" cellpadding="6" cellspacing="0">
  <tr><td ><span class="promo">
  <netui:anchor action="showAddBookPage"> Add Book </netui:anchor><br>
  <netui:anchor action="viewBook"> View Book Details</netui:anchor><br>
    <netui:anchor action="showSearchBookPage"> Search Book</netui:anchor><br>
  </span></td></tr>
</table>
```

Figure 5-2 shows `bookMenu.jsp`. In this JSP, you first include some tag libraries. For instance, this JSP is using the `NetUI` tag library, as introduced in the previous chapter. You're using the `<netui:anchor>` tag to create links. These anchors call an action; by default, they automatically call an action in the Page Flow in the same directory as the JSP. The NetUI anchor is probably one of the simplest tags in this tag library. We'll spare you from seeing all the attributes of the tag in this chapter. However, we recommend you explore the API documentation for the tags and other attributes. If you've used Struts or Java Standard Tag Library (JSTL), you'll see a lot of similarities between those tags and the NetUI tags.

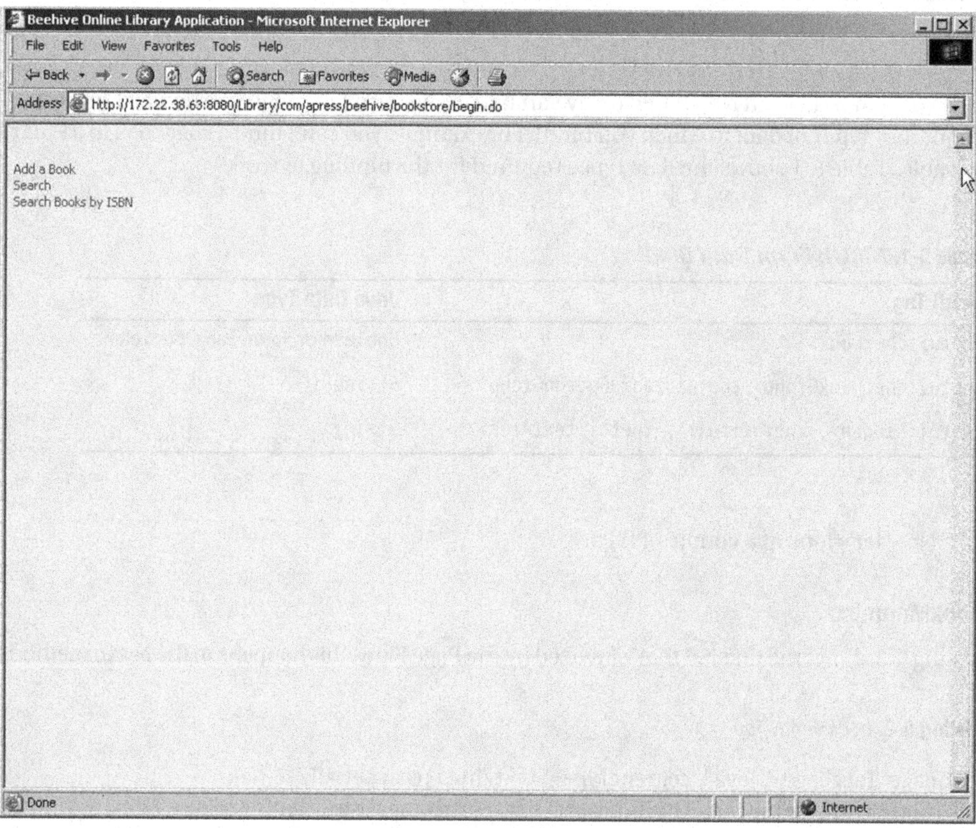


**Figure 5-2.** *bookMenu.jsp*

■ **Tip** Bookmark the tag library documentation at `http://incubator.apache.org/beehive/reference/taglib/index.html`. You'll need it a lot as you read this book and work with Beehive.

## addBook.jsp

Listing 5-4 shows `addBook.jsp` in a browser; it's invoked by the `showAddBookPage` action in the controller.

**Listing 5-4.** *addBook.jsp*

```
<%@ page language="java" contentType="text/html;charset=UTF-8"%>
<%@ taglib uri="http://beehive.apache.org/netui/tags-databinding-1.0"
      prefix="netui-data"%>
<%@ taglib uri="http://beehive.apache.org/netui/tags-html-1.0"
      prefix="netui"%>
<%@ taglib uri="http://beehive.apache.org/netui/tags-template-1.0"
     prefix="netui-template"%>

 <netui-template:template templatePage="librarytemplate.jsp">
    <netui-template:section name="body"> <center>
    <netui:form action="submitForm"
             tagId="addBookForm" genJavaScriptFormSubmit="true">
    <netui-data:declareBundle bundlePath="apress.beehive.resources.template"
           name="catalog"/>
<table border="0" cellpadding="0" cellspacing="0" width="100%">
<tr valign="top">
    <td >${bundle.catalog.addBookTitle} <br>
        Required fields are in <b>bold</b>.</td>
    <td align="right" valign="top"></td>
</tr>
</table><br>

<table border="0" cellpadding="6" cellspacing="0" width="100%">

<tr class="odd" valign="top">
    <td class="text" align="right"><b>Name/Title</b></td>
    <td class="text" ><netui:textBox tagId="name"
         dataSource="actionForm.aBook.title" size="40" styleClass="text"/>
    <netui:error key="addBook.error.requiredTitle"></netui:error></td>
</tr>
<tr class="even" valign="top">
    <td  class="text" align="right"><b>Type</b></td>
    <td class="text" ><netui:select tagId="type"
        dataSource="actionForm.aBook.book_type"
        optionsDataSource="${actionForm.bookTypes}" styleClass="text"/>
    </td>
```

```
</tr>
<tr class="odd" valign="top">
    <td  class="text" align="right"><b>Author</b></td>
    <td class="text" ><netui:textBox tagId="author"
         dataSource="actionForm.aBook.author" size="20" styleClass="text"/>
   </td>
</tr>
<tr class="even" valign="top">
    <td  class="text" align="right"><b>Publication</b> </td>
    <td class="text" ><netui:textBox tagId="publication"
        dataSource="actionForm.aBook.publication" size="20" styleClass="text" />
   </td>
</tr>
<tr class="odd" valign="top">
    <td  class="text" align="right">Publication Date</td>
    <td class="text">
        <table border="0" cellpadding="0" cellspacing="0"><tr>
        <td class="text"><netui:textBox tagId="date"
            dataSource="actionForm.aBook.publication_Date" styleClass="text"
                size="12" maxlength="10"/> </td>
        <td class="text"></td>
        </tr></table></td>
</tr>
<tr class="even" valign="top">
    <td  class="text"  align="right"><b>ISBN #</b></td>
    <td class="text" ><netui:textBox tagId="isbn"
         dataSource="actionForm.aBook.isbn" size="13" styleClass="text"/>
   </td>
</tr>
<tr class="odd" valign="top">
    <td  class="text" align="right"><b>Catalog #</b></td>
     <td class="text" ><netui:textBox tagId="catalog"
          dataSource="actionForm.aBook.catalogNo" size="20" styleClass="text"/>
     </td>
</tr>
<tr class="even" valign="top">
    <td  class="text" align="right">Comments</td>
    <td class="text" ><netui:textArea tagId="comments"
        dataSource="actionForm.aBook.comments"
                                cols="30" rows="6"  styleClass="text"/>
   <netui:error key="addBook.error.invalidLength"></netui:error></td>
</tr>
 <tr class="odd" valign="top">
    <td class="text"  align="right"> </td>
    <td class="text" ><netui:checkBox tagId="stock"
         dataSource="actionForm.aBook.available"/>In Stock</td>
</tr>
```

```
</table> <br>
<netui:button action="addBook" type="submit" styleClass="text" >
        Submit
</netui:button>
<netui:button type="reset" styleClass="text" >
       Reset
</netui:button>

 <br><br>
 <netui:anchor action="begin" styleClass="text" >${bundle.catalog.back2Menu}
  </netui:anchor>
</netui:form>
 </netui-template:section >
</netui-template:template>
```

Figure 5-3 shows addBook.jsp in a browser.

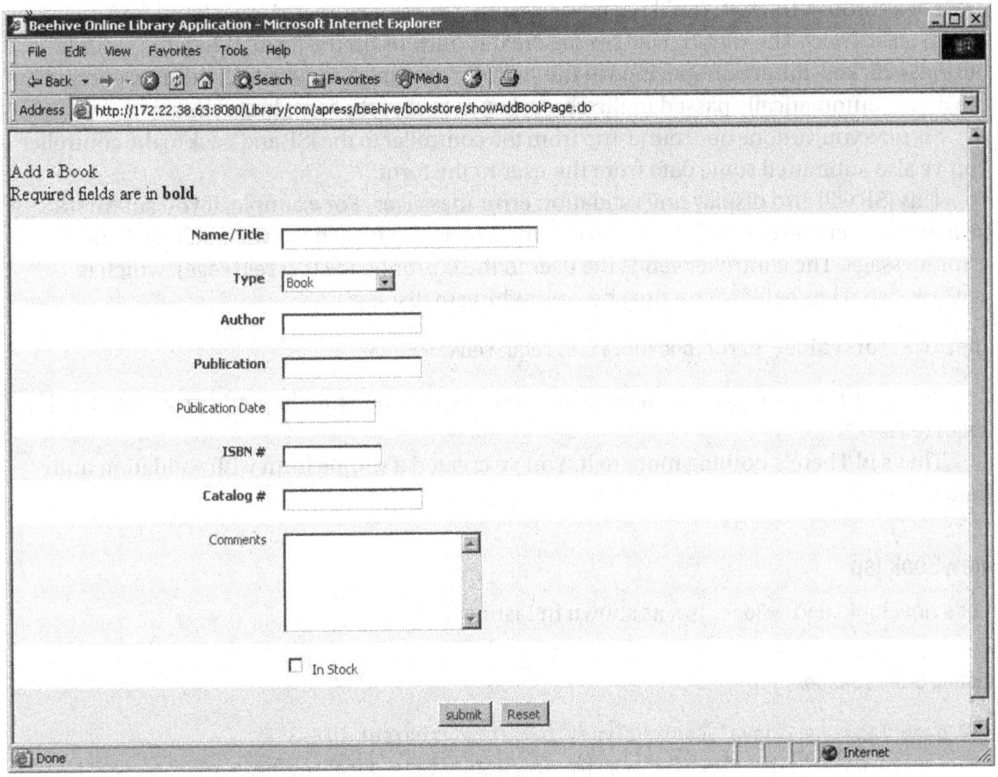

**Figure 5-3.** *addBook.jsp*

In this JSP, you can see several new NetUI tags. The first one of interest is the <netui:form> tag. This tag, as you can imagine, defines a form. You also define what action will be called when the form is submitted. Let's look at the next tag:

```
<netui:textBox tagId="name" dataSource="actionForm.name" size="40"/>
```

This tag is a little more interesting. Essentially, it's displaying a simple textbox on the JSP. However, what's interesting is the dataSource attribute, which provides automatic data binding with the form class you saw earlier. In this case, you're binding this textbox to the name field in the form. The notation actionForm does this binding. You can bind your NetUI tags to fields in a form bean or to variables in your Page Flow, as you'll see next.

In the <netui:select> tag, you're binding the selection the user makes to the type field in the form:

```
<netui:select tagId="type"  dataSource="actionForm.type"
      optionsDataSource="pageFlow.bookTypes" multiple="false" />
```

However, you have another attribute called optionsDataSource, which is bound to the bookTypes field in the Page Flow. The end result of this tag is an HTML <select> with the options populated from the content of the bookTypes variable. (Remember, you populated this in an onCreate method in the Page Flow.) When the user selects a value, this value is stored in the action form variable.

Look through the JSP. You'll see other simple tags such as <netui:textArea> and <netui:checkBox>. The <netui:button> tag creates buttons on the form. When the submit button is clicked, the action specified in the <netui:form> tag is invoked. All the data entered by the user is automatically passed to the controller as part of the form bean class.

So, now you've done one round-trip from the controller to the JSP and back to the controller. You've also submitted some data from the user to the form.

This JSP will also display any validation error messages. For example, if you submit the form without entering a name, the validate method in the form bean will fail. It will add an error message. The controller sends the user to the current page (currentPage), which is addBook.jsp. The <netui:error> tag has something to display:

```
<netui:error value="error.bookDetails.requiredName" />
```

You'll see the error message defined in your messages file, with the key "error.bookDetails.requiredName".

That's it! There's nothing more to it. You've created a simple form with validation and data binding.

## viewBook.jsp

Let's now look at viewBook.jsp, as shown in Listing 5-5.

**Listing 5-5.** *viewBook.jsp*

```
<%@ page language="java" contentType="text/html;charset=UTF-8"%>
<%@ taglib uri="http://beehive.apache.org/netui/tags-databinding-1.0"
      prefix="netui-data"%>
<%@ taglib uri="http://beehive.apache.org/netui/tags-html-1.0"
      prefix="netui"%>
<%@ taglib uri="http://beehive.apache.org/netui/tags-template-1.0"
      prefix="netui-template"%>
```

```
<netui-template:template templatePage="librarytemplate.jsp">
   <netui-template:section name="body">
 <netui:form action="addBook" tagId="viewBook" genJavaScriptFormSubmit="true">
<table border="0" cellpadding="6" cellspacing="0" class="prefbox" width="100%">
<tr>
  <td class="text">

  <table border="0" cellpadding="6" cellspacing="0" width="100%">
   <tr class="odd">
      <td class="text" valign="top" align="right"> Name/Title</td>
      <td class="text" valign="top">
        <netui:label value="${actionForm.aBook.title}" />
      </td>
      <td class="text" valign="top" align="right">Author</td>
      <td class="text" valign="top">
        <netui:label value="${actionForm.aBook.author}" />
      </td>
    </tr>
    <tr class="even">
      <td class="text" valign="top" align="right">Type</td>
      <td class="text" valign="top">
              <netui:label value="${actionForm.aBook.book_type}" />
      </td>
      <td class="text" valign="top" align="right">Publication</td>
      <td class="text" valign="top">
              <netui:label value="${actionForm.aBook.publication}" />
       </td>
    </tr>
    <tr class="odd">
      <td class="text" valign="top" align="right">Publication Date</td>
      <td class="text" valign="top">
            <netui:label value="${actionForm.aBook.publication_Date}" />
      </td>
      <td class="text" valign="top" align="right">ISBN</td>
      <td class="text" valign="top">
              <netui:label value="${actionForm.aBook.isbn}" />
      </td>
    </tr>
    <tr class="even">
      <td class="text" valign="top" align="right">Catalog</td>
      <td class="text" valign="top">
            <netui:label value="${actionForm.aBook.catalogNo}" />
       </td>
    </tr>
    <tr class="odd">
      <td class="text" valign="top" align="right">Comments</td>
      <td class="text" valign="top" colspan="3">
```

```
                <netui:label value="${actionForm.aBook.comments}" />
        </td>
      </tr>
    </table>
</td></tr></table><br>
   <netui:anchor action="begin" styleClass="text" >Back To Menu </netui:anchor>

</netui:form>
</netui-template:section >
</netui-template:template>
```

Figure 5-4 shows viewBook.jsp in a browser. In this JSP, you will see a couple new tags. Look at the name attribute. You use simple HTML to display the text *Name*. Then you use the <netui:label> tag and expressions to bind to the field in the form. Pay close attention to the notation of how to use expressions.

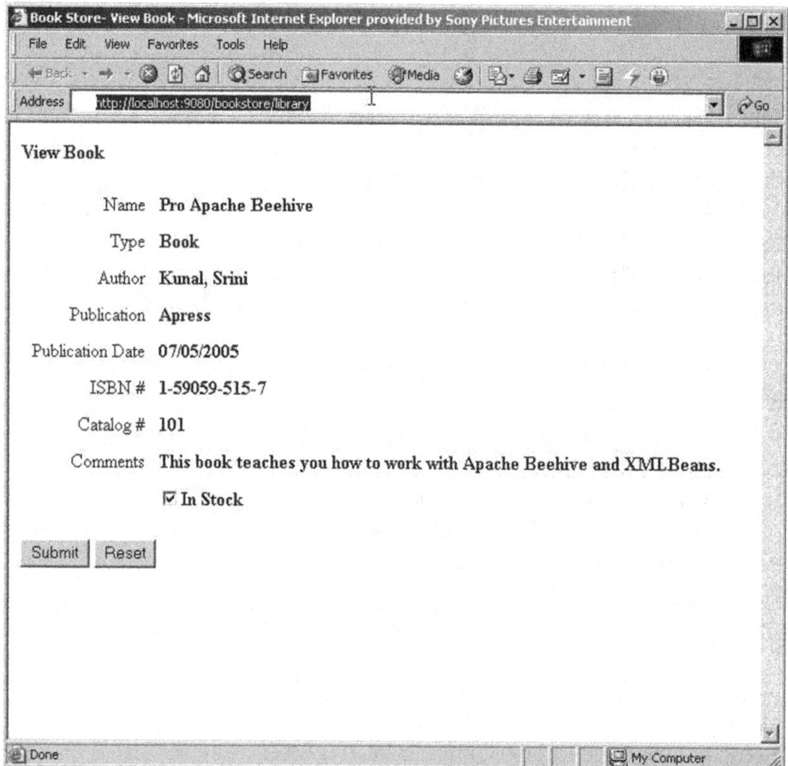


**Figure 5-4.** *viewBook.jsp*

In the next tag, you use a different way of showing labels. Specifically, you use a <netui:label> tag to actually display the label. This is useful, especially if you want to internationalize the application.

When you run this code, click the Reset button. It will clear all the variables in the form.

That's it for the basic bookstore example in this chapter. In the next section, we'll cover each of the NetUI tags in much greater detail. By the end of the next section, you'll become an expert at using NetUI.

# Dissecting NetUI Tags

In Chapter 4, we covered all the available NetUI tags. And we started this chapter by showing how to create a sample bookstore, which is basically a simple NetUI/Page Flow application. We described some of the basic NetUI tags, and we exposed you to some basic tips for how to use these tags. Now it's time to really drill down and dissect each tag. You might remember from Chapter 4 that there are three tag libraries for NetUI tags:

- `NetUI`
- `NetUI-data`
- `NetUI-template`

As mentioned in Chapter 4, if it were up to us, we'd rename the `NetUI` tag library to `NetUI-html`, because that better describes what it contains. Let's start with this tag library.

## Examining the NetUI Tag Library

The following sections cover every tag in the `NetUI` library alphabetically.

### <netui:anchor>

This is a tag you saw earlier. The anchor tag creates links. These links can be links to other sites or to actions in a controller. Listing 5-6 shows some examples of how you can use this tag.

**Listing 5-6.** *Examples of the `<netui:anchor>` Tag*

```
<table border="0" cellpadding="6" cellspacing="0">
  <tr>
    <td> <netui:anchor tagId="link1" action="submitAnchor"> simple anchor
           </netui:anchor>with just an action attribute
    </td>
  </tr>
  <tr>
    <td> <netui:anchor tagId="link2" formSubmit="true">anchor
           </netui:anchor> with action and formSubmit set as true
    </td>
  </tr>
  <tr>
    <td> <netui:anchor  href="javascript:test();" accessKey="t">anchor
           </netui:anchor>with action and location
    </td>
  </tr>
```

```
  <tr>
    <td> <netui:anchor  href="www.yahoo.com" target="_blank" >anchor
         </netui:anchor>with target attribute
    </td>
  </tr>
  <tr>
    <td> <netui:anchor  action="submitAnchor" title="text tip">anchor
           </netui:anchor>with target attribute
    </td>
  </tr>
  <tr>
    <td> <netui:anchor formSubmit="true" onClick="SubmitFromAnchor();
              return false;">Submit</netui:anchor>
    </td>
  </tr>
<netui:anchor formSubmit="true" onClick="SubmitFromAnchor();
</table>
```

These examples are pretty much self-explanatory; they show you how to create simple anchors, use anchors to submit forms, use anchors to invoke JavaScript, and even use anchors to open new windows and create ToolTips. The last example shows you how to invoke JavaScript functions from an anchor tag.

## <netui:area>

This tag creates image maps. It generates an URL-encoded area within an image. Here's an example:

```
<netui:image src="worldMap.jpg" alt="World Map" usemap="#worldmap"/>
<map id="worldmap" name="My World Map">
    <netui:area shape="rect" coords="56,12,80,80"
          href="mapOfIndia.jpg" alt="India on the map"/>
</map>
```

## <netui:attribute>

The `<netui:attribute>` tag creates attributes in other tags. For example:

```
<netui:textBox dataSource="actionForm.name" >
    <netui:attribute name="tagId" value="name"/>
    <netui:attribute name="size" value="10"/>
    <netui:attribute name="title" value="Enter Name"/>
    <netui:attribute name="maxLength" value="5"/>
</netui:textBox>
```

This code snippet shows how to embed the `<netui:attribute>` tag as part of the `<netui:textBox>` tag. We'll discuss the `<netui:textBox>` tag in the upcoming "<netui:textBox>" section. This tag also supports expressions, as follows:

```
<netui:attribute name="id" value="{pageFlow.myInstanceVariable}" />
```

**Note** You can bind any NetUI tag to any variable in the Page Flow or in a form class. Typical JavaBean rules apply. There needs to be a public getter for the variable you want to display in the JSP. If you want the values to get submitted back, you'll obviously need a setter also.

**Note** You can also bind data to the request and session objects by using `request` or `session`, respectively, as the prefix to the name of the attribute.

### <netui:base>

This tag specifies the base URL for each URL on the page. The only attribute for this tag is the target. It isn't required.

### <netui:behavior>

This adds information to the parent tag from the tag that's being rendered currently.

### <netui:bindingUpdateErrors>

This is an important tag. If you've ever worked with the first incarnation of the NetUI tags in WebLogic Workshop, you'll understand why immediately. This tag didn't exist in the original version. The only way to see any binding errors were with glaring error messages on pages and in the command window. So, if something unexpected happened at runtime, users would see these error messages. The tag provides an easy way to show binding errors. You can choose to display all error messages for any binding errors or just specific ones by binding to specific variables. The following examples show both formats:

```
<netui:bindingUpdateErrors />
<netui:bindingUpdateErrors expression="{actionForm.firstName}"/>
```

### <netui:body>

This is a basic tag that renders a body tag in the HTML code. The properties are similar to the ones available in the HTML `<body>` element.

### <netui:button>

This tag creates buttons in the same way as in traditional HTML forms. You've seen a couple examples of this earlier in the chapter. However, this is a good tag to introduce JavaScript handling. Often, you might want to simulate the clicking of a button using JavaScript.

The first step to access any NetUI tag using JavaScript is to define a `tagId` attribute, as follows:

```
<netui:form tagId="myTag" >
```

Once you've defined a tagId attribute, you can access the tag in JavaScript in the following way:

```
document[getNetuiTagName( "myTag", this )]
```

## <netui:checkBox>

This tag defines a single checkbox in your forms. The syntax is pretty simple:

```
<netui:checkBox tagId="check1" title=" Type A" defaultValue="true"
dataSource="actionForm.type"  disabled="true"/>  Checkbox
```

## <netui:checkBoxGroup>

This tag is more interesting than the <netui:checkBox> tag discussed earlier. This tag allows you to create groups of checkbox tags, either using an optionsDataSource attribute or using individual <netui:checkBoxOption> tags.

---

■ **Note** You can't use optionsDataSource and <netui:checkBoxOption> together in the same <netui:checkBoxGroup> tag.

---

The following code is an example of the <netui:checkBoxOption> tag with optionsDataSource:

```
<netui:checkBoxGroup  dataSource="actionForm.selectedStudents"
optionsDataSource="actionForm.studentsMap"
defaultValue="actionForm.selectedStudents" disabled="false"/>
```

---

■ **Note** The <netui:checkBoxGroup> tag doesn't have a tagId attribute.

---

## <netui:checkBoxOption>

This tag can't be used without the <netui:checkBoxGroup> tag. The following is a simple example:

```
<netui:checkBoxGroup  dataSource="actionForm.selectedStudents"
defaultValue="actionForm.selectedStudents" disabled="false">
    <netui:checkBoxOption title="Peter"
              value="actionForm.name" disabled="false"/> Peter
    <netui:checkBoxOption title="John"
              value="actionForm.name" disabled="false"/>  John
</netui:checkBoxGroup>
```

### <netui:configurePopup>

This tag configures a pop-up window that you might want to open to provide some functionality. For example:

```
<netui:anchor action="getCityZipFromNestedPageFlow" popup="true">
    Get a city and ZIP code
    <netui:configurePopup resizable="false" width="400" height="200">
       <netui:retrievePopupOutput tagIdRef="zipCodeField"
           dataSource="outputFormBean.zipCode" />
       <netui:retrievePopupOutput tagIdRef="cityField"
           dataSource="outputFormBean.city" />
    </netui:configurePopup>
</netui:anchor>
```

This example generates a pop-up window to get a city and ZIP code from the user. (We'll explain the `<netui:retrievePopupOutput>` tag in the "netui:retrievePopupOutput" section.)

### <netui:content>

This is another important tag. It's similar to the `<netui:label>` tag you saw earlier. The main difference between the `<netui:content>` tag and the `<netui:label>` tag is the way they handle HTML characters.

For example, consider the following `<netui:content>` tag:

```
<netui:content value="&amp;"/>
```

In the browser, this would produce "&"; if you did a similar thing with the `<netui:label>` tag, you would see "&" instead.

### <netui:divPanel>

You can use this tag with DHTML to generate an HTML `<div>` tag.

### <netui:error>

This tag displays individual field-level validation errors. The syntax is as follows:

```
<netui:error bundleName="com.project.errorMessages" key="actionForm.name "/>
```

In this example, the tag will look at the bundle specified to display an error for the `name` field. It's similar to Struts validation error messages. The `bundle` attribute is optional. If you don't specify a bundle, the tag will look at the bundle specified in the annotations for the controller that calls this JSP. If there's no bundle defined there also, you'll see the key as the error message.

### <netui:errors>

This tag displays all the validation messages. It's similar to the previous tag, except it doesn't have a `value` attribute. For example:

```
<netui:errors bundleName="com.project.errorMessages"></netui:errors>
```

## <netui:exceptions>

This is an interesting tag, especially during development. You might also use it on your error pages. The syntax is as follows:

```
<netui:exceptions showMessage="true" showStackTrace="false" />
```

It takes an exception and shows the message and/or the stack trace for the exception.

## <netui:fileUpload>

This tag uploads files from the JSP. The syntax is quite simple:

```
<netui:fileUpload tagId="inputbox" dataSource="{actionForm.theFile}" />
```

To use this tag, make sure you specify the encoding type in the `<netui:form>` tag, as follows:

```
<netui:form action="uploadFile" enctype="multipart/form-data">
```

## <netui:form>

This is a typical HTML form tag, except for its support for data binding. The form bean used to provide this data binding can be scoped to the controller, the session, or the request using the `scope` attribute.

## <netui:formatDate>

The next three tags go hand in hand. They format the output of other tags appropriately. This example should be pretty self-explanatory:

```
<netui:label value="pageFlow.today" defaultValue="1/1/2005" >
    <netui:formatDate country="US" language="en" pattern="yyyy-MM-dd"/>
</netui:label>
```

The class uses the `SimpleDateFormat` class. See the Javadocs for this class to see how you can create different patterns. The country and language aren't required.

## <netui:formatNumber>

This tag is quite useful. You can use it to format any type of number. The valid values for the type attribute are number, currency, and percent.

The following example formats a number:

```
<netui:label value="555444333333" >
    <netui:formatNumber country="US" language="en" pattern="###,####,###.00"
          type="number"/>
</netui:label>
```

The following example formats currency. The output of this tag is "$99.99".

```
<netui:label value="99.993">
    <netui:formatNumber country="US" language="en" type="currency" />
</netui:label>
```

The following example formats percentages. The output of this tag is "50%".

```
<netui:label value=".50">
    <netui:formatNumber type="percent" />
</netui:label>
```

### <netui:formatString>

This tag formats String objects. You could use it for phone numbers, Social Security numbers, and so on. The following example formats a phone number:

```
<netui:label value="555444333333" >
    <netui:formatString country="US" language="en" pattern="(###)###-####"
          truncate="true"/>
</netui:label>
```

### <netui:hidden>

This is a simple tag to add values to a page that's hidden. You could use it to carry form variables from one page to another but not to display them on the page. Things such as status codes, IDs, and so on, are places where this tag is typically used.

### <netui:html>

This tag builds the HTML tag in a page.

### <netui:image>

This is another simple tag that displays images.

### <netui:imageAnchor>

This tag is similar to the `<netui:anchor>` tag, but it uses an image as the anchor. You probably will use this tag more often than the anchor tag, depending on how your HTML is designed.

### <netui:imageButton>

This tag is similar to the `<netui:button>` tag, but it uses an image as the anchor. You probably will use this tag more often than the button tag, depending on how your HTML is designed. This tag supports rollover images.

### <netui:label>

You've seen this tag several times. It's a simple tag used to display text to users. You can combine it with the `<netui:formatXXXXXX>` tags to apply some formatting to the output text.

### <netui:parameter>

This tag passes parameters to the URL defined in a parent tag. For example:

```
<netui:anchor href="http://www.google.com/search"> Search Google
    <netui:parameter name="q" value="Apache Beehive" />
</netui:anchor>
```

### <netui:parameterMap>

This is similar to the previous tag but can provide multiple parameters to the URL. You can build the map in the controller as a `java.util.Map` class and pass it to the tag using data binding expressions.

### <netui:radioButtonGroup>

The `<netui:radioButtonGroup>` tag is similar to the `<netui:checkBoxGroup>` tag. All the same rules apply.

### <netui:radioButtonOption>

This tag works the same way as the `<netui:checkBoxOption>` tag but is used with the `<netui:radioButtonGroup>` tag.

### <netui:retrievePopupOutput>

The example with the `<netui:configurePopup>` tag asked the user to input some data. This tag gets the data from the pop-up window so that it's accessible on the parent page.

### <netui:rewriteName>

This tag allows an `id` or `name` attribute to participate in URL rewriting, as well as to be available in the JavaScript. For example:

```
<span id="<netui:rewriteName name="foo"/>">
```

### <netui:rewriteURL>

This tag supports URL rewriting. It's similar to the `<netui:rewriteName>` tag.

### <netui:scriptBlock>

This tag generates a block of JavaScript code.

### <netui:scriptContainer>

NetUI tags typically generate a lot of JavaScript themselves. The `<netui:scriptContainer>` tag bundles all the JavaScript into one HTML `<script>` tag. You can simply enclose all your NetUI elements within this tag to achieve this behavior.

This tag is especially useful in portal applications, where each JSP might not have an HTML tag. You'd basically start the `<netui:scriptContainer>` tag after the HTML `<body>` tag and end it before the end of the `<body>` tag.

### <netui:scriptHeader>

This tag will cause the JavaScript to be written with the `<head>` tag of the HTML.

### <netui:select>

You've seen this tag in the earlier `addBook.jsp` example. It corresponds to the HTML `<select>` tag and supports data binding.

Just like in the `<netui:checkBoxGroup>` tag, you can either use an `optionsDataSource` attribute (see the `addBook.jsp` example) or use the `<netui:selectOption>` tag. You can't use both simultaneously.

### <netui:selectOption>

This tag works the same way as the `<netui:checkBoxOption>` tag works but is used with the `<netui:select>` tag.

### <netui:span>

This tag generates an HTML `<span>` tag.

### <netui:textArea>

This is a typical HTML `<textArea>` tag. It supports data binding.

### <netui:textBox>

This is a typical HTML input tag that supports data binding.

### <netui:tree>

This tag generates a navigable tree of `TreeElement` objects. Listing 5-7 shows an example of how to use the different tree tags.

**Listing 5-7.** *Tree Tags in Action*

```
<netui:tree tagId="mytree" dataSource="pageFlow.myTree"
     imageRoot="treeImages" expansionAction="treeState"
         selectionAction="treeState">
     <netui:treeItem title="Root Folder"
               expanded="true"
           action="treeState" target="contentFrame">
        <netui:treeLabel>Root Folder</netui:treeLabel>
          <netui:treeItem title="I"  action="treeState"
                          target="contentFrame">
              <netui:treeLabel>I</netui:treeLabel>
                <netui:treeItem title="A"  action="treeState"
                           target="contentFrame">
                    <netui:treeLabel>A</netui:treeLabel>
                    <netui:treeItem title="1" action="treeState"
                           target="contentFrame">
                     <netui:treeLabel>1</netui:treeLabel>
                      </netui:treeItem>
                    <netui:treeItem title="2" action="treeState"
                            target="contentFrame">
                     <netui:treeLabel>2</netui:treeLabel>
                     </netui:treeItem>
                </netui:treeItem>
                </netui:treeItem>
        </netui:treeItem>
    </netui:tree>
```

## <netui:treeContent>

This tag displays text within the tree. It's similar to the `<netui:content>` tag but specific to a tree.

## <netui:treeHtmlAttribute>

This tag sets attributes on a tree, as follows:

```
<netui:treeHtmlAttribute attribute="name" value="myTree" onSelectionLink="true"/>
```

## <netui:treeItem>

This tag adds a node to a tree. An example was shown with the previous `<netui:tree>` tag example.

## <netui:treeLabel>

This tag adds a label to a given node in a tree, as shown with the previous `<netui:tree>` tag.

## <netui:treePropertyOverride>

This tag overrides properties of `<netui:tree>`.

## Examining the NetUI-data Tag Library

The `NetUI-data` library provides data binding between form beans and the Page Flow. You can use it to display sets of data, to call methods in the Page Flow, to provide pagination, and so on. The following sections cover every tag in this library alphabetically. In the bookstore example, `bookGrid.jsp` has several examples of how to use the tags in this tag library.

### <netui-data:anchorCell>

This generates anchor cells. For example, if you want to make the book title a hyperlink to a detail page, you can use this tag. The following example comes from `bookGrid.jsp`:

```
<netui-data:anchorCell action="getBookDetails" value="${container.item.title}" >
</netui-data:anchorCell>
```

### <netui-data:callMethod>

This tag calls any method in a Page Flow. For example:

```
<netui-data:callMethod object="{pageFlow}"
      method="printHello" resultId="message"
  />
```

This example calls the `printHello` method on the current Page Flow. You can actually use this tag to call a method on any Page Flow by specifying the Page Flow in the object tag. The return value of this method is stored in an attribute called `message`. You can access this attribute from the Page Flow in any other NetUI tag or in a scriptlet.

### <netui-data:callPageFlow>

This tag calls any method in the current Page Flow. It's similar to the previous tag, but it assumes the current Page Flow. If no controller file is found, an `ObjectNotFoundException` is thrown and the tag execution fails. Any return value is stored in the `${pageScope...}` data binding context object under the attribute specified by the `resultId` attribute. For example:

```
<netui-data: callPageFlow method="printHello" resultId="message" />
```

### <netui-data:caption>

This tag displays a caption in any data grid.

### <netui-data:cellRepeater>

This tag renders a single cell within an HTML table. The tag will automatically generate the open and close table, row, and cell tags. In the following sample, the `<netui-data:cellRepeater>` tag creates a table with three columns and as many rows as necessary to display all the items in the data set:

```
<netui-data:cellRepeater dataSource="{pageFlow.itemArray}"
         columns="3" >  Item: <netui:label value="{container.item}"/>
</netui-data:cellRepeater>
```

### <netui-data:configurePager>

This tag provides pagination capabilities to a NetUI data grid. You can specify the action to be called that manages the pagination, the look and feel for the pagination, the number of rows per page, and so on.

### <netui-data:dataGrid>

This tag displays a set of data. For example:

```
<netui-data:dataGrid dataSource="pageFlow.personsList" name="personsGrid">
    <netui-data:header title="header"/>
    <netui-data:footer title="footer"/>
</netui-data:dataGrid>
```

Don't worry about the header and footer tags for now. We'll discuss those in a moment. This `<netui-data:dataGrid>` tag displays all the content for the `personsList` attribute.

### <netui-data:declareBundle>

This tag specifies a resource bundle for internationalization. For example:

```
<netui-data:declareBundle bundlePath="com/foobar/resources/messages"
        name="messages"/>
    <netui:label value="{bundle.messages.messageKey"/>
```

In this example, you simply define a bundle to use and then use a key in the `<netui:label>` tag.

### <netui-data:declarePageInput>

The presence of `<netui-data:declarePageInput>` tags in a JSP file helps indicate the type of data expected at runtime. The information about the incoming data will let you know of any data dependencies a given JSP may have on the controller file. Here's an example:

```
<netui-data:declarePageInput name="myData"
            type="myPageFlow.MyPageFlowController.MyData"/>
```

In `bookGrid.jsp` you can see an example of how you're using this in the bookstore application. You declare a `ResultSet` object to be an input to that JSP:

```
<netui-data:declarePageInput name="rs" type="java.sql.ResultSet"/>
```

### <netui-data:footer>

This renders a footer to a data grid.

### <netui-data:getData>

This tag evaluates an expression and places the result into the `javax.servlet.jsp.PageContext` object so that it's available to the JSP scriptlets. For example:

```
<netui-data:getData resultId="myData" value="{form.myData}"/>
```

You can now access this data from the `pageContext` using the `getAttribute` method.

### <netui-data:header>

This renders a header to a data grid.

### <netui-data:headerCell>

This renders a table header cell or the equivalent of a <th> HTML tag. This needs to be wrapped in the <netui-data:header> tag. The following examples are available in bookGrid.jsp:

```
<netui-data:headerCell headerText="Author" />
<netui-data:headerCell headerText="Title"/>
<netui-data:headerCell headerText="ISBN"/>
<netui-data:headerCell headerText="Publication"/>
<netui-data:headerCell headerText="Type"/>
```

### <netui-data:imageAnchorCell>

This tag renders a cell in a table that has an image that serves as an anchor or link.

### <netui-data:imageCell>

This is similar to the previous tag, but it doesn't generate an anchor. The image source is specified by the source attribute in the tag.

### <netui-data:message>

This tag generates customizable messages for your page. It's especially useful for error messages. See the following example:

```
<%
   pageContext.setAttribute("errorMessage",
    new String("Password must be atleast {0} characters
       and at most {1} characters."));
%>

<netui-data:message value="{pageContext.errorMessage }"
         resultId="message">
  <netui-data:messageArg value="6"/>
  <netui-data:messageArg value="10"/>
</netui-data:message>

<netui:error value="{pageContext.message}" key={actionForm.password} />
```

In this example, you use the <netui-data:message> tag and the <netui-data:messageArg> tag to build a dynamic error message for a validation failure.

### <netui-data:messageArg>

This tag passes arguments to the <netui-data:message> tag described previously.

### <netui-data:methodParameter>

This tag passes parameters to the <netui-data:callPageFlow> tag, as follows:

```
<netui-data:callPageFlow  method="getStateName"  resultId="stateValue"
                object="apress.beehive.databinding.Controller">
     <netui-data:methodParameter value="${container.item.state}"/>
</netui-data:callPageFlow>
```

### <netui-data:pad>

This tag provides some padding in an HTML table. The <netui-data:pad> tag has the ability to turn an irregular data set in the <netui-data:repeater> tag into a regular data set by using the maxRepeat, minRepeat, and padText attributes.

### <netui-data:renderPager>

This tag actually renders the links that allow you to paginate through the results, as defined by the <netui-data:configurePager> tag.

### <netui-data:repeater>

This tag generates the HTML for a set with a variable number of rows. You need to combine several tags need to achieve this functionality. This tag defines the set that you want to iterate over. For example:

```
<netui-data:repeater dataSource="pageFlow.persons" defaultText="No Persons Found">
```

This is just the start. We'll use the next three tags covered to generate the table completely:

```
<netui-data:repeater dataSource="{pageFlow. persons }">
    <netui-data:repeaterHeader />
    <netui-data:repeaterItem>
        <li><netui:label value="{container.item. firstName },
               {container.item.lastName}, {container.item.email} "/>
        </li>
     </netui-data:repeaterItem>
     <netui-data:repeaterFooter />
 </netui-data:repeater>
```

We'll discuss the other tags in the following sections.

### <netui-data:repeaterFooter>

This tag generates a footer in the <netui-data:repeater> tag.

### <netui-data:repeaterHeader>

This tag generates a header in the <netui-data:repeater> tag.

### <netui-data:repeaterItem>

This tag is what actually renders the data in the `<netui-data:repeater>` tag. As shown in the previous example, you use this tag to iterate over the list of people and display individual items in the data set. The individual item is available using the `{container.item}` data binding expression.

### <netui-data:rows>

This is just a container tag for a set of data rows.

### <netui-data:serializeXML>

This tag serializes an XMLBean into the output of a JSP in order to move data to the browser for data binding. We'll revisit this tag when we talk about XMLBeans in Chapter 8.

### <netui-data:spanCell>

This tag renders a cell in a column. The following examples are available in `bookGrid.jsp`:

```
<netui-data:spanCell value="${container.item.isbn}"/>
<netui-data:spanCell value="${container.item.publication}"/>
<netui-data:spanCell value="${container.item.book_type}"/>
```

### <netui-data:templateCell>

This tag is used in data grids to render a templated cell in a table.

## Examining the NetUI-template Tag Library

The following sections cover every tag in the `NetUI-template` library alphabetically. Look at `libraryTemplate.jsp` and `books.jsp` while reading these sections. We use snippets from these files to describe the `NetUI-template` tag library.

### <netui-template:attribute>

This tag defines any property placeholder that you need as part of your template. For example, in the template JSP, you could define this:

```
<head>
    <title>
        <netui-template:attribute name="title"/>
    </title>
</head>
```

In the JSP that actually becomes the content for this template, you'd set a value for the attribute. You do this using the `<netui-template:setAttribute>` tag described later.

### <netui-template:divPanel>

This tag creates an HTML <div> tag that may contain additional tags. Only a single section will be visible at a time.

### <netui-template:includeSection>

This tag defines a section to include as part of the template. Listing 5-8, which you'll see in a moment, shows an example of this tag.

### <netui-template:section>

This tag actually defines the section. For example, if in the main template file you use the <netui-template:includeSection> tag to define a section called body, then the JSP that becomes the body needs to be defined using this tag. For example, books.jsp specifies which template you're using and what section of that template this JSP is part of. For example:

```
<netui-template:template templatePage="librarytemplate.jsp">
<netui-template:section name="body">
```

### <netui-template:setAttribute>

If you have an attribute defined in your template, you can set the value using this tag. For example, in books.jsp you might want to override the default title using this:

```
<netui-template:setAttribute name="title" value="Book List"/>
```

### <netui-template:template>

The <netui-template:template> tag is the parent tag for any template. Listing 5-8 shows the libraryTemplate.jsp example.

**Listing 5-8.** *libraryTemplate.jsp*

```
<%@ page language="java" contentType="text/html;charset=UTF-8"%>
<%@ taglib uri="http://beehive.apache.org/netui/tags-databinding-1.0"
      prefix="netui-data"%>
<%@ taglib uri="http://beehive.apache.org/netui/tags-html-1.0"
      prefix="netui"%>
<%@ taglib uri="http://beehive.apache.org/netui/tags-template-1.0"
      prefix="netui-template"%>

<netui-data:declareBundle
     bundlePath="apress.beehive.resources.template" name="catalog"/>
```

```
<netui:html>
    <head>
        <title>
            <netui-template:attribute name="title" defaultValue="Bookstore" />
        </title>
        <link rel="stylesheet" type="text/css"
             href="../../../../resources/beehive/version1/css/main.jsp" />
    </head>
    <netui:body>
         <br/>
            <div>
                <br/>
                <netui-template:includeSection name="body"/>
            </div>
    </netui:body>
</netui:html>
```

In this example, you're defining a template file that will form the wrapper for all the JSPs in the bookstore application. You define a single section called body using the `<netui-template:includeSection>` tag.

# Introducing Shared Flows

*Shared flows* are a way for controllers in NetUI to share code. Think of them as a utility class or a parent class in object-oriented programming. You can build several shared flows, each for different functions. For example, you could have one shared flow for all database access and another one for all the exception handling logic. For the bookstore example, we've created a shared flow. The definition of the shared flow is as follows:

```
@Jpf.Controller
public class BookSharedFlow extends SharedFlowController {
```

We won't go into the methods in this shared flow at this time, because they contain several methods for Web Services and Controls that you'll see in later chapters. For now, it's sufficient for you to assume that you can place any actions, exception handling code, simple Java methods, and so on, in this class. You'll then be able to access these methods from other Page Flows.

## Accessing Methods of the Shared Flow from Your Page Flow

To access methods declared in the shared flow, you need to declare the shared flow in your Page Flow class. Here's how we've done it in BookController:

```
@Jpf.Controller (
         sharedFlowRefs = {
        @Jpf.SharedFlowRef(name="booksharedFlow",
               type=com.apress.beehive.bookstore.BookSharedFlow.class)
},
        messageBundles = {
        @Jpf.MessageBundle(bundlePath = "apress.beehive.messages.bookstore")
        }

        )
  public class BookController extends PageFlowController {
    @Jpf.SharedFlowField(name = "booksharedFlow")
    private com.apress.beehive.bookstore.BookSharedFlow _sharedFlow = null;
```

Once you've declared the shared flow in your controller, you can call methods on the shared flow just like you would on any other Java class. The name attribute in the shared flow annotation is important; you'll need to use it if you want to access data or methods from the shared flow in your JSP.

## Accessing Methods of the Shared Flow from Your JSP

You can also access any data in a shared flow or execute methods in a shared flow from a JSP. To access data from a shared flow, you can use the following syntax:

```
<netui-data:repeater dataSource="sharedFlow.sharedFlowName.myData">
```

The sharedFlowName name refers to the value in the annotation's name attribute for the shared flow in the controller.

In a similar way, you can invoke actions defined in your shared flows. Just use sharedFlow.sharedFlowName.methodName in the appropriate NetUI tags that you've learned about in this chapter.

# So, What's Next?

This chapter showed you how to set up and run the bookstore application that you'll be expanding as you read this book. This chapter also focused on the NetUI tag libraries. We showed you how to use all the tags and provided some pointers on their usage.

This technology is new and changing fast. Even as we're writing this book, we're seeing some changes. Thus, if you find something new or that something doesn't quite work as it's described, please let us know so that in future publications of this book we can make those changes.

Now you can move on to Chapter 6, the world of Controls.

CHAPTER 6

# Using Controls

In this chapter, you'll explore the concept of Controls. The chapter begins with an explanation of the Control architecture and demonstrates when and where you should consider using them. We'll also talk about the different types of Controls that come with Apache Beehive, show you the API, and teach you how to build your own Controls. In addition, we'll dig into the specifics of the out-of-the-box Controls, such as the Database Control, EJB Control, and Timer Control.

## Introducing Controls

A *Control* is nothing more than a Java object that encapsulates some business logic or controls access to some resource such as a database or external application. The Control then exposes a common API, which allows developers to access this business logic or the external resource as though they were using a Plain Old Java Object (POJO).

**Note** Controls, like other Beehive technologies, were introduced by BEA in the WebLogic Workshop product. The motivation behind Controls is to write code in a service-oriented manner. Controls abstract any platform considerations and encapsulate any services or other Controls that the Control consumes. BEA WebLogic Workshop comes bundled with several types of Controls to access databases, EJBs, JMS queues, and so on. It also provides an extensibility model that allows developers to implement their own Controls for business logic and resources that aren't accessible by the built-in Controls that ship with the product. Think of these Controls as a proof of concept for this new technology.

The Apache Beehive runtime environment manages Controls quite similarly to how the EJB container manages an EJB. However, this runtime environment is a lightweight layer packaged as a set of JAR files that you can include with your application server. The runtime layer provides services such as transaction management, state management, asynchrony, and other services.

**Note** You don't need an EJB container to run Controls unless they are EJB Controls. In this chapter, you will deploy a Database Control on Tomcat and an EJB Control on JBoss.

A Java Control is packaged just like any other Java class, except that the extension is `.jcs` (which stands for Java Control Source). Java Controls are extensible, and the extension is typically packaged as a `.jcx` (Java Control Extension) file. A Java Control may be invoked from a Web Service, a Page Flow, a plain old Java class, or another Java Control. However, a Java Control is not network addressable unless you wrap it using a Web Service.

---

■ **Caution** A Java Control is not network addressable. To invoke a Java Control from outside the application, you can expose it using a Web Service.

---

You should first understand the anatomy of a Control.

## Understanding the Control Architecture

Beehive's Control architecture provides a common framework and configuration model for how enterprise resources can be exposed to clients. It doesn't replace existing resource access models; it provides a unifying layer on top of them to provide consistency and simplification.

Figure 6-1 shows the anatomy of a Control at a high level.

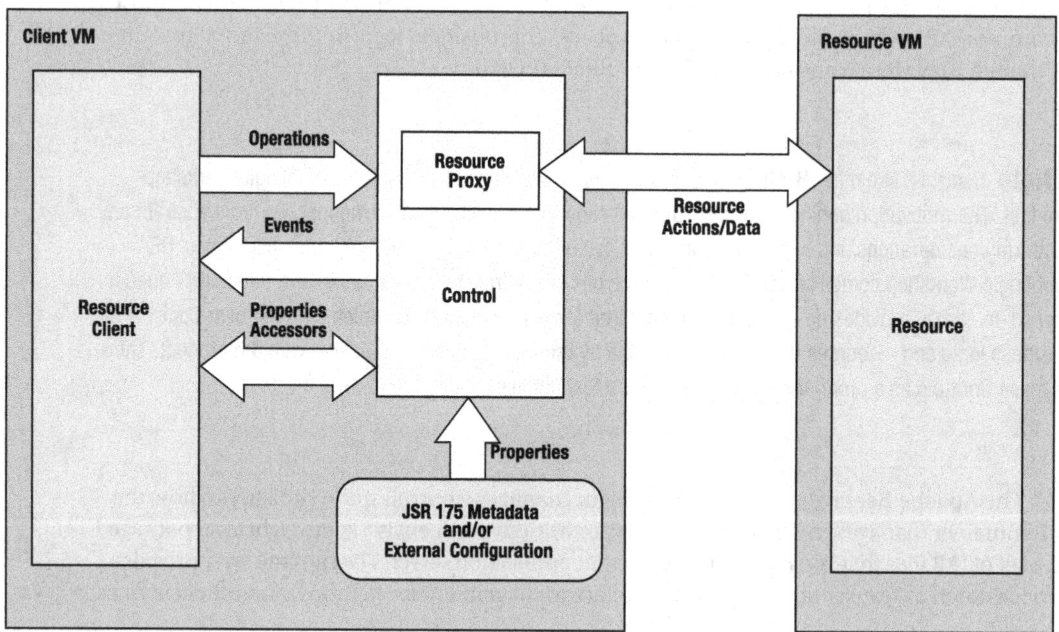


**Figure 6-1.** *Control architecture from the Apache Beehive Web site*

The Control architecture employs a unique variant of the Inversion of Control (IoC) design pattern based on JSR 175 metadata. This enables a Control implementation class to declaratively specify the events or services it requires to provide its semantics. Another advantage is consistency—the Control compiler provides both verification and code generation services to ensure that the resulting implementation provides consistent APIs and behaviors for clients, tools, and application deployers or administrators.

### Understanding the Resource

The resource shown on the right side of Figure 6-1 is the external resource that a Control is trying to access. Think of the resource as a database, external application, or some Java classes that contain some business processes. If the resource is a set of Java classes, they need not be in the same VM as the Control. The communication between the resource proxy and the resource could be RMI, Web Service calls (SOAP over HTTP), local Java invocation, or any other communication protocols.

### Understanding JSR 175 Metadata or External Configuration

Access to this resource can be parameterized using JSR 175 metadata annotations. In addition, the configuration of this resource is enabled for deploy-time binding. These configuration properties include things such as JNDI names, usernames and passwords, and so on.

### Understanding the Resource Proxy

The *resource proxy* that is part of the Control is typically EJB `home` or `remote` stubs, Web Service proxies, or some session information. The Control runtime manages the life cycle and state of this proxy. This runtime management, along with the external configuration, is used to "control" the resource.

The resource proxy uses the `onAcquire` and `onRelease` methods to manage the resource. The `onAcquire` event will fire once and only once, prior to the invocation of any operation. This method is a good place to write code related to acquiring any connections, sessions, and so on, that are needed for the life cycle of this Control instance. Once the `onAcquire` method fires, you're also guaranteed that an `onRelease` event will be executed when the resource scope ends. The `onRelease` event becomes like the `finally` block in the `try-catch` statement. This method is where you release any resources acquired in the `onAcquire` method.

For example, let's say you were implementing a Control to connect to some proprietary system. You would implement the `onAcquire` method to obtain a connection to this system, and you would release the connections in the `onRelease` method. A closer-to-home example is if you were actually writing a Database Control to connect to Oracle. In the `onAcquire` method, you would write the code to obtain the connection from the connection pool. In the `onRelease` method, you would make sure you close the connection.

You'll actually see some code for this later in this chapter, in Listing 6-3.

### Understanding the Resource Client

The *resource client* is the code that calls this resource. This needs to be in the same VM as the resource and is typically a Web Service, another Control, a Page Flow, or just some other Java object.

## Understanding Operations and Events

*Operations* and *events* provide two-way communication between the client and the Control. The set of operations that the client can call on the Control are exposed using a public interface. The Control then defines a set of callbacks or events. This is done using the callback interface, which is defined as an inner class to the public interface that exposes the operations. Listing 6-1 shows an example to make this clearer.

**Listing 6-1.** *HelloWorld Control*

```
@ControlInterface
public interface HelloWorldControl
{
    public void sayHelloWorld() throws IllegalStateException;

    @EventSet
    public interface Callback
    {
        public void printHelloWorld(String name);
    }
}
```

---

**Caution** This HelloWorld example is not built to actually compile and run. We're using it purely as a means to explain the concepts. Later in the chapter we provide examples that you can compile, deploy, and execute.

---

In this example, the method that the Control exposes is `sayHelloWorld`. The Control then fires an event called `printHelloWorld` that is returned. We'll get to the `name` parameter in the next section.

## Accessing the Properties

In Listing 6-1, you can see that the `printHelloWorld` callback event requires a single parameter called `name`. You can configure this property in several ways. For example, when the client is actually using the Control, then you can declare the property as follows:

```
@HelloWorldControl(name="John Doe")
public HelloWorldControl myHelloWorldControl;
```

Another mechanism to set the properties is to use an external XML file, as follows:

```
< helloWorldControl:HelloWorld
        xmlns:helloWorldControl=
            "http://openuri.org/com/myco/ helloWorldControl ">
          < helloWorldControl:name>John Doe</ helloWorldControl:name>
</ helloWorldControl:HelloWorld >
```

## Looking at the Control Authoring Model

In the following sections, you'll learn how you can write your own Controls from scratch. If you don't plan to do so and want to learn how to use the out-of-box Controls with Beehive, you can skip to the "Dissecting Common Controls" section later in this chapter.

### Creating a Control

Earlier in this chapter, we showed you the overall architecture of how a Control is used. Before you can write your own Control, you need to understand the architecture of a Control in a little more detail. Let's take the Control box from Figure 6-1 and blow it up, as shown in Figure 6-2.

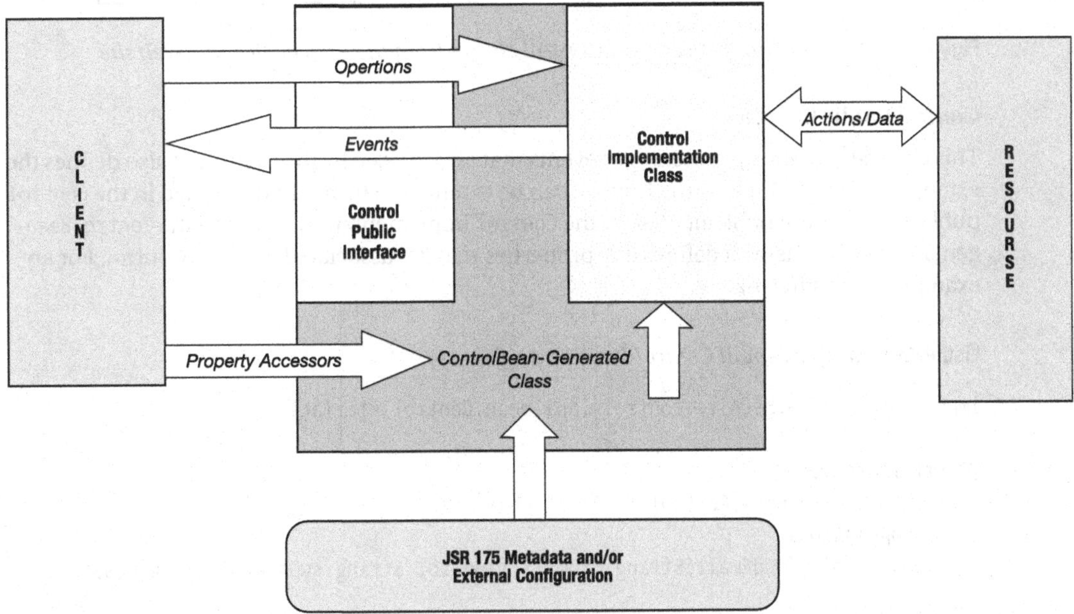


**Figure 6-2.** *Elements of a Control from the Apache Beehive Web site*

Concentrate on the shaded box. That is the heart of the Control itself. Basically, it defines three sections:

- `Control` public interface
- `Control` implementation class
- `ControlBean`-generated class

A picture speaks a thousand words. Figure 6-3 shows another diagram from the Beehive Web site and explains the relationship between the three classes mentioned previously.

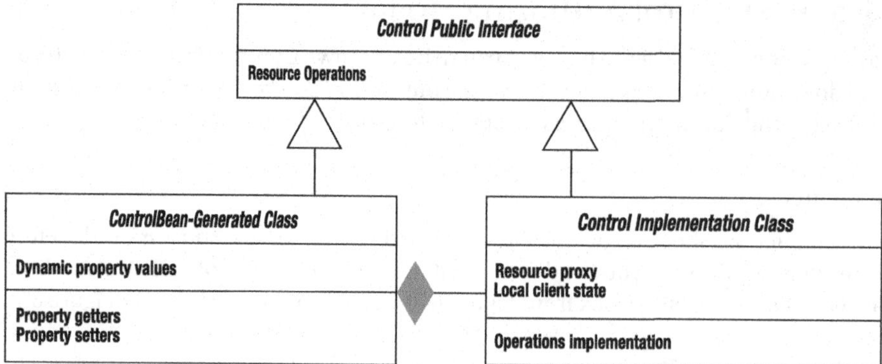


**Figure 6-3.** *Relationships between the Control classes from the Apache Beehive Web site*

## Control Public Interface

This class defines the operations and events that are exposed by the Control. It also defines the extensibility model for how the Control can be extended. The methods defined in the `Control` public interface are implemented by the `Control` implementation class and the `ControlBean`-generated class. Lastly, it defines any properties that are associated with the Control. For an example, see Listing 6-2.

**Listing 6-2.** *Sample E-mail Control Public Interface*

```
import org.apache.beehive.controls.api.bean.ControlInterface;

@ControlInterface
public interface EmailControl {
    // operations
    public void sendEmail(String from, String to, String subject, String message);

    @EventSet
    public interface Callback    {
        /**
         * The onMessage event is delivered to a registered
         * client listener whenever a
         * message has been sent by the Control.
         * @param msg the message that was sent
         */
        public void onEmailSent(String msg);
    }
     // PROPERTIES
    @PropertySet
    @Target({FIELD, TYPE})
```

```
    public @interface Connection    {
        public String factoryName();
        public boolean transacted() default true;
        public int acknowledgeMode()  default  Session.CLIENT_ACKNOWLEDGE;
    }
}
```

---

**Caution** This `EmailControl` example is not built to actually compile and run. We're using it purely as a means to explain the concepts. Later in the chapter we'll provide examples that you can compile, deploy, and execute.

---

Listing 6-2 defines a simple e-mail Control that has one method and one event. The send e-mail method takes in a few `String` parameters. The callback has an `onEmailSent` event that fires when the e-mail is sent. It also defines one property called `Connection`. This obtains a connection to the e-mail system, typically using the Simple Mail Transfer Protocol (SMTP).

### Control Implementation Class

This class provides the implementation details of the operations defined in the public interface. See Listing 6-3 for an example.

**Listing 6-3.** *Sample E-mail Control Implementation Class*

```
import org.apache.beehive.controls.api.bean.ControlImplementation;
import org.apache.beehive.controls.api.bean.Extensible;
import org.apache.beehive.controls.api.context.ControlBeanContext;
import org.apache.beehive.controls.api.context.ResourceContext;
import org.apache.beehive.controls.api.events.Client;
import org.apache.beehive.controls.api.events.EventHandler;

import javax.mail.*;
import javax.mail.event.TransportListener;
import javax.mail.internet.InternetAddress;
import javax.mail.internet.MimeMessage;

@ControlImplementation
public class EmailControlImple implements EmailControl
{
    /**
     * The peer BeanContext instance associated with the Control
     */
    @Context ControlBeanContext context;
```

```
    /**
     * The client callback event router for this Control
     */
    @Client Callback client;

    /**
     * The fields are used to hold transient e-mail resources
     * that are acquired and held for
     * the resource scope associated with the Control
     */
    transient Session _session;

   /**
     * The Resourceontext instance associated with the Control
     */
    @Context ResouceContext resourceContext;

    /*
     * The onAcquire event handler
     * This method will be called prior to any operation with
     * a given resource scope. It is responsible for
     * obtaining the connection, session, destination, and appropriate
     * writer instance, for use within the operation.
     */
    @EventHandler(
      field="resourceContext",
      eventSet=ResourceContext.ResourceEvents.class,
      eventName="onAcquire"
    )

    public void  onBeanAcquire()    {
        java.util.Properties mailProps = new java.util.Properties();
        mailProps.put("mail.smtp.host", "my.smtp.server.com");
        mailProps.put("mail.transport.protocol", "smtp");
        mailProps.put("mail.store.protocol", "imap");
         _session = Session.getDefaultInstance(mailProps, null);

      // exception handling not shown.....

    }

    /*
     * The onRelease event handler for the associated context
     * This method will release all resource acquired by onAcquire.
     */
```

```
    @EventHandler (
      field="resourceContext",
      eventSet=ResourceContext.ResourceEvents.class,
      eventName="onRelease"
    )

    public void onRelease()
    {
        try
        {
              if (_session != null)
              {
                 _session.close();
                 _session = null;
            }
        }
        catch (Exception ex)
        {
            throw new ControlException("Unable to release Email  resource", ex);
        }
    }

    /**
     * Sends a simple Email  to the Control's destination
     * @param text the contents of the TextMessage
     */
    public void sendEmail (String from, String to,
                String subject, String message)
                          throws EmailException
    {
        try
        {
Message message = new MimeMessage(mSession);
            message.setFrom(new InternetAddress(from));
            message.setRecipients(Message.RecipientType.TO,
                    InternetAddress.parse(to));
            message.setSubject(subject);
            message.setContent(message, "text/plain");
            message.setSentDate(new java.util.Date());
            Transport transport = mSession.getTransport();
            transport.connect();
            transport.send(message);
            transport.close();
            message=null;
        }
```

```
        catch (javax.mail.internet.AddressException aex)
        {
            throw new EmailException(aex);
        }
        catch (javax.mail.NoSuchProviderException nspe)
        {
            throw new EmailException(nspe);
        }
        catch (javax.mail.MessagingException mex)
        {
            throw new EmailException(mex);
        }
    }
}
```

This example is implementing the `EmailControl` using the Java Mail API to send an e-mail message. Notice that it's defining the `onAcquire` and `onRelease` methods to connect to the e-mail servers.

### ControlBean-Generated Class

This is a JavaBean class that's automatically generated by the Control's compiler based on the `Control` public interface and the `Control` implementation class. Since this is a generated class, we won't show you the code for it here.

## Creating a Control Extension

A *Control extension* is useful when you need to add functionality to some Control. For example, let's say you wanted to set up a synchronous queue using JMS for the e-mails to be sent. You might want to extend the e-mail Control shown earlier in the chapter to add this functionality. Here's how this might look at a high level:

```
import org.apache.beehive.controls.api.bean.ControlExtension;

@ControlExtension
public interface EmailQueue extends EmailControl
{
    // your custom code
}
```

In this example, you could override the `sendEmail` method to actually write the e-mails to a JMS queue, and the queue could then send the e-mails one by one.

## Using Control Composition

This is an interesting concept. You can actually combine the functionality in more than one Control to create another Control on top of them. For example, let's assume you have two Controls—a JMS Control and the e-mail Control shown earlier in this chapter. I've talked about how you might extend the e-mail Control to build in a JMS queue. This, however, would mean you'd have to pretty much write all the JMS-related code in this Control extension. However, since you also have a JMS Control, you could create a class that would combine the JMS Control with the e-mail Control to provide the same functionality that the extended `EmailQueue` Control does. Listing 6-4 shows some pseudocode for this.

**Listing 6-4.** *Control Composition: E-mail and JMS*

```
public class EmailQueue
{
    @Control @Destination(Name="EmailQueue")
    JMSQueueBean emailQueue;

    @Control @Destination(Name="Email")
    EmailControlBean email;

    public void queueEmail
            (String from, String to, String subject, String message)
    {
                  // custom code
    }
}
```

This example creates a simple Java class that combines the functionality of the two Controls. You could also create a Control on top of the two Controls if you want to do so. Let's look at some more interesting pseudocode. Listing 6-5 shows two JMS Controls being combined with the e-mail Control.

**Listing 6-5.** *Control Composition: E-mail and JMS with Priority*

```
public class PriorityEmailQueue
{
    @Control @Destination(Name="EmailQueue")
    JMSQueueBean emailQueue;

    @Control @Destination(Name="PriorityQueue")
    JMSQueueBean priorityQueue;


    @Control @Destination(Name="Email")
    EmailControlBean email;
```

```
    public void queueEmail
            (String from, String to, String subject,
              String message, boolean highPriority)
    {
            if (highPriority)
            {
                    // send email on priorityQueue
            }
            else
            {
                    // send email on emailQueue
            }
    }
}
```

### Packaging a Control

Controls are packaged as JAR files so that they can be easily distributed. A manifest file inside the JAR describes all the Controls that are in it. This can be read by tools such as Pollinate and Workshop to create a graphical palette of Controls that are available to you.

Beehive also ships with a rich Controls Packaging API that primarily helps in creating good documentation on how to use the Control and the features of the Control. This might not be suitable for you if you're just writing a few small Controls to use on your project. However, if you're building Controls to expose functionality within a product you're selling, then leveraging this API may be useful. You can learn more about the API on the Beehive wiki at `http://wiki.apache.org/beehive/Controls/ControlPackaging`.

## Using a Control

In the following sections, you'll learn how you can use the HelloWorld Control you saw in Listing 6-1.

### Understanding the Control Client Model

Two basic models exist for using a Control: programmatic and declarative. The two models offer the same basic functionality. Let's take a look at each of them.

#### Programmatic Model

In the programmatic model, the client must take responsibility for instantiating the Control and working with the events that get thrown. This is typically good for experienced programmers who are comfortable working with events and JavaBeans. Here's how the programmatic model would work with `HelloWorldControl`:

```
HelloWorldControl myHelloWorldControl =
   (HelloWorldControl)Controls.instantiate(classloader, "HelloWorldControl");
myHelloWorldControl.addHelloWorldControlEventListener(
     new HelloWorldControlEventListener ()    // anonymous event handler class
     {
         public void sayHelloWorld(String name)
         {
             // event handling code
         }
     }
);
```

### Declarative Model

In this model, the creation of the Control and event routing are automatically handled for you. This model is easier and faster to use and is ideal for developers who like to use a rich set of tools to program.

Here's how the declarative model would work with `HelloWorldControl`:

```
@HelloWorldControl(name="John Doe")
               HelloWorldControl myHelloWorldControl;
public void myHelloWorldControl _sayHelloWorld(String name) {
   // event handling code
}
```

The question you might ask is, if the declarative model requires less code and is easier to use, why would anyone use the programmatic model? The key difference is that if you use the declarative model, then the resources accessed by the Control must be available in that runtime environment or else the instantiation of the Control will fail. This sort of becomes a prerequisite to the server start-up.

When using the programmatic model, on the other hand, you have control to test whether the resource is available and can decide how to proceed.

For example, let's say the application depends on one Oracle database and occasionally connects to some e-mail server to send e-mail. The application can still run if the e-mail server is down, but not if the database is down. In this scenario, you might decide to use the declarative model for the Database Control and the programmatic model for the e-mail Control.

## Instantiating a Control

Controls use *lazy instantiation*, which means that an instance of the Control is not actually created until the client actually invokes one of the methods on the Control. Once instantiated, the Control will exist until the client releases the reference on the Control. When the client terminates, all the Controls that were used by that client are terminated.

# Dissecting Common Controls

In the following sections, you'll learn about several Controls that ship with Apache Beehive. It was important for the Beehive team to provide some out-of-the-box Control implementations to jump-start development. BEA WebLogic Workshop shipped with several Controls, including a Database Control, JMS Control, EJB Control, Web Service Control, and Timer Control. Currently, these have been released into ControlHaus to foster more community support for authoring these Controls. To learn more about ControlHaus, visit `http://www.controlhaus.com/`.

---

■ **Tip** You'll see several interesting examples of Controls at ControlHaus, such as an Amazon Control, Google Control, EBay Control, PayPal Control, and so on. You'll also find technology-specific Controls such as a Hibernate Control and an XFire Control that uses XMLBeans.

---

At the time of writing, the Beehive wiki mentioned that the Beehive team might consider making these part of Beehive. Just to get you started with using Controls, we'll now explain some of the Controls that are available freely or packaged with Apache Beehive. We'll start with the Database Control.

## Using the Database Control

We'll use the Database Control from the ControlHaus project as an example. You can find the JAR file in the Beehive distribution under `lib\controls\jdbc-control.jar`.

You can use a Database Control to encapsulate access to a relational database. It's somewhat like an entity EJB where some of the database logic is encapsulated for you—but you should not confuse it with an entity EJB. The verdict on the value of an entity EJB might even be 50/50, and we don't really want to dig into those issues now. That is a topic for its own book. The primary similarity between a Database Control and an entity EJB is that you don't have to understand JDBC to work with a database.

Since you'll be using the Database Control implementation from ControlHaus, you need to implement the `JdbcControl` interface. The methods are used to execute regular SQL statements against a database. There's no restriction on the types of SQL statements you can execute using a Database Control. Each method in a Database Control has a single SQL statement associated with it. This is defined using a JSR 175 metadata annotation.

---

■ **Note** The Beehive samples also provide an implementation of the Database Control called `DatabaseControl`. You might find it interesting to go through that example also. We won't cover it in this book.

---

In the `@SQL` metadata annotation, you can specify parameters that are replaced with runtime values. These parameters match the signature of the methods, thus the replacement happens automatically using Java reflection. You'll see examples of this in just a minute, but first refer to the "Getting Ready to Use the Database Control Example" sidebar to set up a database that you can use with the Database Control you'll work with next.

## GETTING READY TO USE THE DATABASE CONTROL EXAMPLE

To use the Database Control example, you'll need to download and install a database. In this example, we're using MySQL. However, there's no reason why you couldn't use any other database such as PointBase, SQL Server, or Oracle.

1. First, you'll need to download and install MySQL 4.1 from `http://dev.mysql.com/downloads/mysql/4.1.html`.

2. We recommend downloading a version that has the installer. Once you've installed MySQL, open a command prompt. You can do this from the Start menu by clicking Run, typing **cmd**, and then clicking Enter. Once the command prompt is open, change to the MySQL directory (for example, `c:\mysql`).

3. Now, type the following:

   ```
   mysql -h localhost -u root -p test
   ```

4. You'll be asked for a password. Just click Enter to use a blank password.

5. You'll see `mysql>` as the prompt; enter the following SQL commands:

   ```
    GRANT ALL PRIVILEGES ON *.* TO beehiveuser@localhost
       ->   IDENTIFIED BY 'password' WITH GRANT OPTION;
    create database bookstoredb;
    use bookstoredb ;

   create table book_Detail (
   book_id varchar(20),
   title varchar(50),
   book_type varchar(50),
   author varchar(100),
   publication varchar(100),
   isbn varchar(15),
   publication_date date,
   comments varchar(300),
   available char(1));
   ```

6. This will create the user `beehiveuser`, the database `bookstoredb`, and the table `book_Detail` in that database. The next step is a few changes to the Tomcat configuration. You need to modify the `server.xml` file, which can be found under the `conf` directory of your Tomcat installation.

7. Add the following `<context>` element, before the `</host>` element in `server.xml`. You make this change to configure the datasource to your MySQL database in Tomcat. You can also find this change in the `server.xml.changes.txt` file in the code download in the `chapter6\dbControlExample` directory:

   ```
   <Context path="/Library" docBase="Library"
                             debug="5" reloadable="true" crossContext="true">
              <Logger className="org.apache.catalina.logger.FileLogger"
                           prefix="localhost_library_log." suffix=".txt"
                           timestamp="true"/>
   ```

*Continued*

```
<Resource name="jdbc/bookstoreDS"
                 auth="Container"
                 type="javax.sql.DataSource"/>

            <ResourceParams name="jdbc/bookstoreDS">
              <parameter>
                <name>factory</name>
                <value>
                     org.apache.commons.dbcp.BasicDataSourceFactory
                </value>
              </parameter>

              <!-- Maximum number of dB connections in pool. Make sure
               you configure your mysqld max_connections large
               enough to handle all of your db connections.
               Set to 0 for no limit.
                   -->
              <parameter>
                <name>maxActive</name>
                <value>100</value>
              </parameter>

         <!-- Max # of idle dB connections to retain in pool
                   Set to -1 for no limit.  See also the DBCP
                  documentation on this and the
                  minEvictableIdleTimeMillis
                   configuration parameter.
                   -->
              <parameter>
                <name>maxIdle</name>
                <value>30</value>
              </parameter>

              <!-- Maximum time to wait for a dB connection to become
                     available in ms, in this example 10 seconds.
                  An Exception is thrown if this timeout
                   is exceeded.  Set to -1 to wait indefinitely.
                   -->
              <parameter>
                <name>maxWait</name>
                <value>10000</value>
              </parameter>

              <!-- MySQL dB username and
                      password for dB connections  -->
              <parameter>
```

*Continued*

```
                    <name>username</name>
                       <value>beehiveuser</value>
                      </parameter>
                      <parameter>
                       <name>password</name>
                       <value>password</value>
                      </parameter>

                <!-- Class name for the official MySQL Connector/J driver -->
                      <parameter>
                         <name>driverClassName</name>
                         <value>com.mysql.jdbc.Driver</value>
                      </parameter>

                      <!-- The JDBC connection url for
                           connecting to your MySQL dB.
                           The autoReconnect=true argument to the url
                           makes sure that the
                           mm.mysql JDBC Driver will
                           automatically reconnect if mysqld closed the
                           connection.  mysqld by default closes idle
                               connections after 8 hours.
                           -->
                      <parameter>
                        <name>url</name>
                        <value>
                     jdbc:mysql://localhost:3306/bookstoredb?
                        autoReconnect=true
                       </value>
                      </parameter>
                     </ResourceParams>
        </Context>
```

8. You should also download the MySQL Connector/J to be able to connect from MySQL to Java. You can download MySQL Connector/J 3.1 from `http://dev.mysql.com/downloads/connector/j/3.1.html` and make sure it's being referred to in the classpath when you run the application. To do this in Tomcat, you can copy the `mysql-connector-java-3.1.7-bin.jar` file in the `<tomcat-home>/common/lib` directory.

9. Now, create a directory called `library` under `$tomcat_home$/webapps/`. This is where you'll deploy the application. In the code download, copy all the files and directories under `chapter6\dbControlExample` to this directory. Build the application using `build.xml` found under `$tomcat_home$/webapps/library/web-inf/src`.

10. Start the Tomcat server. You can see the application in action by going to `http://localhost:8080/Library/com/apress/beehive/bookstore`.

## Creating the Bookstore Database Control

In this section, you'll extend the bookstore example that was introduced in Chapter 5 to actually store books in the database. To do this, you'll use a Database Control. Let's first glance at the code for the Control, and then we'll dissect the pieces of it individually. You can find the code shown in Listing 6-6 in the code download in the `chapter6\dbControlExample\WEB-INF\src\apress\beehive\controls\bookstoredb.jcs` directory.

**Listing 6-6.** *Bookstore Database Control*

```
package apress.beehive.controls.bookstoredb;

import org.apache.beehive.controls.system.jdbc.JdbcControl;
import org.apache.beehive.controls.api.bean.ControlExtension;
import com.apress.beehive.bookstore.vo.Book;
import java.sql.SQLException;
import java.sql.ResultSet;

@ControlExtension
@JdbcControl.ConnectionDataSource(
         jndiName="java:/bookstoreDS")

public interface BookDBControl extends JdbcControl {

    @JdbcControl.SQL(statement=" ", maxRows = 1)
    public void addBook() ;

    @JdbcControl.SQL( statement=
            "select title from book where author_name={name}",
                    maxRows = 10)
    public String [] getAllBooksTitlesForAuthor(String name);

    @JdbcControl.SQL( statement=
           "select isbn from book_detail",
                maxRows = 5)
    public String[] getISBNCodes();

    @JdbcControl.SQL(statement=
           "SELECT * FROM book_detail WHERE book_id={book_Id}",
                 maxRows = 1)
    public Book getBookDetails(int book_Id) throws SQLException;

    @JdbcControl.SQL(statement=
           "SELECT * FROM book_detail WHERE book_type= {type}  ",
                maxRows = 10)
      public ResultSet findBooksByAuthorAndType(String author,
                        String type) throws SQLException;

    static final long serialVersionUID = 1L;
}
```

The first line in Listing 6-6 is a metadata annotation that defines this file to be a Control extension. The next line defines the information for the JDBC datasource that this Control will use. The next line is the class definition. Notice that `BookDBControl` extends from `JdbcControl` that's currently part of ControlHaus. Now, you've defined several methods that perform SQL operations. For this example, you'll be implementing only the `select` or `read` methods from the database. We'll show a different implementation of the `Add` methods using EJB Controls in the next section. Look at the `getAllBooksTitlesForAuthor` method. In this method, you'll define a SQL statement to get all books for a given author. Notice that the parameter passed to the method `name` is used to perform runtime substitution into the SQL statement defined in the annotation.

## Using the Bookstore Database Control

You'll now modify the Page Flow example from Chapter 5 to leverage the Control you just defined. You can find the complete code for the Page Flow in the code download at `chapter6\dbControlExample\com\apress\beehive\bookstore\BookController.jpf`.

---

■ **Note** In this controller, you're using the Database Control and EJB Control that we'll explain later in this chapter. For now, you can ignore the usage of the EJB Control.

---

In the controller, you define the Database Control in the same way as you would any class variable. You use the `@control` metadata annotation, as follows:

```
@Control
 public BookDBControl dbcontrol;
```

Once you've defined the Control as a class variable, you can use it in your action methods. Let's look at a quick example:

```
@Jpf.Action(
    forwards = {
        @Jpf.Forward(name = "success", path = "viewBook.jsp")
    })
protected Forward getBookDetails()throws SQLException
{
    BookForm form =new BookForm();
    String bookId = this.getRequest().getParameter("bookId");
   Book abook= dbcontrol.getBookDetails(Integer.parseInt(bookId) );
    form.setaBook(abook);
   return new Forward("success", form);
}
```

Only one line is really important in this snippet. Notice that the Database Control is being used just as any other Java class. There's nothing special from a usage perspective. As a client of the Control, you did not need to know *anything* about JDBC. This really is the value of the Control architecture.

## Using the EJB Control

You'll use the EJB Control from the ControlHaus project as an example. You can find the JAR file in the Beehive distribution under `lib\controls\ejb-control.jar`.

An EJB Control encapsulates all the baggage of using EJBs. This includes the JNDI lookup, `home` interface lookup, and the invocation of methods on the `remote` interfaces. Using an EJB Control, you can work with an EJB just like you would a plain old Java class. Just like with a Database Control, the client will not have to know anything about EJBs.

You'll now see a quick example of how to use an EJB Control. Since Tomcat is not an EJB container, we'll use JBoss. Please read the "Getting Ready to Use the EJB Control Example" sidebar to learn how to set up JBoss for this example. Once you have JBoss set up and the application deployed, you can use the EJB Control. (However, we recommend you just use any application server you're comfortable with. As for the two authors of this book, one of us used JBoss and the other one used WebLogic.)

The code for the EJB that we'll use is available at `chapter6\dbControlExample\src`. However, for this example, you can just use the `libraryejb.jar` file found under `chapter6\dbControlExample\dist`.

### GETTING READY TO USE THE EJB CONTROL EXAMPLE

To use the EJB Control example, you'll need to download and install an application server such as JBoss. We've tested this example on JBoss 3.2.6, which you can download at `http://www.jboss.com/downloads/index#as`.

You can read the documentation on how to install and set up JBoss at `http://www.jboss.com/index.html?module=downloads&op=download&authid=ae885bbacae56aeb29c8f068974add90&downloadId=4`.

To build and work with this example, you need to deploy `libraryejb.jar` from the `dist` directory. The next step is to build and deploy the `library.war` file. You can do this using the Ant build script found under `Web-inf/src`. Also, copy the `jboss-j2ee.jar` file into `web-inf/lib`. To deploy these to JBoss, copy both these files (`libraryejb.jar` and `library.war`) to the `jboss-home/server/default/deploy` directory. Also, copy the attached `mysql-ds.xml` to the same directory (`jboss-home/server/default/deploy`).

The `mysql-ds.xml` file contains information for creating the MySQL datasource. This file contains the following:

```
<?xml version="1.0" encoding="UTF-8"?>
<!DOCTYPE jbosscmp-jdbc PUBLIC
"-//JBoss//DTD JBOSSCMP-JDBC 3.0//EN"
"http://www.jboss.org/j2ee/dtd/jbosscmp-jdbc_3_0.dtd">
<datasources>
<local-tx-datasource>
<jndi-name>bookstoreDS</jndi-name>
<connection-url>
        jdbc:mysql://localhost:3306/bookstoredb
</connection-url>
```

*Continued*

```
<driver-class>com.mysql.jdbc.Driver</driver-class>
<use-java-context>false</use-java-context>
<user-name>beehiveuser</user-name>
<password>password</password>
</local-tx-datasource>
</datasources>
```

You also need to copy the JConnector (`mysql-connector-java-3.1.7-bin.jar`) file into the `<jboss-home>/server/default/lib` directory.

### Creating the Bookstore EJB Control

In this example, you're creating an EJB Control to access a session EJB. The session EJB in turn uses a Data Access Object (DAO) to access the database. Let's look at the EJB Control (see Listing 6-7).

**Listing 6-7.** *Bookstore EJB Control*

```
package apress.beehive.conrols.ejbcontrol;

import org.apache.beehive.controls.api.bean.ControlExtension;
import org.apache.beehive.controls.system.ejb.SessionEJBControl;
import org.apache.beehive.controls.system.ejb.EJBControl.EJBHome;
import org.apache.beehive.controls.system.ejb.EJBControl.JNDIContextEnv;
import com.apress.beehive.bookstore.ejb.BookDetailHome;
import com.apress.beehive.bookstore.ejb.BookDetailRemote;
@ControlExtension
@EJBHome(jndiName="BookManager")
@JNDIContextEnv(contextFactory=
        "org.jnp.interfaces.NamingContextFactory",
         providerURL="localhost:1099")

public interface BookDetailEJBControl extends
         SessionEJBControl, BookDetailHome, BookDetailRemote
{
}
```

In Listing 6-7, you can see that you specify the basic properties for the EJB like the JNDO name and the `home` and `remote` interface for the EJB. And that's it. You don't really have to do anything more to use the EJB via this Control.

## Using the Bookstore EJB Control

You'll now modify the Page Flow example introduced in Chapter 5 to leverage the Control you just defined. You can find the complete code for the Page Flow in the code download at chapter6\dbControlExample\com\apress\beehive\bookstore\BookController.jpf.

In the controller, you can define the EJB Control in the same way as you would any class variable. The @control metadata annotation is as follows:

```
@Control
    public BookDetailEJBControl ejbcontrol;
```

Once you've defined the Control as a class variable, you can use it in your action methods. Let's look at the following quick example:

```
    @Jpf.Action(
        forwards = {
            @Jpf.Forward(name = "success",path = "viewBook.jsp")
          },
          validationErrorForward = @Jpf.Forward(name = "failure", navigateTo = ➥
                Jpf.NavigateTo.currentPage)
           )

    protected Forward addBook(BookForm form)
              throws RemoteException,SQLException
    {
       ejbcontrol.insertBookDetail(form.getaBook());
       return new Forward("success", form);
}
```

Only one line is really important in this snippet. Notice that the EJB Control is being used just as any other Java class. There's nothing special from a usage perspective. As a client of the Control, you didn't need to know *anything* about how to use the EJB. Figure 6-4 shows you the add page that's used to add the book using this Control.

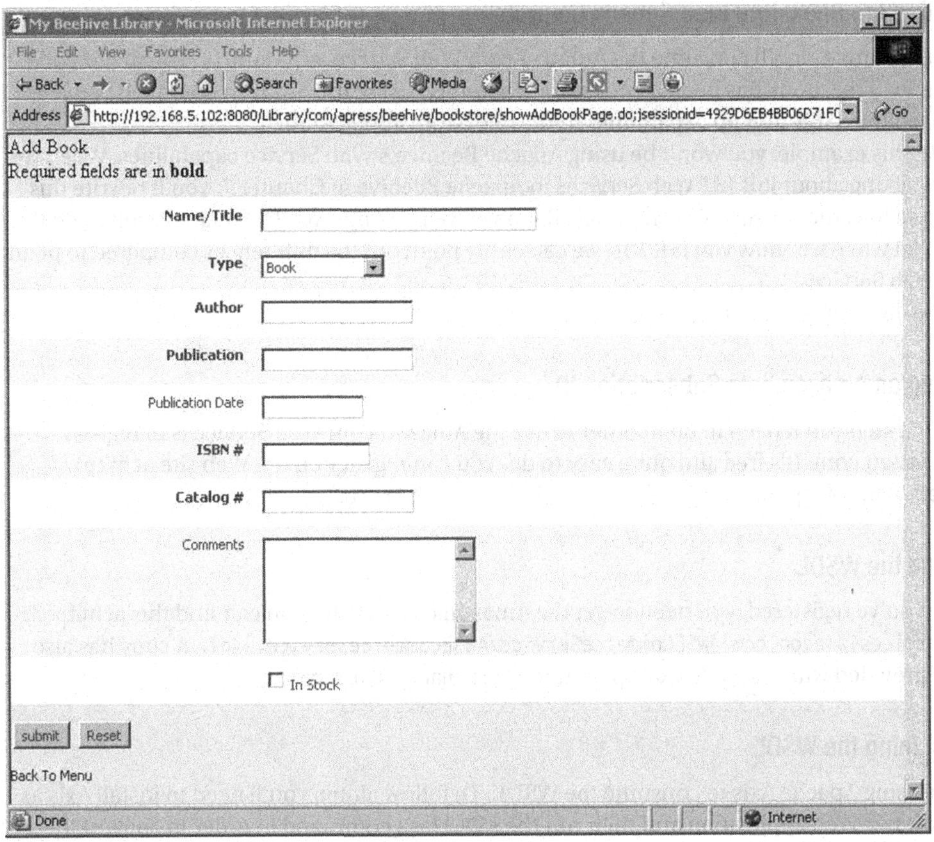

**Figure 6-4.** *Adding a book using the EJB Control*

## Using the Web Service Control

Let's now build a Web Service Control for the bookstore application. A Web Service Control is nothing but a Control that consumes a Web Service.

---

■ **Note** This section assumes you have some level of familiarity with Web Services. We won't go into all the details of Web Service code; rather, we'll focus on how a Control is used as a wrapper to a Web Service.

---

## Creating the Bookstore Web Service Control

In this example, you'll consume the Amazon.com Web Service as a Control. The major code example in this book has been a bookstore. Therefore, using the Amazon.com Web Service, you'll enable ISBN lookup capabilities in the bookstore application.

In this example, you won't be using Apache Beehive's Web Service capabilities. When we get to talking about JSR 181 Web Services in Apache Beehive in Chapter 7, you'll rewrite this example to actually use that technology. For now, we're using Axis. The main reason to do this is so that when we show you JSR 181, we can easily point out the differences compared to plain Axis Web Services.

So, let's jump right in.

### Getting an Amazon.com Subscription ID

The first step you'll need to do in order to use the Amazon.com Web Service is to register on Amazon.com. It's free and quite easy to do. You can register on the Web site at `http://www.amazon.com/gp/aws/registration/registration-form.html`.

### Getting the WSDL

Once you've registered, you need to get the Amazon.com WSDL. You can find this at `http://webservices.amazon.com/AWSECommerceService/AWSECommerceService.wsdl`. A copy has also been provided with the code examples, under the `chapter6` directory.

### Consuming the WSDL

We're using Apache Axis to consume the WSDL. To follow along, you'll need to install Axis as part of your Web application and then run the `WSDL2Java` command in order to convert the WSDL into a set of Java classes you can use. The first thing is to get the libraries from the examples in `chapter6\webservicescontrols\web-inf\lib\wsm`. You'll need the following files:

- `axis.jar`
- `axis-ant.jar`
- `commons-discovery.jar`
- `commons-logging.jar`
- `jaxrpc.jar`
- `saaj.jar`
- `wsdl4j.jar`
- `log4j-1.2.8.jar`

---

**Note** To learn more about Apache Axis, visit the Apache Axis Web site at `http://ws.apache.org/axis/`.

---

Copy these into your Web application. Now, run the following commands from a command prompt:

```
set AXIS_LIB=C:\YOURWEBAPP\lib\wsm
set CLASSPATH=%AXIS_LIB%\axis.jar;%AXIS_LIB%\axis-ant.jar;
            %AXIS_LIB%\commons-discovery.jar;
            %AXIS_LIB%\commons-logging.jar;
            %AXIS_LIB%\jaxrpc.jar;
            %AXIS_LIB%\saaj.jar;
            C:c:\<<BEEHIVE_HOME\lib\common\log4j-1.2.8.jar;
            %AXIS_LIB%\wsdl4j.jar
java org.apache.axis.wsdl.WSDL2Java --server-side
         --noWrapped -v -W
          -p com.amazon.xml.AWSECommerceServer AWSECommerceService.wsdl
```

You'll see that several Java source files get generated. These will be under the `WEB-INF/src` directory of your Web application. The package structure will be `com/amazon/xml/AWSECommerceServer`.

Don't be shocked. About 50–60 Java files are generated. That is the complexity of actually consuming a Web Service. Luckily, you don't have to write those classes yourself.

## Writing the Java Control

The next step is to actually write the Java Control. Let's first define the `Control` interface. You'll define two methods. The first method, `lookupISBN`, gets the details of a book, given the ISBN. The second method, `searchBook`, gets a URL pointing to the book details on Amazon.com, given the ISBN.

Listing 6-8 shows the `Control` interface.

**Listing 6-8.** *Bookstore Web Service Control Interface*

```
package apress.beehive.controls.javacontrol;

import com.amazon.xml.AWSECommerceServer.Items;
import org.apache.beehive.controls.api.bean.ControlInterface;

import java.rmi.RemoteException;

@ControlInterface
public interface AmazonControl
{
    public Items[] lookupISBN(String isbn) throws RemoteException;
    public String searchBook(String isbn)throws RemoteException;
}
```

The interesting part is the Control implementation. Listing 6-9 shows the code for the implementation.

**Listing 6-9.** *Bookstore Web Service Control Implementation*

```
package apress.beehive.controls.javacontrol;

import com.amazon.xml.AWSECommerceServer.*;
import org.apache.beehive.controls.api.bean.ControlImplementation;

import java.io.Serializable;
import java.rmi.RemoteException;

@ControlImplementation
        public class AmazonControlImpl implements AmazonControl, Serializable {
    AWSECommerceServiceLocator locator =
                            new AWSECommerceServiceLocator();

    public Items[] lookupISBN(String isbn) throws RemoteException {
        try {
            System.out.println("Given ISBN is " + isbn);
            AWSECommerceServicePortType type
               = locator.getAWSECommerceServicePort();
            String itemId[] = {isbn.trim()};
            ItemLookup lookup = new ItemLookup();
            lookup.setAssociateTag("***** "); // fill in your AWS id
            lookup.setSubscriptionId("*****");// fill in your AWS id
            ItemLookupRequest lookupReq = new ItemLookupRequest();
            lookupReq.setMerchantId("All");
            lookupReq.setItemId(itemId);
            lookupReq.setResponseGroup(new String[]
               {"Medium", "OfferFull", "Variations", "Images"});
            ItemLookupRequest[] requests = lookup.getRequest();
            requests = new ItemLookupRequest[1];
            requests[0] = lookupReq;
            lookup.setRequest(requests);
            ItemLookupResponse response = type.itemLookup(lookup);
            Items[] items = response.getItems();
            if (items != null && items.length > 0) {
                System.out.println("Number of results "+ items.length);
                return items;
            }
        } catch (javax.xml.rpc.ServiceException se) {
            throw new RemoteException(se.getMessage());

        }
        return new Items[0];
    }
```

```
    public String searchBook(String isbn) throws RemoteException {
        String amazonUrl = "";
        try {
            System.out.println("book search is " + isbn);
            AWSECommerceServicePortType type = locator.getAWSECommerceServicePort();
            String itemId[] = {isbn.trim()};
            ItemLookup lookup = new ItemLookup();
            lookup.setAssociateTag("***** "); // fill in your AWS id
            lookup.setSubscriptionId("*****");// fill in your AWS id
            ItemLookupRequest lookupReq = new ItemLookupRequest();
            lookupReq.setMerchantId("All");
            lookupReq.setItemId(itemId);
            lookupReq.setResponseGroup(new String[]
                  {"Medium", "OfferFull", "Variations", "Images"});
            ItemLookupRequest[] requests = lookup.getRequest();
            requests = new ItemLookupRequest[1];
            requests[0] = lookupReq;
            lookup.setRequest(requests);
            ItemLookupResponse response = type.itemLookup(lookup);
            Items[] items = response.getItems();
            if (items != null && items.length > 0) {
                System.out.println("number of results " + items.length);
                for (int i = 0; i < items.length; i++) {
                    Item[] itemvalues = items[i].getItem();
                    if (itemvalues != null) {
                        for (int j = 0; j < itemvalues.length; j++) {
                            System.out.println("URL :" +
                                itemvalues[j].getDetailPageURL());
                            amazonUrl = itemvalues[0].getDetailPageURL();
                        }
                    }
                }
            }
        } catch (javax.xml.rpc.ServiceException se) {
            throw new RemoteException(se.getMessage());

        }
        return amazonUrl;
    }
}
```

If you've worked with Web Services, the implementation of the two methods should look familiar. It isn't in the scope of this book to dive into the details. We'll touch on Web Services again in the context of JSR 181 in Chapter 7, and you'll see how that code differs from the Web Service code in Listing 6-4.

---

■ **Note** You'll need to replace the Associate Tag and Subscription ID with your AWS ID from Amazon.com.

---

In both methods, you're calling the Amazon.com Web Service to get data back. Now you have a Control that consumes a Web Service. You've gained all the advantages of a Control and covered the complexities associated with Web Services.

All the code for Listing 6-3 and Listing 6-4 is available under `chapter6\wsControlExample\WEB-INF\src\apress\beehive\controls\javacontrol`.

## Using the Bookstore Web Service Control

You've consumed the Web Service. You've written a Control to wrap the Web Service. Now, let's write a client that calls the Control. In this section, you'll expand on the bookstore controller that you've been working with throughout this book. The complete code is available in `chapter6\wsControlExample\com\apress\beehive\bookstore`. You'll see snippets of it that are related to the Amazon.com Control you just created.

The first step obviously is to declare the Control, as follows:

```
@Control
        public AmazonControl amazon;
```

Listing 6-10 shows an action that calls one of the methods in the Amazon Control.

**Listing 6-10.** *searchAWS Action from BookStoreController*

```
@Jpf.Action(
            forwards = {
            @Jpf.Forward(name = "success", path = "amazonResults.jsp")
            })
            protected Forward searchAWS(AmazonSearchForm form)
                    throws RemoteException {
        System.out.println("ISBN is " + form.getIsbn());
        String url = amazon.searchBook(form.getIsbn());
        form.setUrl(url);
        System.out.println("url" + form.getUrl());
        Items [] resultItems =  amazon.lookupISBN(form.getIsbn());
        ArrayList resultsList = new ArrayList();
        if(resultItems!=null && resultItems.length>0)
        {
             for (int i = 0; i < resultItems.length; i++) {
             Item[] itemvalues = resultItems[i].getItem();
                    if (itemvalues != null) {
                        for (int j = 0; j < itemvalues.length; j++) {
                            Book aBook = new Book();
                            String [] authors=
                                itemvalues[j].getItemAttributes().getAuthor();
                            StringBuffer authorBuffer=new StringBuffer();
```

```
                        if(authorBuffer!=null) {
                        for( int k=0;k<authors.length;k++)
                        {
                           authorBuffer.append(authors[k]);
                           authorBuffer.append(" ");

                        }
                        }
                         aBook.setTitle(
                            itemvalues[j].getItemAttributes().getTitle());
                        aBook.setPublication(
                          itemvalues[j].getItemAttributes().getPublisher());
                        aBook.setAuthor(authorBuffer.toString());
                        aBook.setIsbn(
                           itemvalues[j].getItemAttributes().getISBN());
                        aBook.setPrice(
                          itemvalues[j].getItemAttributes().getListPrice()
                                 .getFormattedPrice());
                        aBook.setPages(
                              itemvalues[j].getItemAttributes()
                                          .getNumberOfPages().intValue());

                        System.out.println("Authors :
                             "+ authorBuffer.toString());
                        System.out.println("ISBN :
                            "+ itemvalues[j].getItemAttributes().getISBN());
                         System.out.println("Label :
                            "+ itemvalues[j].getItemAttributes().getLabel());
                         System.out.println("Price : "
                             + itemvalues[j].getItemAttributes().
                                 getListPrice().getFormattedPrice());
                         System.out.println("No of pages : "
                            + itemvalues[j].getItemAttributes()
                                          .getNumberOfPages());
                         System.out.println("publisher : "
                             + itemvalues[j].getItemAttributes()
                                         .getPublisher());
                         System.out.println("Title : "
                            + itemvalues[j].getItemAttributes().getTitle());
                        resultsList.add(aBook);
                    }
                }
            }
        }
        form.setBooksList(resultsList);
        return new Forward("success", form);
}
```

Listing 6-10 looks long and tedious but is really simple. All you're doing is getting an ISBN from the user, submitting it to the Control using a couple lines of code, and then preparing the results to be displayed in the browser. You use the `searchBook` method in the Control to get the URL to the book and the `lookupISBN` method to get the details of the book.

This action is called from `searchAmazon.jsp`. Figure 6-5 shows you this JSP, and Listing 6-11 shows the code.

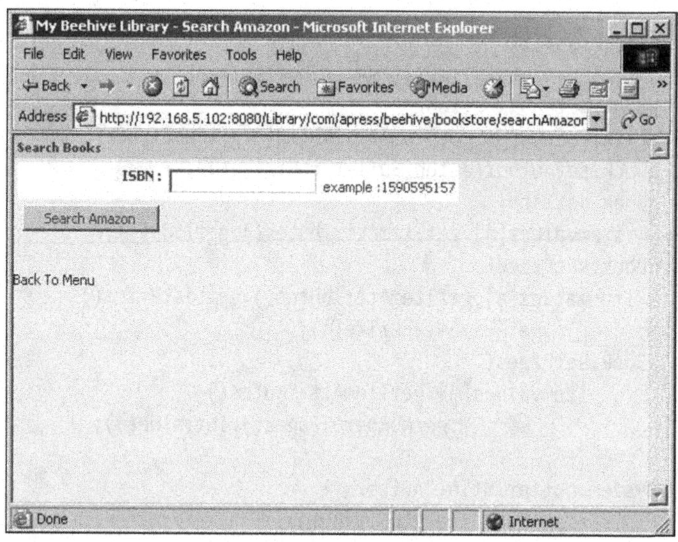


**Figure 6-5.** *searchAmazon.jsp*

**Listing 6-11.** *searchAmazon.jsp*

```
<%@ page language="java" contentType="text/html;charset=UTF-8"%>
<%@ taglib uri=http://beehive.apache.org/netui/tags-databinding-1.0
                 prefix="netui-data"%>
<%@ taglib uri="http://beehive.apache.org/netui/tags-html-1.0" prefix="netui"%>
<%@ taglib uri=http://beehive.apache.org/netui/tags-template-1.0
                   prefix="netui-template"%>
<netui:html>
    <head>
        <title>
            My Beehive Library - Search Amazon
        </title>
    </head>
```

```
<body>
<link rel="stylesheet" type="text/css"
        href="../../../../resources/beehive/version1/css/main.jsp" />
<netui:form action="searchAWS" tagId="amazonSearch"
        genJavaScriptFormSubmit="true">
    <table border="0" cellpadding="3" cellspacing="0" width="100%" >
            <tr><td class="corpsubhead"><span class="promo"><B>
                            Search Books</b></span></td></tr>
            <tr><td colspan="2" class="promo">

            <table border="0" cellpadding="2" cellspacing="0">
                <tr class="odd" valign="top">
                    <td  class="text" align="right"><b> ISBN  : </b></td>
                    <td class="text" ><netui:textBox tagId="isbn"
                     dataSource="actionForm.isbn" size="20" styleClass="text"/>
                                 example :1590595157</td>
                            </tr>
                 <tr>
                         <td>
                   <netui:button action="searchAWS"
                                                type="submit"
                                               styleClass="text" >
                                                  Search Amazon
                                      </netui:button>
                                 </td>
                            </tr>
                     </table>
           </td></tr>
    </table>
  <BR><BR>
  <netui:anchor action="begin" styleClass="text" >Back To Menu </netui:anchor>
  </netui:form>
    </body>
</netui:html>
```

In Listing 6-11, you can see a simple example of a couple NetUI tags that call the searchAWS action and provide the action with the ISBN. You've seen this sort of JSP in Chapter 5, so we won't get into the details here.

Once you enter an ISBN and click Search Amazon, the action shown in Listing 6-10 is called. You're then taken to the amazonResults.jsp page, as shown in Figure 6-6. Listing 6-12 shows the code for this JSP.

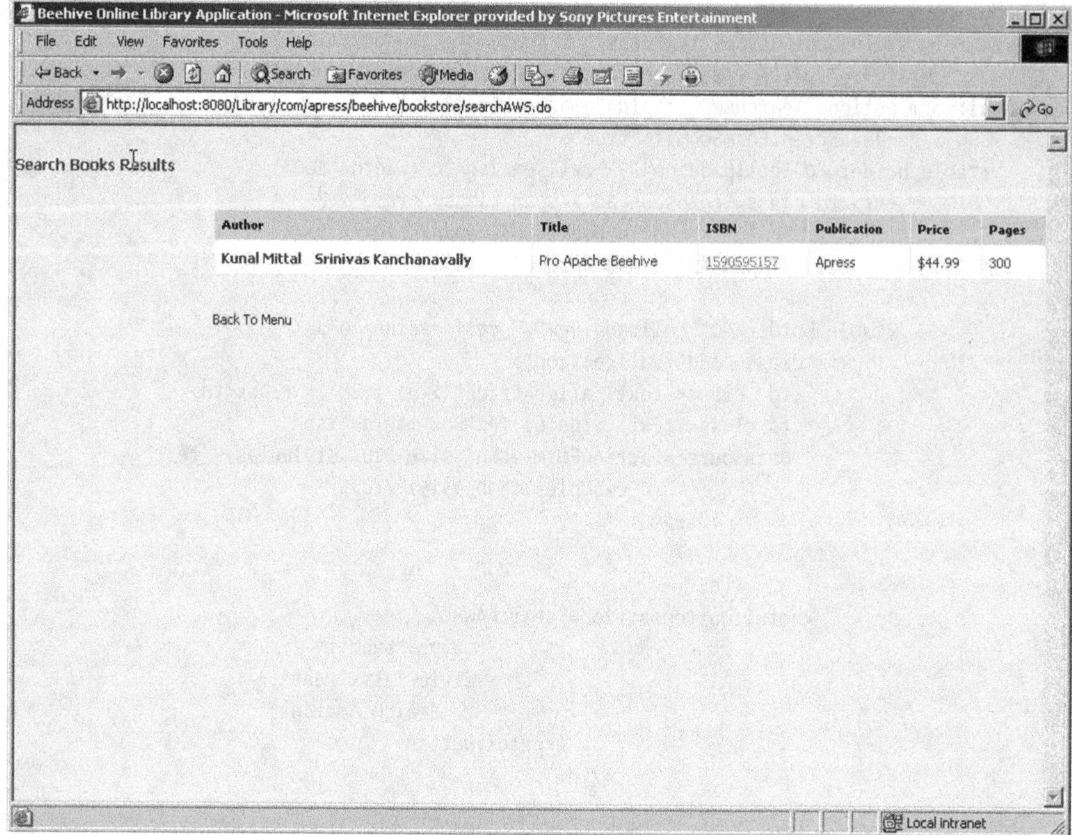


**Figure 6-6.** *amazonResults.jsp*

Listing 6-12 is another example of a NetUI JSP page. We're just showing the code here as a reference. Chapter 5 covered all the details of the NetUI tags. In Chapter 5, when we talked about all these NetUI tags and the controller, you really had no backend to the bookstore system; lots of stuff was just hard-coded. Now, you've actually seen different types of Controls that provide the business layer, or backend, to the bookstore system that you're building as part of this book.

**Listing 6-12.** *amazonResults.jsp*

```
<%@ page language="java" contentType="text/html;charset=UTF-8"%>
<%@ taglib uri="http://beehive.apache.org/netui/tags-databinding-1.0"
               prefix="netui-data"%>
<%@ taglib uri="http://beehive.apache.org/netui/tags-html-1.0" prefix="netui"%>
<%@ taglib uri="http://beehive.apache.org/netui/tags-template-1.0"
              prefix="netui-template"%>
<head>
<title>Amazon search results</title>
```

```
</head>
<netui:form tagId="searchresultsForm" action="searchAWS">

<table border="0" cellpadding="0" cellspacing="0" width="100%">
  <tr valign="top">
       <td class="text"><span class="promotitle">
        Search Books Results</span></td>
          <td class="text">
            <br>


<br><br>
 <% String toggle="odd"; %>
<netui-data:repeater dataSource="actionForm.booksList" defaultText="No Books Found">
 <netui-data:repeaterHeader>
    <table border="0" cellpadding="6" cellspacing="1" width="100%">
    <tr class="sort" valign="bottom">
        <td class="sort"><b>Author</b></td>
        <td class="sort"><b>Title</b></td>
        <td class="sort"><b>ISBN</b></td>
        <td class="sort"><b>Publication</b></td>
        <td class="sort"><b>Price</b></td>
         <td class="sort"><b>Pages</b></td>
    </tr>
 </netui-data:repeaterHeader>
 <netui-data:repeaterItem>
     <%if(toggle.equals("odd")) {
            toggle="even"; %>
        <tr class="odd">
     <% } else {
        toggle="odd";%>
        <tr class="even">
     <%} %>

    <td class="text"><b><netui:label value="${container.item.author}" /></b></td>

           <td class="text"><netui:label value="${container.item.title}" /></td>
           <td class="text"><netui:anchor href="${actionForm.url}" target="_blank" >
            <netui:content value="${container.item.isbn}" /> </netui:anchor></td>
             <td class="text">
                   <netui:label value="${container.item.publication}" />
              </td>
    <td class="text"><netui:label value="${container.item.price}" /></td>
    <td class="text"><netui:label value="${container.item.pages}" /></td>
  </tr>
  </netui-data:repeaterItem>
      <netui-data:repeaterFooter>
           </table>
```

```
        </netui-data:repeaterFooter>
    </netui-data:repeater>
 <BR><BR>
  <netui:anchor action="begin" styleClass="text" >Back To Menu </netui:anchor>
</netui:form>
```

Clicking the ISBN link shown in Figure 6-6, you'll be taken directly to the details of the book on the Amazon.com Web site, as shown in Figure 6-7. This link is what you get using the searchBook method in the Amazon Control that you wrote.

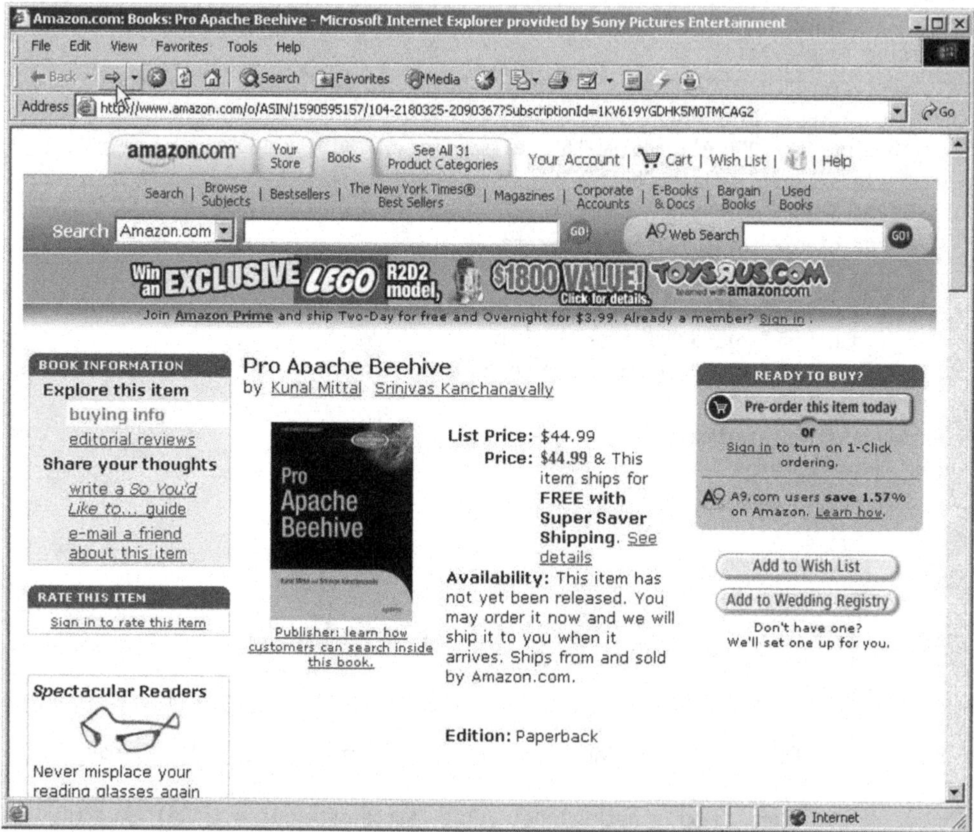


**Figure 6-7.** *The book listing on Amazon.com*

## So, What's Next?

In this chapter, you learned about the power and value of Controls. You saw examples of how Controls and NetUI/Page Flows work together. In this chapter, you also looked at some Web Service–related code that was based on Apache Axis. The next piece of technology in the Apache Beehive project is Web Services. Web Services are based on the JSR 181 standard, and they use metadata annotations like Controls and NetUI do. In the next chapter, you'll learn about JSR 181 and Web Services in Beehive.

CHAPTER 7

# Working with Beehive Web Services and JSR 181

In this chapter, you'll explore the Web Service capabilities that are part of Apache Beehive. You already learned a little bit about Web Services in Chapter 6. In this chapter, you'll learn about JSR 181, Web Services Metadata for the Java Platform, which allows you to expose Web Services using metadata annotations. This concept is similar to all the metadata annotations you've seen thus far.

We'll start the chapter by explaining JSR 181 and the different annotations it provides. We'll then cover the details of the Apache Beehive implementation of JSR 181, including showing some Web Service code.

Apache Beehive Web Services provide full support for JSR 181 and leverage Apache Axis for its SOAP implementation.

## Introducing JSR 181

The Web Service capabilities in Apache Beehive revolve around the JSR 181 annotations. We introduced these in Chapter 3 of this book.

---

**Further Reading** You can read more about JSR 181 at `http://www.jcp.org/en/jsr/detail?id=181`.

---

Using the eight annotations in JSR 181, you can easily expose any Java class as a Web Service. With the Apache Beehive implementation, you get twelve annotations, including the eight from JSR 181. These annotations will determine how WSDL defines pieces of the Java code.

For example, to expose your Java class as a Web Service, change the signature of the class to look like this:

```
@WebService public class MyClass {
```

Just add the `@WebService` annotation to define that this class will be a Web Service.

Now you can expose a method within this class in your Web Service by using the `@WebMethod` annotation:

```
@WebMethod public String myMethod() {
```

Last, you need to define the parameters for the method using the `@WebParam` annotation. You can also name your return value using the `@WebResult` annotation, like so:

```
@WebResult(name="myReturnValue")
@WebMethod public String myMethod(@WebParam String myParam) {
```

The following are the twelve annotations available in Apache Beehive. (The first eight are part of the JSR 181 specification; Apache Beehive introduced the last four.)

- `@WebService`: This specifies that the class is to be exposed as a Web Service.
- `@WebMethod`: This specifies that the method is to be exposed as a Web Service operation.
- `@WebParam`: This specifies that the parameter will be exposed in the Web Service.
- `@WebResult`: This maps the return value to a WSDL element.
- `@OneWay`: This specifies that the method defined by the `@WebMethod` annotation has only an input message or parameter but no return value. The JSR 181 processor in Beehive will report an error if the method has a return value or `@WebResult` annotation associated with it.
- `@SOAPBinding`: This binds the Web Service to SOAP. This specifies whether the Web Service is a document-style or RPC Web Service.
- `@HandlerChain`: This defines `@SOAPMessageHandlers` that are shared across Web Services.
- `@SOAPMessageHandlers`: This is a collection of `SOAPMessageHandler` annotations. The order of execution is the order in which the `SOAPMessageHandler` annotations appear.
- `@SOAPMessageHandler`: This defines any protocol handler that's executed before and after the methods of the Web Service are executed.
- `@SecurityRoles`: This specifies the security roles that have access to the Web Service, either at the Web Service level or at the Web method (operation) level.
- `@SecurityIdentity`: This defines the identity that the Web Service assumes as it's running. By default, the Web Service runs as the authenticated user. However, this annotation allows the developer to override this if required.
- `@InitParam`: This specifies any initialization parameters for the Web Service.

Now that you've seen all the JSR 181 annotations, it's time to understand how JSR 181 works.

## The JSR 181 Process

Let's take a look at the JSR 181 process. In other words, how do you go about building Web Services using JSR 181? What are your responsibilities as a developer, and what happens behind the scenes for you? Take a look at Figure 7-1.

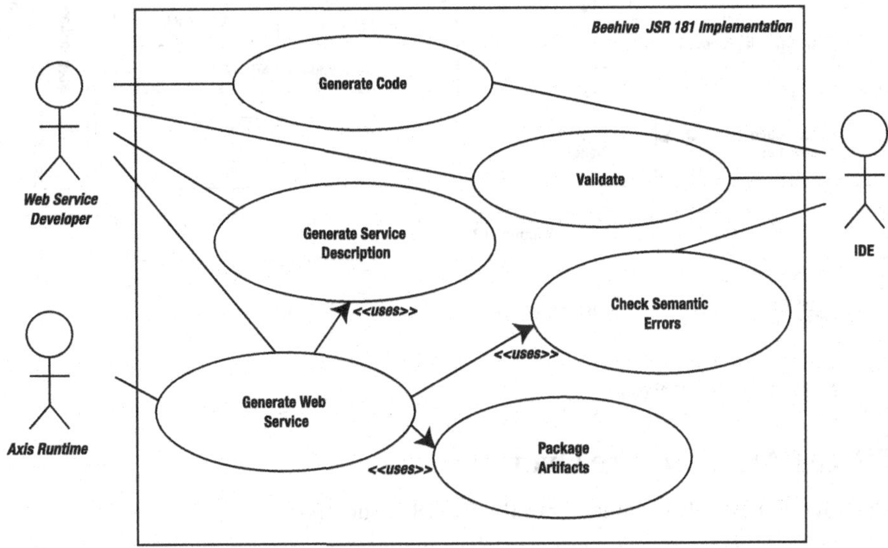


**Figure 7-1.** *Use case for JSR 181 Web Service*

Figure 7-1 shows a simple use case diagram that explains the Beehive JSR 181 implementation. It has three actors: you, the Web Service developer; the Axis runtime engine; and some IDE, such as Eclipse Pollinate. We'll show you one more figure, and then we'll explain both of these in detail. Take a look at Figure 7-2, which shows the JSR 181 runtime processor.

Now we'll explain Figure 7-1 and 7-2 at the same time. The Web Service developer is involved in several use cases, as shown in Figure 7-1. These are Generate Code, Generate Service Description, Generate Web Service, and Validate. All of these use cases either are command-line tools exposed by the JSR 181 runtime processor, are provided as functions in the Pollinate IDE, or are both.

---

■ **Note** The processor can also run as a stand-alone tool (from the command line) to manually generate the artifacts required for a Web Service that can be deployed.

---

Take the use cases in Figure 7-1, and map them to elements in Figure 7-2. The Generate Code and Generate Web Service use cases correspond to the Source Code Generator. The Generate Service Description is the WSDL handler in Figure 7-2. The Validate use case maps to the Validator. Now map the use cases for the IDE and Axis runtime to the corresponding elements in Figure 7-2.

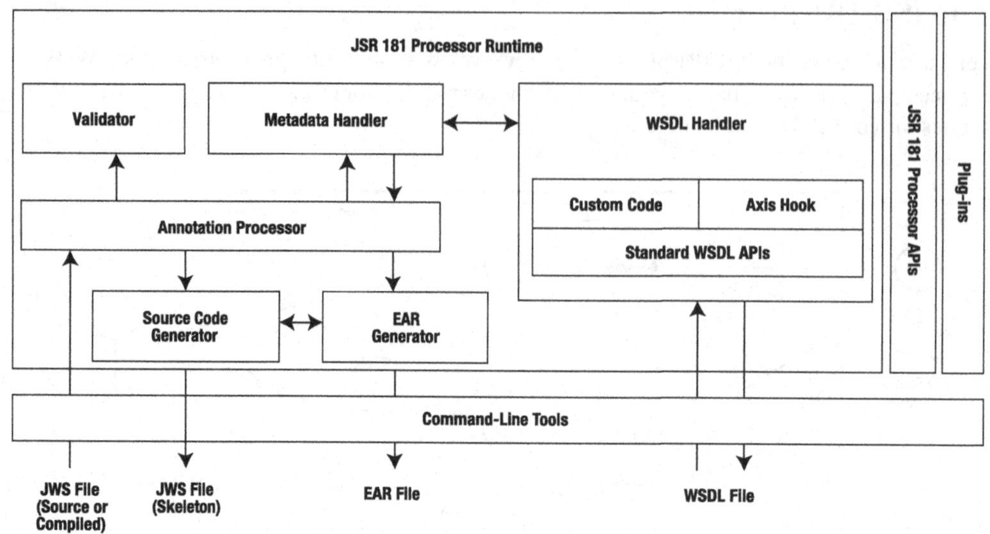


**Figure 7-2.** *JSR 181 runtime processor*

## The JSR 181 Architecture Overview

Figure 7-3 shows the overall architecture of the JSR 181 processor.

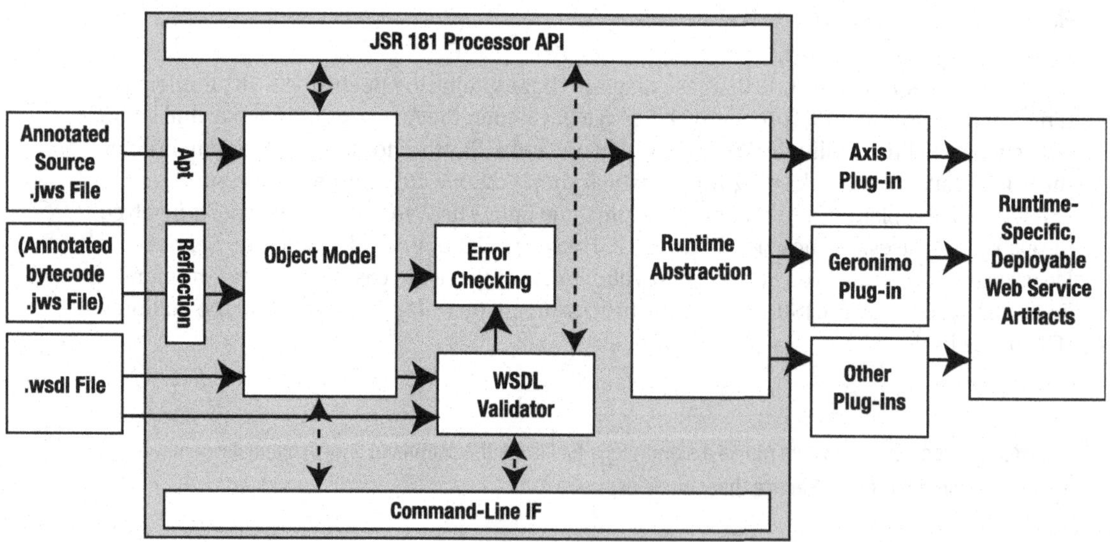


**Figure 7-3.** *JSR 181 architecture*

### Building the Web Service

While working with JSR 181, you have two potential starting points. You can start with a WSDL file, or you can start with a Java source file that's built using the JSR 181 annotations. Both options result in the generation of the Web Service. WSDL validator and code validation features are provided as part of JSR 181 to make sure the generated Web Service is in sync with the WSDL that's exposed. You can do this using API calls or the command-line interface.

As mentioned, you can start working with the JSR 181 processor using either a Java source file or a WSDL file. To start with Java, you need an annotation Java Web Service (JWS) file (either source code or compiled bytecode). You can also have several XML Schemas or Java files that define messages or data types that are used by the JWS file.

To start with WSDL, all you need to provide is a valid WSDL file. The JSR 181 processor has a validator that will let you know if your WSDL isn't valid.

### Working with the Output Files

Depending on which input files you start with, you'll end up with a different set of artifacts at the end.

In other words, if you start with Java, you'll get deployable code that's the Java Web Service. This will include a WSDL and several Java files or JARs that contain all the code for the Web Service.

If you start with WSDL, you'll end up with an annotated JWS file skeleton that you need to implement. The method signatures will conform to the WSDL, but obviously you'll need to implement your business logic.

### Deploying the Web Service

You have a couple deployment options for your Web Service:

- You can build and deploy the Web Service in an EAR file.
- You can use JSR 109, Implementing Enterprise Web Services, for deploying Web Services.
- You can copy the annotation Java Web Service source to the appropriate directories for a runtime such as Axis. When the first request is sent to the Web Service, the Axis runtime will automatically invoke the JSR 181 processor.

Without further delay, let's start writing a Web Service using JSR 181.

# Writing Your First Web Service

You'll now look at a simple HelloWorld Web Service and use it to understand the fundamentals. We'll show how to write the Web Service, deploy it, and then test it. You'll use Java code in the form of a JWS file.

## Writing the Web Service

Listing 7-1 shows you a simple Java Web Service: the HelloWorld Web Service.

**Listing 7-1.** *HelloWorld Web Service*

```
package apress.beehive;
import javax.jws.WebMethod;
import javax.jws.WebService;
import javax.jws.WebParam;

@WebService
public class HelloWorld {

    @WebMethod
    public String sayHelloWorld() {
        return "Hello World";
    }

    @WebMethod
    public String sayHelloWorldInParam( @WebParam String name )
    {
        if (name.equals("") )
            { name = "World"; }

        return "Hello, " + name + "!";
    }

    public String notExposedOverTheWeb()
    {
        return "Not a Web Service method!";
    }
}
```

In this example, you're exposing a simple HelloWorld Web Service. You use the `@WebService` annotation to denote that this Java class is a Web Service. It has three methods, but only two of them are exposed as Web Services. Can you figure out which ones? Last, only one of the three methods has a parameter that's exposed in the Web Service. All this has to do with simple annotations.

## Deploying the Web Service

You now need to compile and deploy the Web Service. You can use `ant` and the `build.xml` file under the `chapter7/web-inf/src` directory:

```
ant -f C:\beehive_projects\chapter7\code\WEB-INF\src\build.xml
        -Dto.dir=%CATALINA_HOME%\webapps clean build deploy
```

## Testing the Web Service

Now you can run the Web Service using the Tomcat container. Visit the `index.jsp` page: `http://localhost:8080/<<WebAppName>>/index.jsp`.

Once there, click the *Validate* link for an evaluation of the resources available to your Web Service. Click the *WSDL* link to see the Web Service's WSDL. Click the *sayHelloWorld()* link to see a SOAP response from the Web Service's `sayHelloWorld()` method.

You can also test the `sayHelloWorldInParam` Web Service method using the following URL: `http://localhost:8080/<<WebAppName>>/HelloWorld.jws?method=sayHelloWorldInParam&name➥ =kunal`.

That's it! You've written and tested a simple Web Service. Now let's expose a Web Service for your bookstore application.

# Exposing a Web Service from the Bookstore Application

The following sections will show you how to extend the bookstore example to expose a Web Service. This Web Service will use the Controls you've been using in previous chapters. We'll show you how to write the Web Service, set up the Web application configuration to deploy the Web Service, and then test the Web Service. In addition, we'll show you the WSDL file for the Web Service.

## Writing the Web Service

Listing 7-2 shows the code for the bookstore Web Service.

**Listing 7-2.** *Bookstore Web Service*

```
package apress.beehive.controls.wscontrol;

import org.apache.beehive.controls.api.bean.Control;

import javax.jws.*;
import javax.jws.soap.SOAPBinding;
import java.rmi.RemoteException;
import java.sql.SQLException;

import com.apress.beehive.bookstore.vo.BookDetailDocument;
import com.apress.beehive.bookstore.vo.Book;

@WebService (name="LibraryWebService",
        targetNamespace="http://wscontrol.controls.beehive.apress",
        serviceName="LibraryService")
        @SOAPBinding(style = SOAPBinding.Style.RPC, use = SOAPBinding.Use.ENCODED)
        public class MyBookWebService {

    @Control
        public apress.beehive.controls.javacontrol.AmazonControl amazon;
```

```
@Control
        public
          apress.beehive.controls.ejbcontrol.BookDetailEJBControl ejbcontrol;

@WebMethod(operationName = "getGreeting" )
 @WebResult(name="greetings")
   public String sayHello() {
    return "Hello world!";
}

/** example to show the usage of @Oneway annotation
 * This is used for methods which does not return anything
 * As a side effect, a @OneWay method can not
 * throw checked exceptions and obviously
 * cannot have any OUT/INOUT parameters.
 *
 */
@WebMethod(operationName = "printHello", action="urn:printHello1")
 @Oneway
     public void printHello(String name) {
      System.out.println("Hello"+ name +"!!" );
   }

@WebMethod
        public String addBook(@WebParam(name = "book")
              Book newBook)
                throws RemoteException,SQLException
{
   return ejbcontrol.insertBookDetail(this.getBookDetail(newBook));
}

@WebMethod
        public String getAmazonURLForBook
           (@WebParam(name = "bookISBN") String isbn)
               throws RemoteException {
    return amazon.searchBook(isbn);
}

// I have given this method to show that a JWS file
// can have non_webservice methods
 private BookDetailDocument.BookDetail getBookDetail(Book book) {
     BookDetailDocument.BookDetail bd =
         BookDetailDocument.Factory.newInstance().addNewBookDetail();
    bd.setAuthor(book.getAuthor());
    bd.setAvailable(book.isAvailable());
    bd.setBookId(book.getBook_Id());
    bd.setBookType(book.getBook_type());
```

```
        bd.setCatalogNo(book.getCatalogNo());
        bd.setComments(book.getComments());
        bd.setIsbn(book.getIsbn());
        bd.setPrice(book.getPrice());
        bd.setPages(book.getPages());
        bd.setPublication(book.getPublication());

        return bd;
    }
}
```

We'll first point out that Listing 7-2 uses an XMLBean. You can ignore this for now; we'll cover XMLBeans in detail in Chapter 8. For now, just concentrate on the pieces of code that relate to Web Services. For instance, notice the different annotations in the source code. You'll see that a single Java file can contain annotations for Web Services as well as Controls. This example uses two Controls that are declared as instance variables. We'll talk about the Web Service annotations now to walk you through how to create the Web Service.

The first annotation is the `@WebService` annotation:

```
@WebService (name="LibraryWebService",
      targetNamespace="http://wscontrol.controls.beehive.apress",
      serviceName="LibraryService")
```

Name this Web Service `LibraryWebService`. This is simple enough. All you're doing is telling the JSR 181 processor that this Java source file needs to be converted to a Web Service.

The next annotation in this example is the `@SOAPBinding` annotation:

```
@SOAPBinding(style = SOAPBinding.Style.RPC, use = SOAPBinding.Use.ENCODED)
```

The `@SOAPBinding` annotation defines the type of Web Service. Using this annotation, you define the style of Web Service.

The next annotation is the `@WebMethod` annotation. You'll see a couple examples of this annotation in the source code:

```
@WebMethod(operationName = "getGreeting" )
```

In this example, you're defining that the method defined below this annotation should be exposed as a Web Service method. The Web Service operation name should be `getGreeting`.

The next annotation is the `@WebResult` annotation. The example from the source code is as follows:

```
@WebResult(name="greetings")
```

In this example, you're basically defining that the return value from the method should be called `greetings`.

The code example has another method that uses the `@WebMethod` annotation. However, it also adds a new annotation called `@OneWay`:

```
@WebMethod(operationName = "printHello", action="urn:printHello1")
 @Oneway
```

This annotation is used for methods that aren't supposed to return anything. Thus, this method can obviously not have any OUT parameters. Lastly, as a side affect, this method can't throw any checked exceptions.

In the next method, you'll see an example of the @WebParam annotation:

```
@WebMethod
        public String addBook(@WebParam(name = "book")
               Book newBook) throws RemoteException,SQLException
```

Here, you're defining a method called addBook that takes in a parameter called newBook. However, because you define the name=book option, in the WSDL the parameter name will be book. If you deleted (name="book") from the signature, then the parameter name in the WSDL would be newBook.

Notice that the last method that uses XMLBeans doesn't have any JSR 181 annotations. Like you saw in the HelloWorld example, this is a method that won't get exposed as a Web Service.

## Setting Up to Run the Web Service

To run the Web Service, you need to make sure the code shown in Listing 7-3 is in your web.xml file. Copy and paste the code into web.xml or use the sample web.xml from the chapter7/web-inf directory.

**Listing 7-3.** *web.xml for Web Services*

```
<listener>
  <listener-class>
       org.apache.axis.transport.http.AxisHTTPSessionListener
  </listener-class>
</listener>

<servlet>
  <servlet-name>AxisServlet</servlet-name>
  <display-name>Apache-Axis Servlet</display-name>
  <servlet-class>
     org.apache.axis.transport.http.AxisServlet
  </servlet-class>
</servlet>

<servlet>
  <servlet-name>AdminServlet</servlet-name>
  <display-name>Axis Admin Servlet</display-name>
  <servlet-class>
     org.apache.axis.transport.http.AdminServlet
  </servlet-class>
  <load-on-startup>100</load-on-startup>
</servlet>
```

```
<servlet>
  <servlet-name>SOAPMonitorService</servlet-name>
  <display-name>SOAPMonitorService</display-name>
  <servlet-class>
      org.apache.axis.monitor.SOAPMonitorService
  </servlet-class>
  <init-param>
    <param-name>SOAPMonitorPort</param-name>
    <param-value>5001</param-value>
  </init-param>
  <load-on-startup>100</load-on-startup>
</servlet>

<servlet-mapping>
  <servlet-name>AxisServlet</servlet-name>
  <url-pattern>/servlet/AxisServlet</url-pattern>
</servlet-mapping>

<servlet-mapping>
  <servlet-name>AxisServlet</servlet-name>
  <url-pattern>*.jws</url-pattern>
</servlet-mapping>

<servlet-mapping>
  <servlet-name>AxisServlet</servlet-name>
  <url-pattern>/services/*</url-pattern>
</servlet-mapping>

<servlet-mapping>
  <servlet-name>SOAPMonitorService</servlet-name>
  <url-pattern>/SOAPMonitor</url-pattern>
</servlet-mapping>
```

The only other setup you have to do in order to run the Web Service is to copy the `server-config.wsdd` file from the `chapter7\web-inf` directory into the `web-inf` directory of your Web application.

## Deploying the Web Service

You now need to compile and deploy the Web Service. You can use `ant` and the `build.xml` file under the `chapter7/web-inf/src` directory:

```
ant -f C:\beehive_projects\chapter7\code\WEB-INF\src\build.xml
        -Dto.dir=%CATALINA_HOME%\webapps clean build deploy
```

## Looking at the WSDL

When you compile this Web Service and run it through the JSR 181 processor, you'll generate a WSDL file. Listing 7-4 shows the WSDL file for this Web Service.

**Listing 7-4.** *WSDL File for the Bookstore Web Service*

```
<?xml version="1.0" encoding="UTF-8"?>
<wsdl:definitions targetNamespace=http://wscontrol.controls.beehive.apress
xmlns:apachesoap=http://xml.apache.org/xml-soap
xmlns:impl=http://wscontrol.controls.beehive.apress
xmlns:intf="http://wscontrol.controls.beehive.apress"
xmlns:soapenc=http://schemas.xmlsoap.org/soap/encoding/
xmlns:tns1=http://lang.java
xmlns:wsdl=http://schemas.xmlsoap.org/wsdl/
xmlns:wsdlsoap=http://schemas.xmlsoap.org/wsdl/soap/
xmlns:xsd="http://www.w3.org/2001/XMLSchema">
<!--WSDL created by Apache Axis version: 1.2RC3
Built on Feb 28, 2005 (10:15:14 EST)-->
 <wsdl:types>
  <schema targetNamespace=
          http://wscontrol.controls.beehive.apress
          xmlns="http://www.w3.org/2001/XMLSchema">
   <import namespace="http://lang.java"/>
   <import namespace="http://schemas.xmlsoap.org/soap/encoding/"/>
   <complexType name="Book">
    <sequence>
     <element name="author" nillable="true" type="xsd:string"/>
     <element name="available" nillable="true" type="xsd:boolean"/>
     <element name="book_Id" nillable="true" type="xsd:int"/>
     <element name="book_type" nillable="true" type="xsd:string"/>
     <element name="catalogNo" nillable="true" type="xsd:string"/>
     <element name="comments" nillable="true" type="xsd:string"/>
     <element name="isbn" nillable="true" type="xsd:string"/>
     <element name="pages" nillable="true" type="xsd:int"/>
     <element name="price" nillable="true" type="xsd:string"/>
     <element name="publication" nillable="true" type="xsd:string"/>
     <element name="publication_Date" nillable="true" type="xsd:string"/>
     <element name="title" nillable="true" type="xsd:string"/>
    </sequence>
   </complexType>
   <complexType name="IOException">
    <sequence/>
   </complexType>
   <complexType name="RemoteException">
    <complexContent>
     <extension base="impl:IOException">
      <sequence>
       <element name="cause" nillable="true" type="xsd:anyType"/>
```

```
      <element name="message" nillable="true" type="xsd:string"/>
     </sequence>
    </extension>
   </complexContent>
  </complexType>
  <complexType name="SQLException">
   <sequence>
    <element name="SQLState" nillable="true" type="xsd:string"/>
    <element name="errorCode" nillable="true" type="xsd:int"/>
    <element name="nextException" nillable="true" type="impl:SQLException"/>
   </sequence>
  </complexType>
 </schema>
</wsdl:types>
 <wsdl:message name="getAmazonURLForBookRequest">
    <wsdl:part name="bookISBN" type="soapenc:string"/>
 </wsdl:message>
 <wsdl:message name="printHelloRequest">
    <wsdl:part name="name" type="soapenc:string"/>
 </wsdl:message>
 <wsdl:message name="SQLException">
    <wsdl:part name="SQLException" type="impl:SQLException"/>
 </wsdl:message>
 <wsdl:message name="RemoteException">
    <wsdl:part name="RemoteException" type="impl:RemoteException"/>
 </wsdl:message>
 <wsdl:message name="addBookResponse">
    <wsdl:part name="result" type="xsd:string"/>
 </wsdl:message>
 <wsdl:message name="getAmazonURLForBookResponse">
    <wsdl:part name="result" type="xsd:string"/>
 </wsdl:message>
 <wsdl:message name="getGreetingRequest">
 </wsdl:message>
 <wsdl:message name="getGreetingResponse">
    <wsdl:part name="greetings" type="xsd:string"/>
 </wsdl:message>
 <wsdl:message name="addBookRequest">
    <wsdl:part name="book" type="impl:Book"/>
 </wsdl:message>
 <wsdl:portType name="LibraryWebService">
    <wsdl:operation name="addBook" parameterOrder="book">
       <wsdl:input message="impl:addBookRequest" name="addBookRequest"/>
       <wsdl:output message="impl:addBookResponse" name="addBookResponse"/>
       <wsdl:fault message="impl:SQLException" name="SQLException"/>
       <wsdl:fault message="impl:RemoteException" name="RemoteException"/>
    </wsdl:operation>
    <wsdl:operation name="getGreeting">
```

```
      <wsdl:input message="impl:getGreetingRequest" name="getGreetingRequest"/>
      <wsdl:output message="impl:getGreetingResponse" name="getGreetingResponse"/>
   </wsdl:operation>
   <wsdl:operation name="printHello" parameterOrder="name">
      <wsdl:input message="impl:printHelloRequest" name="printHelloRequest"/>
   </wsdl:operation>
   <wsdl:operation name="getAmazonURLForBook" parameterOrder="bookISBN">
      <wsdl:input message="impl:getAmazonURLForBookRequest"
                name="getAmazonURLForBookRequest"/>
      <wsdl:output message="impl:getAmazonURLForBookResponse"
                   name="getAmazonURLForBookResponse"/>
      <wsdl:fault message="impl:RemoteException" name="RemoteException"/>
   </wsdl:operation>
</wsdl:portType>
<wsdl:binding name="LibraryWebServiceSoapBinding" type="impl:LibraryWebService">
   <wsdlsoap:binding style="rpc"
            transport="http://schemas.xmlsoap.org/soap/http"/>
   <wsdl:operation name="addBook">
      <wsdlsoap:operation soapAction=""/>
      <wsdl:input name="addBookRequest">
         <wsdlsoap:body
                  encodingStyle=http://schemas.xmlsoap.org/soap/encoding/
                  namespace=http://wscontrol.controls.beehive.apress
                  use="encoded"/>
      </wsdl:input>
      <wsdl:output name="addBookResponse">
         <wsdlsoap:body
                 encodingStyle="http://schemas.xmlsoap.org/soap/encoding/"
                 namespace=http://wscontrol.controls.beehive.apress
                 use="encoded"/>
      </wsdl:output>
      <wsdl:fault name="SQLException">
         <wsdlsoap:fault encodingStyle="http://schemas.xmlsoap.org/soap/encoding/"
                name="SQLException"
                namespace=http://wscontrol.controls.beehive.apress
                use="encoded"/>
      </wsdl:fault>
      <wsdl:fault name="RemoteException">
         <wsdlsoap:fault encodingStyle="http://schemas.xmlsoap.org/soap/encoding/"
               name="RemoteException"
               namespace=http://wscontrol.controls.beehive.apress
               use="encoded"/>
      </wsdl:fault>
   </wsdl:operation>
   <wsdl:operation name="getGreeting">
      <wsdlsoap:operation soapAction=""/>
      <wsdl:input name="getGreetingRequest">
```

```
          <wsdlsoap:body encodingStyle=http://schemas.xmlsoap.org/soap/encoding/
              namespace=http://wscontrol.controls.beehive.apress
              use="encoded"/>
        </wsdl:input>
        <wsdl:output name="getGreetingResponse">
          <wsdlsoap:body encodingStyle=http://schemas.xmlsoap.org/soap/encoding/
                namespace=http://wscontrol.controls.beehive.apress
                use="encoded"/>
        </wsdl:output>
      </wsdl:operation>
      <wsdl:operation name="printHello">
        <wsdlsoap:operation soapAction="urn:printHello1"/>
        <wsdl:input name="printHelloRequest">
          <wsdlsoap:body encodingStyle=http://schemas.xmlsoap.org/soap/encoding/
                 namespace=http://wscontrol.controls.beehive.apress
                 use="encoded"/>
        </wsdl:input>
      </wsdl:operation>
      <wsdl:operation name="getAmazonURLForBook">
        <wsdlsoap:operation soapAction=""/>
        <wsdl:input name="getAmazonURLForBookRequest">
          <wsdlsoap:body encodingStyle=http://schemas.xmlsoap.org/soap/encoding/
                   namespace=http://wscontrol.controls.beehive.apress
                   use="encoded"/>
        </wsdl:input>
        <wsdl:output name="getAmazonURLForBookResponse">
          <wsdlsoap:body encodingStyle=http://schemas.xmlsoap.org/soap/encoding/
                    namespace=http://wscontrol.controls.beehive.apress
                    use="encoded"/>
        </wsdl:output>
        <wsdl:fault name="RemoteException">
          <wsdlsoap:fault encodingStyle=http://schemas.xmlsoap.org/soap/encoding/
                   name="RemoteException"
                   namespace=http://wscontrol.controls.beehive.apress
                   use="encoded"/>
        </wsdl:fault>
      </wsdl:operation>
    </wsdl:binding>
    <wsdl:service name="LibraryService">
      <wsdl:port binding="impl:LibraryWebServiceSoapBinding"
           name="LibraryWebService">
        <wsdlsoap:address location=
             "http://192.168.5.101:8080/Library/apress/beehive/controls/wscontrol/
                    MyBookWebService.jws"/>
      </wsdl:port>
    </wsdl:service>
</wsdl:definitions>
```

As an exercise, take this WSDL file and generate a Web Service from it. Compare the JWS file that's generated to the one you wrote in Listing 7-2.

You can also see this WSDL at `http://localhost:8080/Library/apress/beehive/controls/wscontrol/MyBookWebService.jws?wsdl`.

Figure 7-4 shows the WSDL.

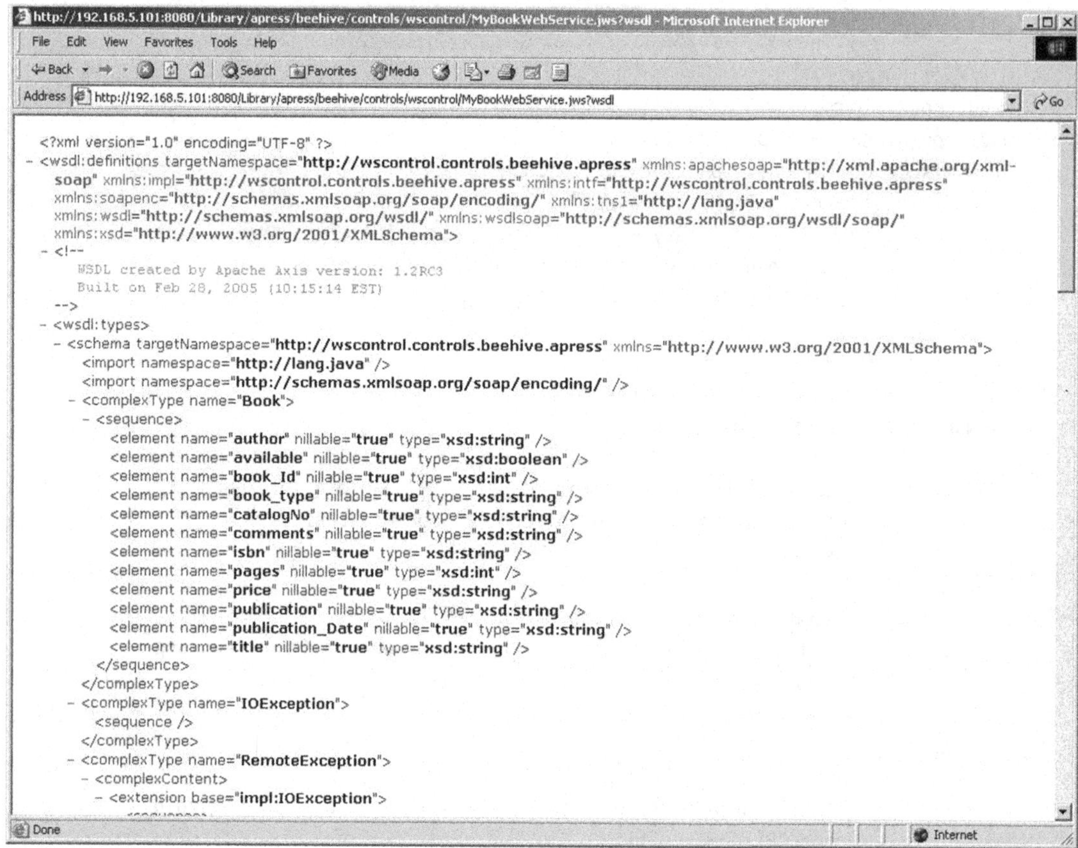


**Figure 7-4.** *JSR bookstore WSDL*

## Running the Web Service

You can run the Web Service at `http://localhost:8080/Library/apress/beehive/controls/wscontrol/MyBookWebService.jws`.

We'll now show the execution of some of the methods. Figure 7-5 shows the call to the `getGreeting` method. The URL to call this method is `http://localhost:8080/Library/apress/beehive/controls/wscontrol/MyBookWebService.jws?method=getGreeting`.

Similarly, you can call the other methods you exposed. To see what an error message from the Web Service looks like, call a method but misspell the name. Enter the URL `http://localhost:8080/Library/apress/beehive/controls/wscontrol/MyBookWebService.jws?method=getAmazonURLForBoo&bookISBN=1590595157`.

Figure 7-6 shows the error message.

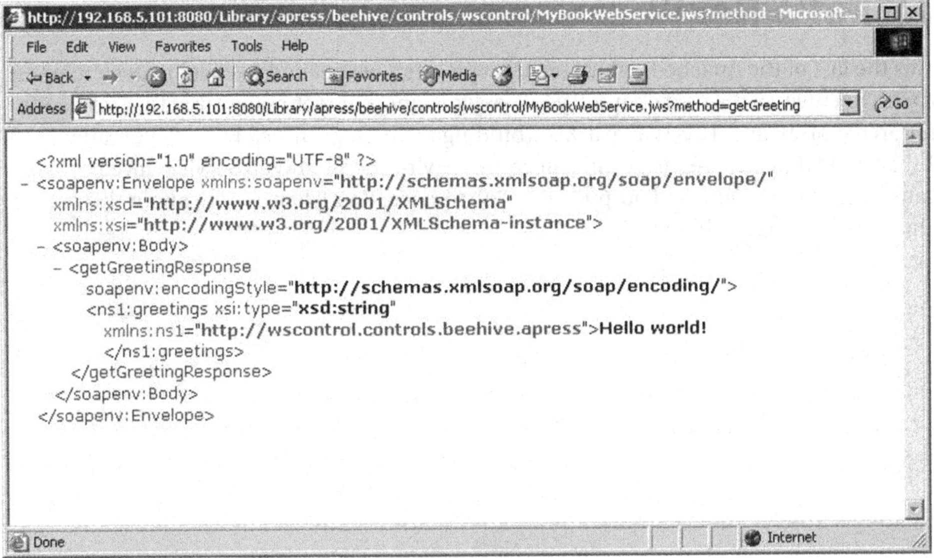


**Figure 7-5.** *Calling the* `getGreeting` *method on the Web Service*

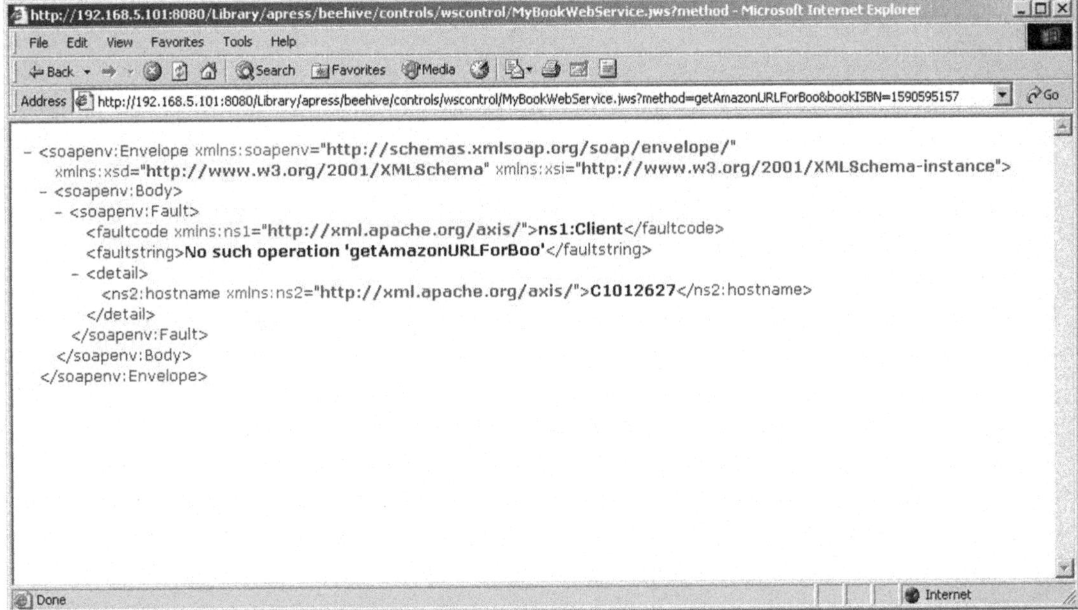


**Figure 7-6.** *SOAP fault from the Web Service*

## So, What's Next?

This was the last of the Apache Beehive technologies that we needed to cover to get you up to speed with Beehive. In the next chapter, you'll explore another technology that BEA released to open source, XMLBeans. This is a Java-XML binding technology, much like an OR mapper but for XML files. XMLBeans are interesting, because they're useful in Web Service development. You can use them as inputs and outputs to a Web Service. You'll learn more about this as you turn the page to the next chapter.

CHAPTER 8

# Using XMLBeans

BEA originally introduced the XMLBeans technology as part of the WebLogic Workshop product, and BEA donated the technology to the Apache Incubator and Apache XML projects in September 2003.

You can think of XMLBeans as an Object-Relational (OR) mapper except for XML files rather than relational databases. In fact, the XMLBeans technology allows you to access an XML file just like you would any Java object or JavaBean. In other words, it's an XML-Java binding tool.

In this chapter, we'll assume you've worked with XML in the past and are familiar with concepts such as XML Schemas, XQuery, XPath, and so on. Don't worry if you aren't an expert at these, though, as the XMLBeans technology hides the complexity of these technologies.

This chapter will show you how to work with XMLBeans and use them in your applications.

---

**Note** If you want to contribute to the XMLBeans open-source project, see Appendix C for details.

---

## What's XML-Java Binding?

XML-Java binding is the process of manipulating XML files as if they were Java objects. Conversely, you might want to convert a Java object into its corresponding XML document format. With XML-Beans, this is easy. Behind the scenes, you always have a copy of the XML file, so you can switch back and forth from accessing the data in XML and accessing it in Java. Before the invention of XML-Java binding, it was tedious and time-consuming to first read in an XML file, manipulate it in Java, and then write out an XML file. This process not only involved a lot of code but also was processing intensive.

Figure 8-1 shows how the typical XML-Java binding technology works. It really acts like a middleman, taking care of the marshalling and unmarshalling between the JavaBean and the XML file.

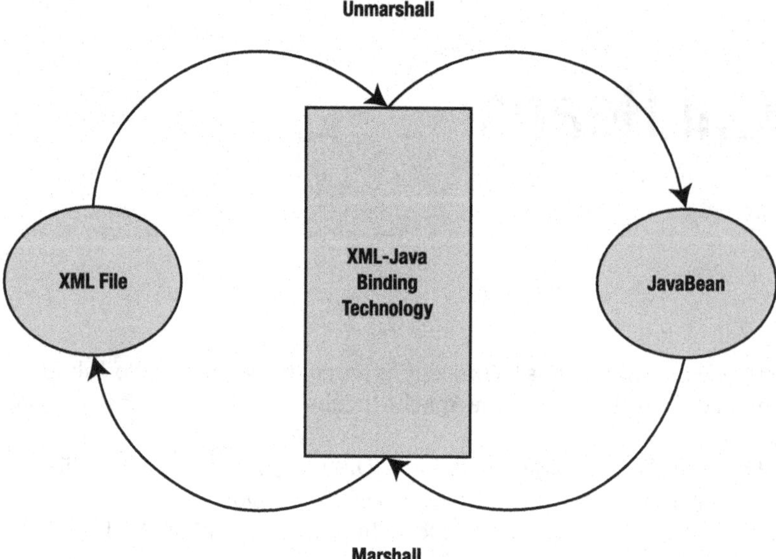


**Figure 8-1.** *XML-Java binding*

The Java Document Model (JDOM) technology was among the first to introduce some concepts of XML-Java binding. JDOM is a new API for reading, writing, and manipulating XML from within Java code.

While deciding to write this chapter, we searched for other XML-Java binding tools and found several:

- Betwixt (`http://jakarta.apache.org/commons/betwixt/`)
- JAXB (`http://java.sun.com/xml/jaxb/`)
- Castor (`http://www.castor.org/`)
- JaxME (`http://ws.apache.org/jaxme/`)
- Jakarta Digester (`http://jakarta.apache.org/commons/digester/`)
- JDOM (`http://www.jdom.org`)
- Enhydra Zeus (`http://zeus.objectweb.org/`)

From this list, Castor and JAXB are the most well-known technologies. Castor is quite an interesting technology. It provides not only XML-Java data binding but also Java-SQL binding like a typical OR tool. In addition, Castor supports runtime introspection capabilities; it will attempt to match elements and attributes of XML to classes and fields of a Java class. Java Architecture for XML Binding (JAXB) is a technology from Sun that provides some basic capabilities.

Still, the XMLBeans technology, while the newest, is probably the most advanced of the XML-Java binding technologies. All the technologies mentioned in the previous list are great, but in our experience XMLBeans is the easiest to use and offers the best set of features and performance. We won't provide a detailed comparison of all these technologies in this chapter; if you've used any of these before, you'll be able to draw your own conclusions as you learn more about XMLBeans in this chapter.

---

■ **Note** A great comparison of different XML-Java binding technologies is available at `https://bindmark.dev.java.net/current-results.html`. This study uses XMLBeans 1.0.3, but XMLBeans 2.0 has made improvements in the areas that XMLBeans 1.0.3 fell short.

---

■ **Note** The most current release of XMLBeans at the time of writing is 2.0.0-beta1, released on February 24, 2005.

---

## XMLBeans As an XML-Java Binding Technology

We're assuming you've worked with XML parsers in the past. As such, you probably already know the differences between SAX and DOM. For example, you probably know that one of the differences is that DOM is much more memory intensive because it provides faster and more flexible access to the XML file. XMLBeans does well on performance by doing incremental unmarshalling and providing `xget` methods to access built-in schema data types. Using XMLBeans, you'll always have full access to the XML file, including all the comments and rules such as the order of the elements. This is definitely a significant advantage of XMLBeans over other data binding technologies.

However, the biggest advantage of XMLBeans is that it provides complete support for XML Schemas. JAXB and Castor, the two closest competitors to XMLBeans, don't have this level of support for XML Schemas. Using XMLBeans, you can access *any* XML Schema with the same level of simplicity and without several different tools.

# XMLBeans Overview

The XMLBeans technology provides intuitive ways to handle XML that make it easier for you to access and manipulate XML data and documents in Java. The technology allows you to treat XML and Java objects as one. You never lose the native XML structure underneath, and XML and Java objects are internally kept in sync.

Using XMLBeans, you can use any XML file that conforms to an XML Schema and manipulate it just as if it were a JavaBean, using getters and setters. XML documents are treated as first-class data objects accessed in a JavaBean-like manner. As a developer, you don't have to write any code to read in the XML file, validate it, manipulate it, and write it back. All this heavy lifting is taken care of for you behind the scenes. What's even better is that in this translation you don't lose the relationships. For example, suppose you have an XML Schema and a corresponding XML file that represents a book. Also, imagine that this file contains an element called `Author` that has a one-to-many relationship with `book`. This is because a book can have multiple authors, as shown in Listing 8-1.

**Listing 8-1.** *Sample XML File for a Book*

```
<book>
    <title>Pro Apache Beehive</title>
        <authors>
            <author>Kunal Mittal</author>
            <author>Srinivas Kanchanvally</author>
        </authors>
    <isbn>1590595157</isbn>
</book>
```

When you work with this file using XMLBeans, the corresponding Java classes will maintain this relationship. Listing 8-2 shows some pseudo-Java code to work with this XML file. Don't try to cut and paste the code in Listing 8-2, though; we'll show you some working code later in this chapter. The code in Listing 8-2 merely illustrates the simplicity of XMLBeans.

**Listing 8-2.** *Pseudo-Java Code to Work with the* `Book.xml` *File*

```
MyBook doc = MyBook.Factory.newInstance();
Book book = doc.addNewBook();
book.setTitle("Pro Apache Beehive");
book.setIsbn("1590595157");
String[] authors = new String[2];
authors[0] = new String("Kunal Mittal");
authors[1] = new String("Srinivas Kanchanavally");
book.setAuthors(authors);
```

That's how simple it is to work with XML files using XMLBeans! You'll see a much more detailed example in the next section.

## DOWNLOAD AND INSTALL XMLBEANS

To work with XMLBeans, you'll need JDK 1.4 or above and Ant installed. Appendix A covers all the information you need to get started with XMLBeans. You can also find the latest version of XMLBeans and instructions on how to use it at `http://xmlbeans.apache.org/documentation/conInstallGuide.html`.

If you need full support for XQuery and XPath, you'll need to download the Saxon XQuery processor (version 8.2 or later) at `http://sourceforge.net/projects/saxon`.

A practical and important use of XMLBeans is creating Web Services with them. Typically in a Web Service you're exchanging SOAP messages in XML format between the Web Service and the Web Service client. Using XMLBeans to consume these messages makes the overall interaction between the Web Services easy to write.

## Data Types in XMLBeans

As you're working with XML Schemas and XMLBeans, it's important to understand the available data types. Each data type in an XML Schema has a corresponding data type in XMLBeans that maps to a Java data type. This helps provide complete support for XML Schemas using XMLBeans. The hierarchy of XMLBeans types mirrors the hierarchy of the schema types themselves. XML Schema types all inherit from `xs:anyType`. XMLBeans types inherit from `XmlObject`. Figure 8-2 shows you a graphical view of the hierarchy.

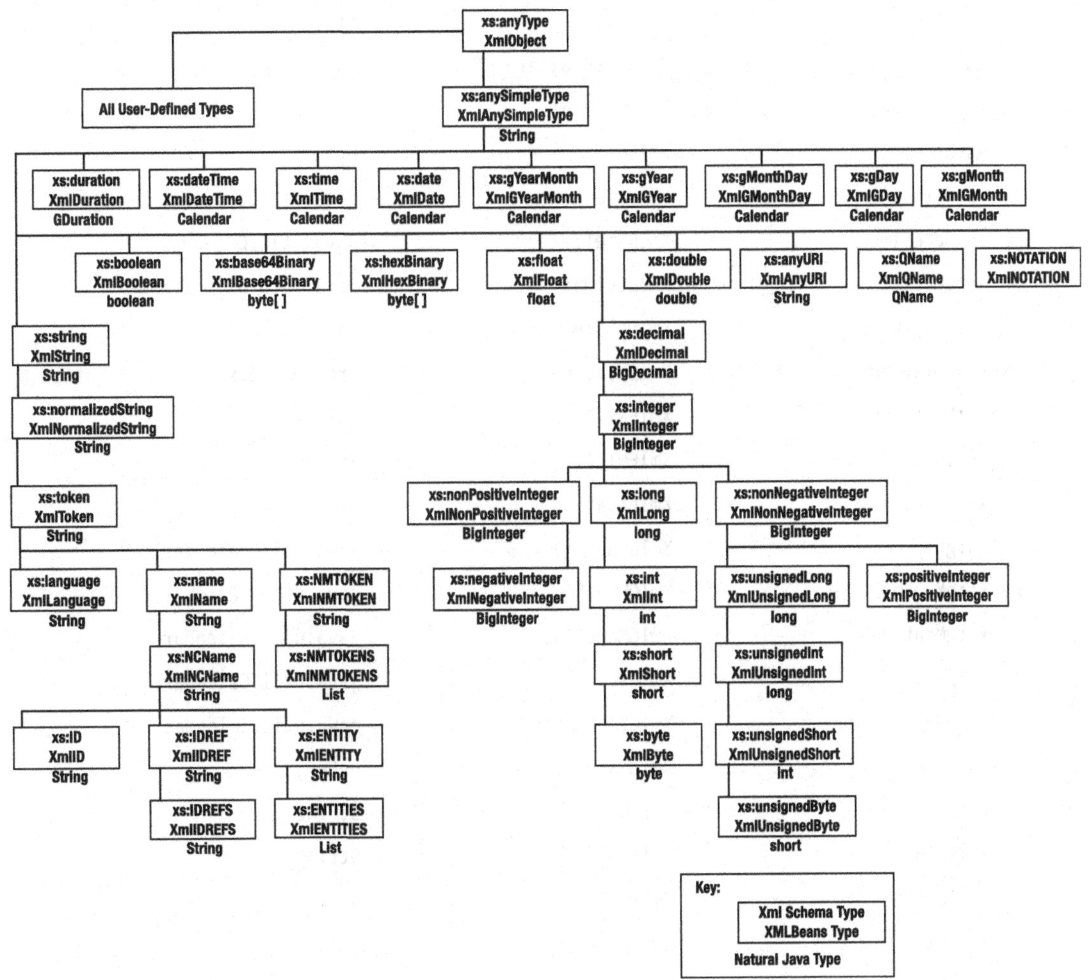


**Figure 8-2.** *Hierarchy of data types in XML Schemas and XMLBeans*

Each of the 46 built-in schema types is represented by an XMLBeans type provided with XMLBeans. Table 8-1 provides an easy reference to the data type mappings.

**Table 8-1.** *Data Type Mappings in XMLBeans*

| Built-in Schema Type | XMLBeans Type | Natural Java Type* |
|---|---|---|
| xs:anyType | XmlObject | org.apache.xmlbeans.XmlObject |
| xs:anySimpleType | XmlAnySimpleType | String |
| xs:anyURI | XmlAnyURI | String |
| xs:base64Binary | XmlBase64Binary | byte[] |
| xs:boolean | XmlBoolean | boolean |
| xs:byte | XmlByte | byte |
| xs:date | XmlDate | java.util.Calendar |
| xs:dateTime | XmlDateTime | java.util.Calendar |
| xs:decimal | XmlDecimal | java.math.BigDecimal |
| xs:double | XmlDouble | double |
| xs:duration | XmlDuration | org.apache.xmlbeans.GDuration |
| xs:ENTITIES | XmlENTITIES | String |
| xs:ENTITY | XmlENTITY | String |
| xs:float | XmlFloat | float |
| xs:gDay | XmlGDay | java.util.Calendar |
| xs:gMonth | XmlGMonth | java.util.Calendar |
| xs:gMonthDay | XmlGMonthDay | java.util.Calendar |
| xs:gYear | XmlGYear | java.util.Calendar |
| xs:gYearMonth | XmlGYearMonth | java.util.Calendar |
| xs:hexBinary | XmlHexBinary | byte[] |
| xs:ID | XmlID | String |
| xs:IDREF | XmlIDREF | String |
| xs:IDREFS | XmlIDREFS | String |
| xs:int | XmlInt | int |
| xs:integer | XmlInteger | java.math.BigInteger |
| xs:language | XmlLanguage | String |
| xs:long | XmlLong | long |
| xs:Name | XmlName | String |
| xs:NCName | XmlNCNAME | String |
| xs:negativeInteger | XmlNegativeInteger | java.math.BigInteger |

**Table 8-1.** *Data Type Mappings in XMLBeans*

| Built-in Schema Type | XMLBeans Type | Natural Java Type* |
|---|---|---|
| xs:NMTOKEN | XmlNMTOKEN | String |
| xs:NMTOKENS | XmlNMTOKENS | String |
| xs:nonNegativeInteger | XmlNonNegativeInteger | java.math.BigInteger |
| xs:nonPositiveInteger | XmlNonPositiveInteger | java.math.BigInteger |
| xs:normalizedString | XmlNormalizedString | String |
| xs:NOTATION | XmlNOTATION | Not supported |
| xs:positiveInteger | XmlPositiveInteger | java.math.BigInteger |
| xs:QName | XmlQName | javax.xml.namespace.QName |
| xs:short | XmlShort | short |
| xs:string | XmlString | String |
| xs:time | XmlTime | java.util.Calendar |
| xs:token | XmlToken | String |
| xs:unsignedByte | XmlUnsignedByte | short |
| xs:unsignedInt | XmlUnsignedInt | long |
| xs:unsignedLong | XmlUnsignedLong | java.math.BigInteger |
| xs:unsignedShort | XmlUnsignedShort | int |

* *All Java types inherit from* `java.lang`, *unless otherwise noted.*

# Working with XMLBeans

Let's now dive in and actually work with XMLBeans. In the following sections, you'll learn how to use an XML Schema to generate the XMLBeans Java code and use it in your applications.

## Working with an XML Schema

The starting point for working with XMLBeans is usually an XML Schema. An XML Schema (XSD file) is an XML document that defines a set of rules to which other XML documents must conform. It provides a data model that allows you to define the contents of your XML file, including complex relationships, data types, the order, and validation rules. Running an XML file through a schema validator, with the schema as input, you can quickly determine whether the XML file is valid. In the Java layer, custom code needs to be written to perform this validation, which is now hidden behind XMLBeans for you.

Throughout this book, you've been building a simple bookstore application. You'll now expand on this application using XMLBeans. You'll define an XML Schema to represent a book object; see Listing 8-3.

**Listing 8-3.** *XML Schema for the Bookstore Sample Application*

```
<xs:schema
   xmlns:xs="http://www.w3.org/2001/XMLSchema"
   xmlns:bk="http://beehive.apress.com/bookstore/vo"
   targetNamespace="http://beehive.apress.com/bookstore/vo"
   elementFormDefault="qualified">

  <xs:element name="bookDetail">
    <xs:complexType>
      <xs:sequence>
       <xs:element name="book_Id" type="xs:int"/>
       <xs:element name="title" type="xs:string"/>
       <xs:element name="book_type" type="xs:string"/>
       <xs:element name="author" type="xs:string"/>
       <xs:element name="publication" type="xs:string"/>
       <xs:element name="publication_Date" type="xs:date"/>
       <xs:element name="catalogNo" type="xs:string"/>
       <xs:element name="isbn" type="xs:string"/>
       <xs:element name="price" type="xs:string"/>
       <xs:element name="comments" type="xs:string"/>
       <xs:element name="pages" type="xs:int"/>
       <xs:element name="available" type="xs:boolean"/>
      </xs:sequence>
    </xs:complexType>
  </xs:element>

  <xs:complexType name="publisher">
    <xs:sequence>
      <xs:element name="name" type="xs:string"/>
      <xs:element name="address" type="xs:string"/>
    </xs:sequence>
    </xs:complexType>

  <xs:complexType name="author">
    <xs:sequence>
      <xs:element name="description" type="xs:string"/>
      <xs:element name="name" type="xs:string"/>
    </xs:sequence>
  </xs:complexType>
 </xs:schema>
```

---

■ **Note** You can either build your XML Schema or take an existing XML file and generate a base schema from it. You can do this using tools such as XMLSpy from Altova or the <oXygen/> XML editor.

---

Listing 8-4 shows a sample XML file that conforms to this schema.

**Listing 8-4.** *Sample XML File for the* `bookDetails.xsd` *Schema*

```
<?xml version="1.0" encoding="UTF-8"?>
<bookDetail xmlns="http://beehive.apress.com/bookstore/vo"
     xmlns:xsi="http://www.w3.org/2001/XMLSchema-instance"
     xsi:schemaLocation="http://beehive.apress.com/bookstore/vo
     file:/C:/ /code/chapter8/bookdetails.xsd">
    <book_Id>1</book_Id>
    <title>Pro Apache Beehive</title>
    <book_type>Book</book_type>
    <author>Kunal Mittal, Srinivas Kanchanvally</author>
    <publication>Apress</publication>
    <publication_Date>2005-08-31T00:00:00.0000000-04:00</publication_Date>
    <catalogNo>123</catalogNo>
    <isbn>1590595157</isbn>
    <price>49.99</price>
    <comments>The first book on Apache Beehive</comments>
    <pages>300</pages>
    <available>false</available>
</bookDetail>
```

With XMLBeans, you can validate XML Schemas, generate the XMLBeans code, and use the code directly from the XMLBeans Web site. So, to validate your XML Schema online, go to `http://xmlbeans.webappshosting.com/schemaToolsV2/validate.do`.

To generate XMLBeans online, visit `http://xmlbeans.webappshosting.com/schemaToolsV2/compile.do`.

The final utility provided online from XMLBeans actually generates an XML Schema from an XML file. You can do this at `http://xmlbeans.webappshosting.com/schemaToolsV2/inst2xsd.do`.

We took the XSD shown in Listing 8-3 and ran it through the online schema validator. Figure 8-3 shows the output.

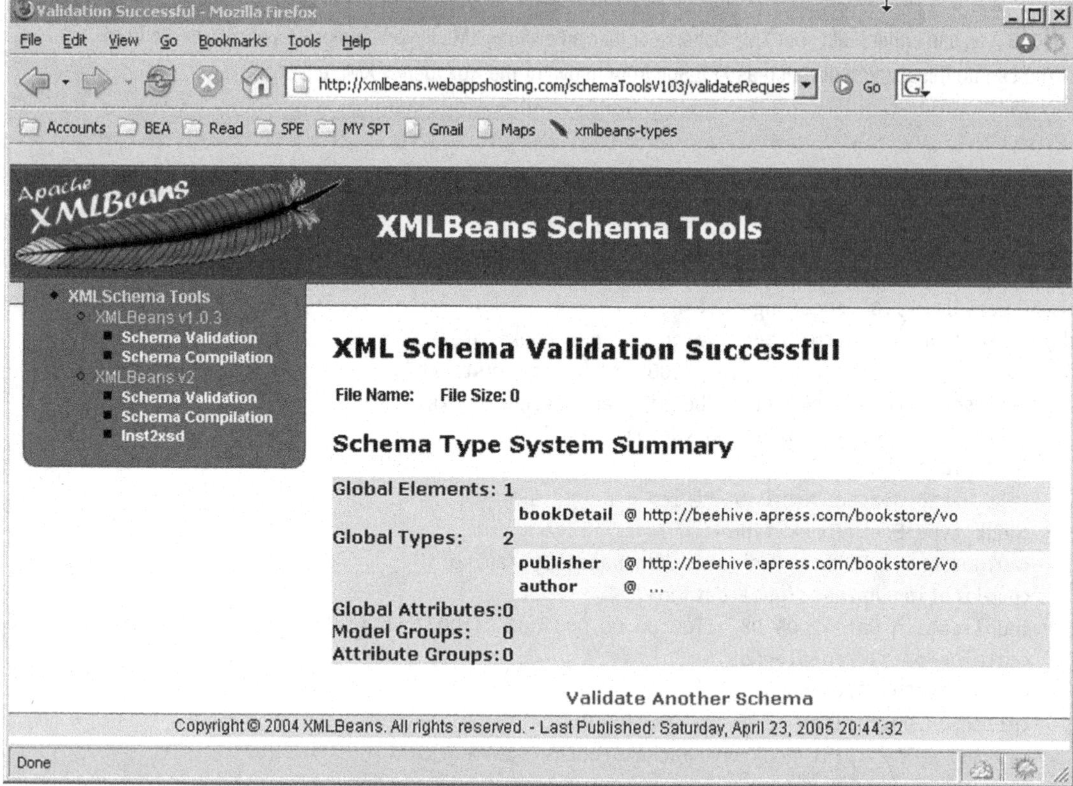


**Figure 8-3.** *Results of schema validator*

## Generating Java Code from the XML Schema

Using XMLBeans, you actually generate Java code to work with the XML Schema. You have two options for compiling your XML Schema into a set of XMLBeans classes. You can use the schema compiler (`scomp`), or you can use the `ant` task provided with XMLBeans.

To run the `scomp` compiler on your schema, use the following command:

```
scomp -out bookstoreXMLBeans.jar bookstore.xsd
```

The output of this command will be a JAR file called `bookstoreXMLBeans.jar` with several class files.

To use the `ant` task, you need to define the task in your build script, like so:

```
<taskdef name="xmlbean"
     classname="org.apache.xmlbeans.impl.tool.XMLBean"
     classpath="<<XMLBeans_Home>>xbean.jar" />
```

In this example, make sure to replace <<XMLBeans_Home>> with the appropriate directory structure. Now you can build your XSD file using the following command:

```
<xmlbean schema="schemas" destfile="Schemas.jar"/>
```

This command will build all the schemas within your `schemas` directory into a JAR file called `Schemas.jar`.

---

■ **Further Reading** For more details on how to use the `ant` task, visit `http://xmlbeans.apache.org/docs/2.0.0/guide/antXmlbean.html`.

---

## Walking Through the Generated XMLBeans Classes

Figure 8-4 shows the contents of the JAR file that's generated from the XML Schema in Listing 8-4.

WinZip - bookdetails.jar

File Actions Options Help

New Open Favorites Add Extract Encrypt View CheckOut Wizard

| Name | Type | Path | Modified |
|---|---|---|---|
| Author$Factory.class | CLASS File | com\apress\beehive\bookstore\vo\ | 4/22/20( |
| Author.class | CLASS File | com\apress\beehive\bookstore\vo\ | 4/22/20( |
| AuthorImpl.class | CLASS File | com\apress\beehive\bookstore\vo\impl\ | 4/22/20( |
| BookDetailDocument$BookDetail$Factory.class | CLASS File | com\apress\beehive\bookstore\vo\ | 4/22/20( |
| BookDetailDocument$BookDetail.class | CLASS File | com\apress\beehive\bookstore\vo\ | 4/22/20( |
| BookDetailDocument$Factory.class | CLASS File | com\apress\beehive\bookstore\vo\ | 4/22/20( |
| BookDetailDocument.class | CLASS File | com\apress\beehive\bookstore\vo\ | 4/22/20( |
| BookDetailDocumentImpl$BookDetailImpl.class | CLASS File | com\apress\beehive\bookstore\vo\impl\ | 4/22/20( |
| BookDetailDocumentImpl.class | CLASS File | com\apress\beehive\bookstore\vo\impl\ | 4/22/20( |
| Publisher$Factory.class | CLASS File | com\apress\beehive\bookstore\vo\ | 4/22/20( |
| Publisher.class | CLASS File | com\apress\beehive\bookstore\vo\ | 4/22/20( |
| PublisherImpl.class | CLASS File | com\apress\beehive\bookstore\vo\impl\ | 4/22/20( |
| TypeSystemHolder.class | CLASS File | schema\system\sAD33296BE2D4EA2D7FA9AF8E938765FF\ | 4/22/20( |
| bookdetails.xsd | XML Schema | schema\src\ | 4/22/20( |
| Author.xsb | XSB File | schema\javaname\com\apress\beehive\bookstore\vo\ | 4/22/20( |
| author.xsb | XSB File | schema\type\http_3A_2F_2Fbeehive_2Eapress_2Ecom_2Fbookstore_2Fvo\ | 4/22/20( |
| author3388type.xsb | XSB File | schema\system\sAD33296BE2D4EA2D7FA9AF8E938765FF\ | 4/22/20( |
| bookDetail.xsb | XSB File | schema\element\http_3A_2F_2Fbeehive_2Eapress_2Ecom_2Fbookstore_2Fvo\ | 4/22/20( |
| BookDetail.xsb | XSB File | schema\javaname\com\apress\beehive\bookstore\vo\BookDetailDocument\ | 4/22/20( |
| bookdetail5e3felemtype.xsb | XSB File | schema\system\sAD33296BE2D4EA2D7FA9AF8E938765FF\ | 4/22/20( |
| bookdetail9609doctype.xsb | XSB File | schema\system\sAD33296BE2D4EA2D7FA9AF8E938765FF\ | 4/22/20( |
| BookDetailDocument.xsb | XSB File | schema\javaname\com\apress\beehive\bookstore\vo\ | 4/22/20( |
| bookdetailelement.xsb | XSB File | schema\system\sAD33296BE2D4EA2D7FA9AF8E938765FF\ | 4/22/20( |
| index.xsb | XSB File | schema\system\sAD33296BE2D4EA2D7FA9AF8E938765FF\ | 4/22/20( |

Selected 0 files, 0 bytes    Total 28 files, 42KB

**Figure 8-4.** *Contents of JAR file after generating XMLBeans classes*

You need to copy this JAR file into `WEB-INF/lib` so your Web application can use it. If you want to use the XMLBeans classes from an EJB or some other layer outside the Web application, you can copy this JAR file into `APP-INF/lib`.

Figure 8-5 shows a class diagram of the generated classes.

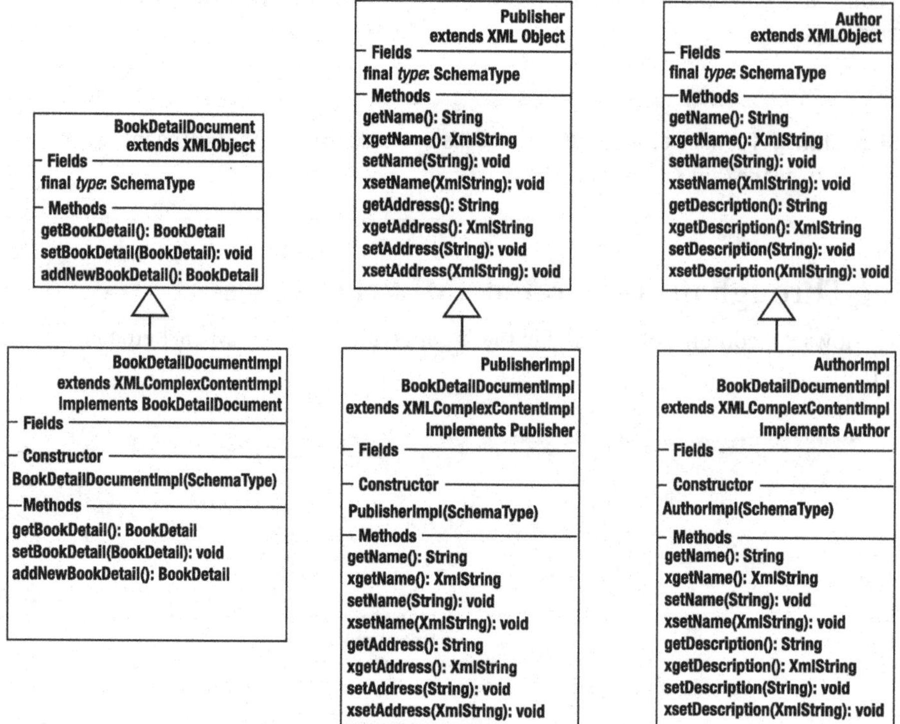


**Figure 8-5.** *Class diagram of the generated XMLBeans classes*

Notice the simplicity of the classes that were generated with simple getters and setters. Standard interfaces with implementing classes were generated that are intuitive to use for someone working with a bookstore application. We're not too fond of code generators, as they typically create classes with generic names and methods that are hard to use. However, in this case, it's quite simple if you have a `BookDetail`, `Author`, and `Publisher` class.

## How to Put Data into the XMLBeans

We'll now walk you through some really simple code that shows how you can use XMLBeans. In the bookstore example, you'll take the `BookValue` object that you've worked with in the past and use it to populate the XMLBean. In the `BookController` shown in Listing 8-5, see the `getBookDetail` method.

**Listing 8-5.** *Populate XMLBeans*

```
private BookDetailDocument.BookDetail getBookDetail(Book book) {
         BookDetailDocument.BookDetail bd =
             BookDetailDocument.Factory.newInstance().addNewBookDetail();
        bd.setAuthor(book.getAuthor());
        bd.setAvailable(book.isAvailable());
        bd.setBookId(book.getBook_Id());
```

```
        bd.setBookType(book.getBook_type());
        bd.setCatalogNo(book.getCatalogNo());
        bd.setComments(book.getComments());
        bd.setIsbn(book.getIsbn());
        bd.setPrice(book.getPrice());
        bd.setPages(book.getPages());
        bd.setPublication(book.getPublication());

        return bd;
    }
```

Notice that the code is really straightforward. You could almost call it boring. It's interesting to remember that you're actually building the XML file shown in Listing 8-4 with this simple code.

## How to Use Get Data from the XMLBeans

Getting data from XMLBeans is the reverse of what you saw in the previous section. You're now taking data from an XML file that's loaded into the XMLBean and populating the `BookValue` object. This code is in the `BookDetailBean.java` EJB class shown in Listing 8-6.

**Listing 8-6.** *Read Data from XMLBeans*

```
private Book getBook(BookDetailDocument.BookDetail bookdetail)
    {
        Book bookObj = new Book();
       bookObj.setBook_Id(bookdetail.getBookId());
        bookObj.setTitle(bookdetail.getTitle());
        bookObj.setAuthor(bookdetail.getAuthor());
        bookObj.setPublication(bookdetail.getPublication());
        bookObj.setBook_type(bookdetail.getBookType());
        bookObj.setCatalogNo(bookdetail.getCatalogNo());
        bookObj.setComments(bookdetail.getComments());
        bookObj.setIsbn(bookdetail.getIsbn());
        bookObj.setPages(bookdetail.getPages());
        bookObj.setPrice(bookdetail.getPrice());
        bookObj.setAvailable(bookdetail.getAvailable());
        return bookObj;
    }
```

Again, the code is simple. Using simple getters, you're accessing data from the XML file using XMLBeans.

# Using XML Cursors

You can use XML cursors to navigate through an XML document. Once you've loaded an XML document, you can create a cursor to navigate through the XML. Think of this cursor as an Iterator that's used to navigate through a Java collection. You can use cursors for XML documents regardless of whether they conform to any XML Schema.

XML cursors allow you to do the following:

- Navigate through an XML document in small steps. Think DOM.
- Manipulate data in the XML document using getters and setters.
- Modify the XML document by inserting, deleting, and moving data.
- Execute XQuery expressions against the XML document.
- Create bookmarks in the XML document for later reference.

## Working with Cursors

Cursors are part of XMLBeans. You can create a cursor on any XML document instance that's part of an `XmlObject` or an inheriting class. So, in the bookstore example, you could create a cursor on `BookDetailDocument` by calling the `newCursor` method on it.

---

■ **Note** You need to call the `dispose` method when you're done working with a cursor.

---

Cursors use `XMLToken` to represent the XML document. We'll explain this in the next section. For now, it's important to remember that an `XMLCursor` moves from token to token. You have methods such as `toParent`, `toFirstAttribute`, `toPrevSibling`, and so on, to move through the XML document. Try the following sample code on your `BookDetail` document as an exercise:

```
XmlCursor bookCursor = xmlDoc.newCursor();
    bookCursor.toFirstChild();
    System.out.println("Token type: " + bookCursor.currentTokenType() +
        " / " + bookCursor.xmlText());
}
```

---

■ **Further Reading** For more information on working with cursors, visit `http://xmlbeans.apache.org/docs/2.0.0/guide/conNavigatingXMLwithCursors.html`.

---

---

■ **Note** For a complete list of methods provided with the `XMLCursor` classes, see the Javadocs at `http://xmlbeans.apache.org/docs/2.0.0/reference/index.html`.

---

## Working with XML Tokens

You can break any XML file up into a set of XMLToken objects so that you can manipulate it using XML cursors.

---

**Note** See the Javadocs for the XMLToken class at http://xmlbeans.apache.org/docs/2.0.0/reference/org/apache/xmlbeans/XmlCursor.TokenType.html.

---

Several types of tokens represent different pieces of an XML document. These are presented by constants in the TokenType class; you can use them to quickly determine the contents of the XML document and navigate through it more easily. Table 8-2 lists the token types.

**Table 8-2.** *List of TokenType Constants*

| Token Type | Switch | Constant Description |
|---|---|---|
| STARTDOC | INT_STARTDOC | Represents the start of the XML. Always the first token. The document element itself is represented by a START token, not the STARTDOC token. |
| ENDDOC | INT_ENDDOC | Represents the end of the XML. Always the last token. |
| START | INT_START | Represents the start of an element. |
| END | INT_END | Represents the end of an element. The END token has no value but marks the element's end. |
| TEXT | INT_TEXT | Represents text. |
| ATTR | INT_ATTR | Represents an attribute. ATTR tokens are allowed to appear after a STARTDOC or START token. |
| NAMESPACE | INT_NAMESPACE | Represents a namespace (xmlns) attribute. Also only allowed after START or STARTDOC tokens. |
| COMMENT | INT_COMMENT | Represents a comment. |
| PROCINST | INT_PROCINST | Represents a processing instruction. |

As you use a cursor to navigate through XML, you can use the XmlCursor.currentTokenType to determine the TokenType.

---

**Further Reading** For more information on working with tokens, visit http://xmlbeans.apache.org/docs/2.0.0/guide/conUnderstandingXMLTokens.html.

---

Taking the sample XML file from Listing 8-4, Figure 8-6 shows you the location for token types in this file.

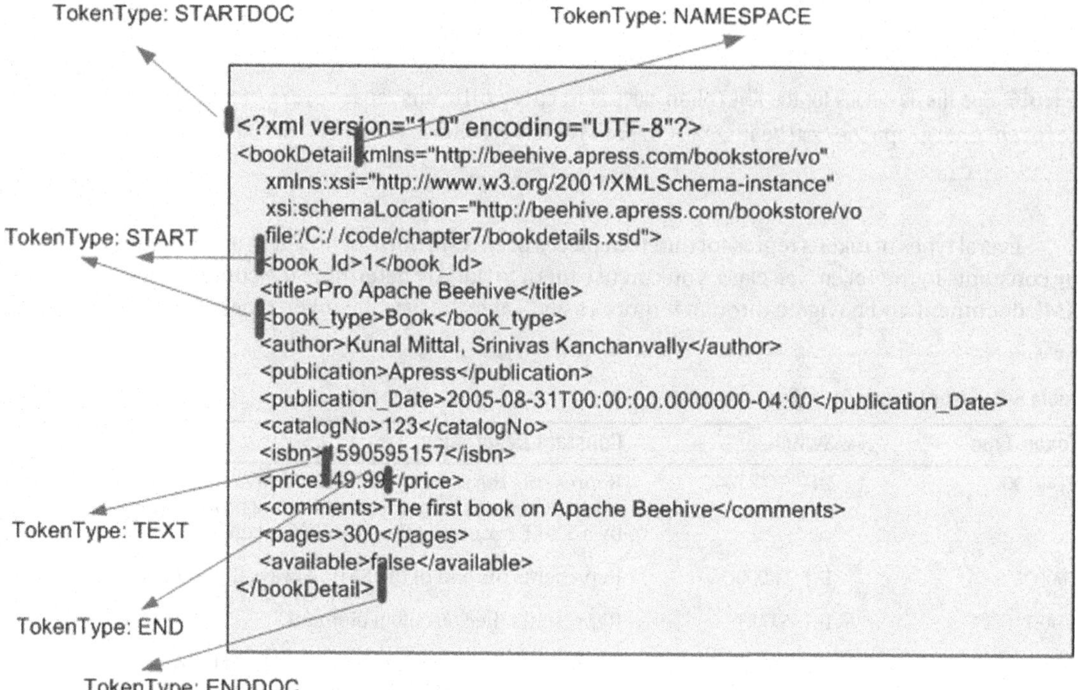


**Figure 8-6.** *Token types in the bookstore XML file*

# Using XMLBeans and Web Services Together

Before we conclude this chapter, we'll explain how you can use Web Services and XMLBeans together. In this book we've talked a lot about the Amazon.com Web Service. We'll again use the Google.com Web Service for this example. We won't provide a complete example, but you should be able to follow through and fill in some of the gaps on your own. First, visit the Google.com Web Service site to create a Google.com account. Similar to what you did in a previous chapter for Amazon.com, you need a key to access the Web Service; you can get this at `http://www.google.com/apis/`.

## Looking at the XML

This section will show you the XML that's sent to the Google.com Web Service and the XML that you get back from it. Listing 8-7 shows the XML file that's sent to the Google.com Web Service. This is straight from the API download on the Google.com Web site.

**Listing 8-7.** *Google.com Search XML*

```
<?xml version='1.0' encoding='UTF-8'?>
<SOAP-ENV:Envelope xmlns:SOAP-ENV="http://schemas.xmlsoap.org/soap/envelope/"
      xmlns:xsi="http://www.w3.org/1999/XMLSchema-instance"
      xmlns:xsd="http://www.w3.org/1999/XMLSchema">
  <SOAP-ENV:Body>
    <ns1:doGoogleSearch xmlns:ns1="urn:GoogleSearch"
         SOAP-ENV:encodingStyle="http://schemas.xmlsoap.org/soap/encoding/">
      <key xsi:type="xsd:string">00000000000000000000000000000000</key>
      <q xsi:type="xsd:string">shrdlu winograd maclisp teletype</q>
      <start xsi:type="xsd:int">0</start>
      <maxResults xsi:type="xsd:int">10</maxResults>
      <filter xsi:type="xsd:boolean">true</filter>
      <restrict xsi:type="xsd:string"></restrict>
      <safeSearch xsi:type="xsd:boolean">false</safeSearch>
      <lr xsi:type="xsd:string"></lr>
      <ie xsi:type="xsd:string">latin1</ie>
      <oe xsi:type="xsd:string">latin1</oe>
    </ns1:doGoogleSearch>
  </SOAP-ENV:Body>
</SOAP-ENV:Envelope>
```

Listing 8-8 shows the XML results for the search described in Listing 8-7. Don't worry about understanding this XML file fully. All we're trying to show you is the complexity of this XML. This makes it a perfect candidate for XMLBeans.

**Listing 8-8.** *Google.com Search Results XML*

```
<?xml version='1.0'     encoding='UTF-8'?>
<SOAP-ENV:Envelope xmlns:SOAP-ENV="http://schemas.xmlsoap.org/soap/envelope/"
        xmlns:xsi="http://www.w3.org/1999/XMLSchema-instance"
        xmlns:xsd="http://www.w3.org/1999/XMLSchema">
  <SOAP-ENV:Body>
        <ns1:doGoogleSearchResponse     xmlns:ns1="urn:GoogleSearch"
                 SOAP-ENV:encodingStyle="http://schemas.xmlsoap.org/soap/encoding/">
          <return xsi:type="ns1:GoogleSearchResult">
                <documentFiltering xsi:type="xsd:boolean">false</documentFiltering>
                <estimatedTotalResultsCount     xsi:type="xsd:int">3
                </estimatedTotalResultsCount>
                <directoryCategories xmlns:ns2="
                http://schemas.xmlsoap.org/soap/encoding/"
                xsi:type="ns2:Array" ns2:arrayType="ns1:DirectoryCategory[0]">
                </directoryCategories>
                <searchTime     xsi:type="xsd:double">0.194871</searchTime>
```

```
<resultElements
      xmlns:ns3="http://schemas.xmlsoap.org/soap/encoding/"
xsi:type="ns3:Array" ns3:arrayType="ns1:ResultElement[3]">
  <item xsi:type="ns1:ResultElement">
        <cachedSize     xsi:type="xsd:string">12k</cachedSize>
        <hostName xsi:type="xsd:string"></hostName>
        <snippet xsi:type="xsd:string"> test </snippet>
        <directoryCategory xsi:type="ns1:DirectoryCategory">
          <specialEncoding xsi:type="xsd:string"></specialEncoding>
          <fullViewableName     xsi:type="xsd:string">
          </fullViewableName>
        </directoryCategory>
        <relatedInformationPresent xsi:type="xsd:boolean">true
        </relatedInformationPresent>
        <directoryTitle xsi:type="xsd:string"></directoryTitle>
        <summary xsi:type="xsd:string"></summary>
        <URL xsi:type="xsd:string">
        http://hci.stanford.edu/cs147/examples/shrdlu/</URL>
        <title xsi:type="xsd:string">
                        &lt;b&gt;SHRDLU&lt;/b&gt;
        </title>
  </item>
  <item xsi:type="ns1:ResultElement">
        <cachedSize     xsi:type="xsd:string">12k</cachedSize>
        <hostName xsi:type="xsd:string"></hostName>
        <snippet xsi:type="xsd:string"> my test snippet</snippet>
        <directoryCategory xsi:type="ns1:DirectoryCategory">
          <specialEncoding xsi:type="xsd:string"></specialEncoding>
          <fullViewableName     xsi:type="xsd:string"
            </fullViewableName>
        </directoryCategory>
        <relatedInformationPresent xsi:type="xsd:boolean">true
        </relatedInformationPresent>
        <directoryTitle xsi:type="xsd:string"></directoryTitle>
        <summary xsi:type="xsd:string"></summary>
        <URL xsi:type="xsd:string">
        http://hci.stanford.edu/winograd/shrdlu</URL>
        <title xsi:type="xsd:string">
             &lt;b&gt;SHRDLU&lt;/b&gt;
         </title>
  </item>
</resultElements>
<endIndex xsi:type="xsd:int">3</endIndex>
<searchTips     xsi:type="xsd:string"></searchTips>
<searchComments xsi:type="xsd:string"></searchComments>
<startIndex     xsi:type="xsd:int">1</startIndex>
```

```
            <estimateIsExact xsi:type="xsd:boolean">true</estimateIsExact>
            <searchQuery xsi:type="xsd:string">
            shrdlu winograd maclisp teletype</searchQuery>
        </return>
      </ns1:doGoogleSearchResponse>
  </SOAP-ENV:Body>
</SOAP-ENV:Envelope>
```

## Creating the XML Schema

You need an XML Schema to be able to generate the XMLBeans. Typically, it's easy to understand the XML Schema from the WSDL file. However, the Google.com WSDL has some subtle complexities that we really don't need to go through for the purposes of this chapter. Listing 8-9 shows you an XML Schema that you can use with the Google.com Web Service. We've placed a copy of this under the Chapter 8 directory; it's called `GoogleSearch.xsd`.

**Listing 8-9.** *Google.com Search XML Schema*

```
<?xml version="1.0"?>
<xsd:schema xmlns="http://www.w3.org/2001/XMLSchema"
        xmlns:typens="urn:GoogleSearch"
        xmlns:xsd="http://www.w3.org/2001/XMLSchema"
        targetNamespace="urn:GoogleSearch">

<xsd:complexType name="DirectoryCategory">
<xsd:all>
  <xsd:element name="fullViewableName" type="xsd:string"/>
  <xsd:element name="specialEncoding" type="xsd:string"/>
</xsd:all>
</xsd:complexType>

<xsd:complexType name="DirectoryCategoryArray">
<xsd:sequence>
    <xsd:element name="DirectoryCategory" type="typens:DirectoryCategory"
                nillable="true" minOccurs="0" maxOccurs="unbounded"/>
</xsd:sequence>
</xsd:complexType>

<xsd:complexType name="GoogleSearchResult">
<xsd:all>
  <xsd:element name="documentFiltering"          type="xsd:boolean"/>
  <xsd:element name="searchComments"             type="xsd:string"/>
  <xsd:element name="estimatedTotalResultsCount" type="xsd:int"/>
  <xsd:element name="estimateIsExact"            type="xsd:boolean"/>
  <xsd:element name="resultElements"
            type="typens:ResultElementArray"/>
  <xsd:element name="searchQuery"                type="xsd:string"/>
  <xsd:element name="startIndex"                 type="xsd:int"/>
```

```
  <xsd:element name="endIndex"                          type="xsd:int"/>
  <xsd:element name="searchTips"                        type="xsd:string"/>
  <xsd:element name="directoryCategories"
            type="typens:DirectoryCategoryArray"/>
  <xsd:element name="searchTime"                        type="xsd:double"/>
</xsd:all>
</xsd:complexType>

<xsd:complexType name="item">
<xsd:all>
  <xsd:element name="summary" type="xsd:string"/>
  <xsd:element name="URL" type="xsd:string"/>
  <xsd:element name="snippet" type="xsd:string"/>
  <xsd:element name="title" type="xsd:string"/>
  <xsd:element name="cachedSize" type="xsd:string"/>
  <xsd:element name="relatedInformationPresent" type="xsd:boolean"/>
  <xsd:element name="hostName" type="xsd:string"/>
  <xsd:element name="directoryCategory" type="typens:DirectoryCategory"/>
  <xsd:element name="directoryTitle" type="xsd:string"/>
</xsd:all>
</xsd:complexType>

<xsd:complexType name="ResultElementArray">
<xsd:sequence>
    <xsd:element name="item" type="typens:item" nillable="true"
            minOccurs="0" maxOccurs="unbounded"/>
</xsd:sequence>
</xsd:complexType>
</xsd:schema>
```

Now you know how to create Web Services using XMLBeans. As an exercise, we recommend you generate the XMLBeans from the examples in this chapter and use the various concepts you've learned throughout this book to generate your own Google.com search page. Make sure you use NetUI, JSR 181 Web Services, Controls, and the XMLBeans that you've generated from following along with the examples in this book.

To get you started, we've generated the XMLBeans from this schema and provided them for you. They live under the Chapter 8 directory in a file called `GoogleSearchXMLBeans.jar`.

## So, What's Next?

You've seen several different technologies so far. Our mission to teach you how to use the technologies within Apache Beehive and XMLBeans is complete. Now it's up to you. You should start using all the technologies you've learned in this book in real-life projects. You should further evaluate these technologies and see which ones can be of value to you on your projects.

We also urge you to actively participate in the developer groups or even contribute to the projects themselves in order to improve Apache Beehive and XMLBeans for the rest of the developer community.

APPENDIX A

# Setting Up Your Development Environment

In this appendix, we'll walk you through the different pieces of software that you'll need to download and install in order to be able to start developing using Apache Beehive and XMLBeans.

## Downloading and Installing the Required Software

Apache Beehive and XMLBeans development needs some minimal software installed on your machine. This includes a JDK, Ant, and a servlet container such as Tomcat.

### Installing J2SE 5 (JDK)

Download and install the latest version of Java 2 Platform, Standard Edition (J2SE). You can download this from the Sun Web site at `http://java.sun.com/j2se/1.5.0/download.jsp`.

Although you can install the JDK in any directory you want, we're assuming you'll install it in `C:\jdk1.5`. If you choose another directory, you'll need to edit the batch files for compiling and running the sample code appropriately. We've added comments to the batch files that describe the changes you'll need to make. This applies to all the software you'll be installing in this appendix.

Next, set the environment variable `JAVA_HOME`. (For example, set it to `JAVA_HOME=C:\jdk1.5`.)

Then modify the environment variable `PATH`. (For example, set it to `PATH=c:\jdk1.5\bin;%PATH%`.)

### Installing Ant 1.6.2

Ant is the build tool used to compile and run Apache Beehive code. Download Ant 1.6.2 from `http://svn.apache.org/repos/asf/incubator/beehive/trunk/external/ant/apache-ant-1.6.2-bin.zip`. You can also download Ant 1.6.2 from `http://ant.apache.org/bindownload.cgi`.

Once you've downloaded the file, you can unzip it on your machine. Ant will be installed in `C:\apache-ant-1.6.2`.

Next, set the environment variable `ANT_HOME`. (For example, set it to `ANT_HOME=C:\apache-ant-1.6.2`.)

Then modify the environment variable `PATH`. (For example, set it to `PATH=C:\apache-ant-1.6.2\bin;%PATH%`.)

## Installing Tomcat 5

This book uses Tomcat 5 as the servlet container. Apache Beehive is also supported on other servlet containers, though. You can check the Beehive wiki for other supported platforms.

Download Tomcat 5 from http://svn.apache.org/repos/asf/incubator/beehive/trunk/external/tomcat/jakarta-tomcat-5.0.25.zip.

Once you've downloaded the file, you can unzip it on your machine. Tomcat will be installed in c:\jakarta-tomcat-5.0.25.

Next, set the environment variable CATALINA_HOME. (For example, set it to CATALINA_HOME=C:\jakarta-tomcat-5.0.25.)

Then modify the environment variable PATH. (For example, set it to PATH=C:\jakarta-tomcat-5.0.25\bin;%PATH%.)

---

■ **Note** If you're planning on using Eclipse Pollinate as an IDE to develop Apache Beehive applications, you'll need to download Apache Tomcat 5.5, not 5. The instructions are almost the same. You can download the latest version at http://jakarta.apache.org/site/downloads/downloads_tomcat-5.cgi.

---

# Downloading and Installing Apache Beehive and XMLBeans

Once you've downloaded the required software, you need to download and install Apache Beehive and XMLBeans.

## Installing the Beehive 1.0.3 Binary Distribution

You can download the latest binary distribution of Beehive (apache-beehive-incubating-1.0-alpha-snapshot.zip) from http://cvs.apache.org/dist/incubator/beehive/v1.0-alpha/bin/. This distribution is an alpha release and isn't intended for creating production-level applications.

Unzip the Beehive distribution file on your machine in C:\.

Next, set the environment variable BEEHIVE_HOME=C:\apache-beehive-incubating-1.0-alpha-snapshot.

Now edit the file beehiveUser.cmd present in C:/apache-beehive-incubating-1.0-alpha-snapshot, and make changes to the following environment variables:

```
BEEHIVE_HOME=C:\apache-beehive-incubating-1.0-alpha-snapshot
JAVA_HOME=C:\jdk1.5
ANT_HOME=C:\apache-ant-1.6.2
CATALINA_HOME=C:\jakarta-tomcat-5.0.25
```

Listing A-1 shows beehiveUser.cmd. After editing beehiveUser.cmd, save and close the file.

**Listing A-1.** *beehiveUser.cmd File*

```
@echo off
REM
REM Customize this file based on where you install various 3rd party components
REM such as the JDK, Ant and Tomcat.
REM

REM the root of Beehive distribution
set BEEHIVE_HOME=c:\apache-beehive-incubating-1.0-alpha-snapshot

REM location of a JDK
set JAVA_HOME=C:\jdk1.5.0

REM location of Ant
set ANT_HOME=c:\apache-ant-1.6.2

REM location of Tomcat
set CATALINA_HOME=c:\jakarta-tomcat-5.0.25

set PATH=%PATH%;%JAVA_HOME%\bin;%ANT_HOME%\bin
```

## Installing the XMLBeans Alpha Binary Distribution

You can install the latest binary distribution of XMLBeans (`xmlbeans-1.0.3.zip`) from `http://www.apache.org/dyn/closer.cgi/xml/xmlbeans`.

Unzip the XMLBeans distribution file on your machine in `C:\`. XMLBeans will be installed in `C:\xmlbeans-1.0.3`.

# Working with Tomcat

In the following sections, we'll walk you through running the Petstore demo that ships with Beehive, located in the Tomcat container.

## Starting Tomcat

Before you can start Tomcat, you need to do a little bit of prep work. You need to add a manager role to Tomcat, which allows you to run deployment-related targets in the Ant file `BEEEHIVE_HOME/ant/runTomcat.xml`. This file is provided as a convenience for managing the Tomcat server.

To do this, edit the file `CATALINA_HOME/conf/tomcat-users.xml` so it appears as shown in Listing A-2. Elements to add are shown in bold type.

**Listing A-2.** *tomcat-users.xml File*

```
<?xml version='1.0' encoding='utf-8'?>
    <tomcat-users>
          <role rolename="tomcat"/>
          <role rolename="role1"/>
          <role rolename="manager"/>
          <user username="tomcat" password="tomcat" roles="tomcat"/>
          <user username="role1" password="tomcat" roles="role1"/>
          <user username="both" password="tomcat" roles="tomcat,role1"/>
          <user username="manager" password="manager" roles="manager"/>
    </tomcat-users>
```

You can start the Tomcat server in two ways. (And you can modify this appropriately if you're using Tomcat 5.5.)

Run the following command to start the Tomcat server:

```
%CATALINA_HOME%\bin\startup.bat
```

or run the following command:

```
C:\startup.bat
```

Alternatively, you can start the Tomcat server by running the `ant` command provided in the Beehive distribution:

```
ant -f %BEEHIVE_HOME%\ant\buildWebapp.xml start
```

## Running the Petstore Sample on Tomcat 5

Copy the `petstoreWeb` folder from `%BEEHIVE_HOME%\samples\petstoreWeb` to another location (say, `C:\beehive\projects`) before proceeding. (The following instructions assume that you've copied the `petstoreWeb` folder into the directory `C:\beehive\projects`.) Also, copy the runtime JARs into the application source.

To copy the runtime JARs into the application source and to compile, run the following Ant target. (You can run this command from anywhere as long as `ant` is in your path.)

```
ant -f  %BEEHIVE_HOME%\ant\buildWebapp.xml
    -Dwebapp.dir= C:\beehive\projects\petstoreWeb
       deploy.beehive.webapp.runtime build.webapp
```

Start Tomcat by running the following Ant command, provided in the `buildWebapp.xml` file:

```
ant -f %BEEHIVE_HOME%\ant\buildWebapp.xml start
```

---

■ **Note** If you use the second of these methods for starting Tomcat, you have to press Ctrl+C in the command shell to enter any further commands.

---

## Deploying the Petstore Sample

To deploy the Petstore application to Tomcat, you need to do the following.

1. Copy BEEHIVE_HOME/samples/petstoreWeb/ to CATALINA_HOME/webapps. This will cause Tomcat to automatically deploy the Web application. Alternatively, you could deploy Beehive manually. If you want to do this, go to step 2; otherwise, skip the rest of the steps in this list.

2. Use Beehive's deploy Ant target to deploy the Petstore application to Tomcat. This requires that the manager role be defined in CATALINA_HOME/conf/tomcat-users.xml with a username/password of manager/manager.

3. Then, run the following Ant command:

```
ant -f %BEEHIVE_HOME%\ant\buildWebapp.xml
    deploy
    -Dwebapp.dir=C:\beehive\projects\petstoreWeb
    -Dcontext.path=petstoreWeb
```

If petstoreWeb is already deployed on the server, run the undeploy target first, like so:

```
ant
  -f %BEEHIVE_HOME%\ant\buildWebapp.xml
  undeploy
  -Dwebapp.dir=C:\beehive\projects\petstoreWeb
  -Dcontext.path=petstoreWeb
```

To see the running application, visit http://localhost:8080/petstoreWeb/Controller.jpf.

# So, What's Next?

You now have all the basic development tools you need in order to start developing using Apache Beehive and XMLBeans. We recommend you jump right into Chapter 3. Make sure you actually complete all the steps outlined in this appendix so that you can try the hands-on examples as you read the rest of the book.

APPENDIX B

# Working with Eclipse and Pollinate

In this appendix, we'll walk you through setting up the Eclipse IDE and the Pollinate plug-in that will allow you to build Apache Beehive applications.

## What's Eclipse?

Eclipse is an open-source software development project that strives to provide a robust, full-featured, industry-standard platform for creating highly integrated tools. Eclipse is widely known for its innovative tools integration platform and rich client application framework. The mission of the Eclipse project is to adapt the Eclipse platform and associated tools to meet the needs of the tool building community so that the vision of Eclipse as an industry platform is realized.

You need to be aware of three projects: the Eclipse project, the Eclipse Tools project, and the Eclipse Technology project. We'll also discuss the Eclipse software development kit (SDK).

### Eclipse Project

The Eclipse project is based around providing an industry-strength yet open-source development platform.

### Eclipse Tools Project

The Eclipse Tools project helps enable diverse tool builders to create best-of-breed tools for the Eclipse platform. In fact, the mission of the Eclipse Tools project is to foster the creation of a wide variety of tools for the Eclipse platform. The Eclipse Tools project provides a single point of coordination for open-source tool developers in order to minimize overlap and duplication, ensure maximum sharing and creation of common components, and promote seamless interoperability between diverse types of tools.

### Eclipse Technology Project

The mission of the Eclipse Technology project is to provide new channels for open-source developers, researchers, academics, and educators to participate in the ongoing evolution of Eclipse.

### Eclipse SDK

The Eclipse SDK consolidates the components produced by three Eclipse subprojects—Platform, Java Development Tools (JDT), and Plug-in Development Environment (PDE)—in a single download.

Together these pieces provide a feature-rich environment that allows developers to efficiently create tools that integrate seamlessly into the Eclipse platform.

## Downloading and Installing Eclipse

To launch Eclipse, you should download and install a JDK. The developer kit will include a Java runtime that you can use to launch Eclipse. Eclipse requires version 1.3 or 1.4 of a J2SE JRE.

---

■ **Note** Eclipse 3.0 is an important milestone in the evolution of Eclipse. The platform has a truly impressive list of features. The most important new features can be grouped into several key areas: Java tools, Swing integration, and the rich client platform.

---

You can download Eclipse from any of the listed mirror sites available at `http://www.eclipse.org/downloads/index.php` or from the main Eclipse download site also provided at this site.

The name of the file is `eclipse-SDK-3.1M4-win32.zip`. Unzip the file into any directory, for example, `c:\eclipse`. The `c:\eclipse` directory then becomes the home directory for Eclipse.

You use `eclipse.exe` for launching Eclipse.

On Windows, the Annotation Processing Tool (APT) is located in the `tools.jar` file. So, for Windows, you'll need to launch Eclipse with a command line like this:

```
<eclipse-home>\eclipse.exe -vm <Java-Home>\jre\bin\javaw
      -vmargs -Xbootclasspath/a: <Java-Home>\\lib\tools.jar
```

where `<eclipse-home>` is where you installed Eclipse and `<Java-Home>` is where you installed JDK 1.5.

## Using the Eclipse Workbench

When you launch Eclipse, the first thing you'll see is a dialog box that allows you to select where your workspace should be located. This is the directory where your work will be stored. Click OK to pick the default location.

After you choose this location, you'll see the Eclipse IDE, which is known as the *workbench* (see Figure B-1). You can have multiple workbench windows open simultaneously.

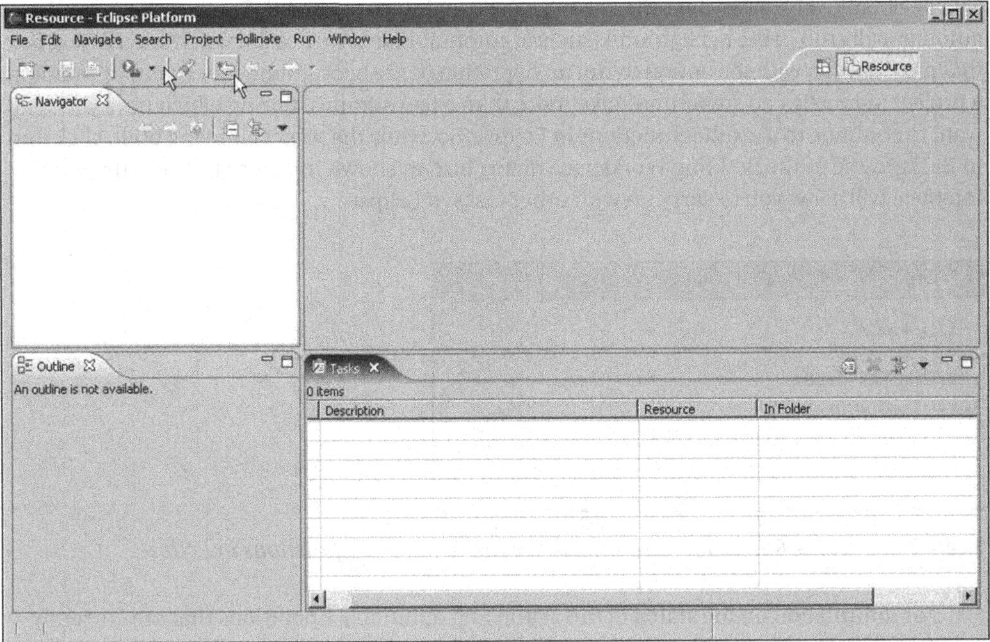


**Figure B-1.** *The Eclipse workbench*

## Importing Files

You can import files into the workbench by doing any of the following:

- Dragging and dropping from the file system
- Copying and pasting from the file system
- Using the Import wizard

## Processing in the Background

When you want to build several projects at once, you can select Project ➤ Build All, as shown in Figure B-2. You can also choose to build just one project or the working set.

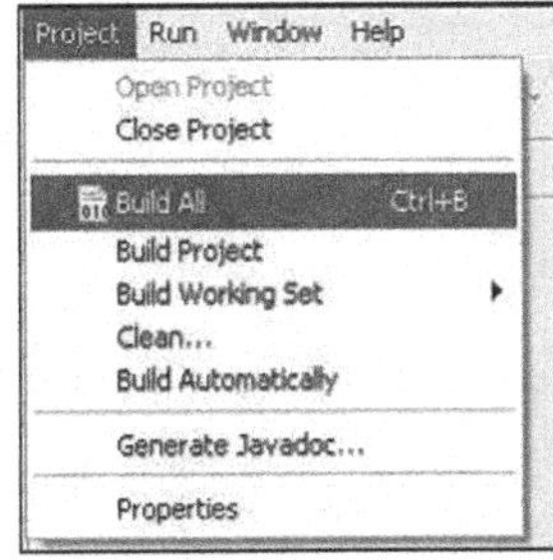


**Figure B-2.** *Building all Eclipse projects*

By default, all Eclipse operations run in the user interface thread. Some of the operations automatically run in the background (such as autobuild). In many cases, you'll see a dialog box that provides you with the option to run an operation in the background. For example, building a project manually can sometimes take more than a few minutes, during which time you may want to continue to use other functions in Eclipse. So, while the project is being built, click Run in Background in the Building Workspace dialog box, as shown in Figure B-3, and the user interface will allow you to carry on with other tasks in Eclipse.

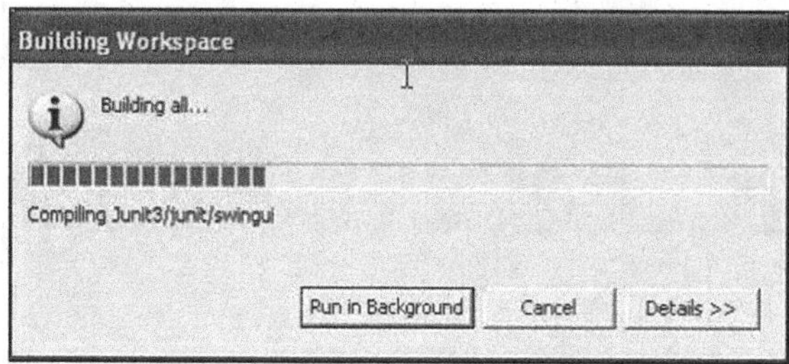


**Figure B-3.** *Clicking Run in Background allows you to use other functions in Eclipse.*

For information on the status of the action and additional operations that are currently running, click Details. The Details panel displays the status information of the operation at hand as well as any additional operations that may be running simultaneously, as shown in Figure B-4.

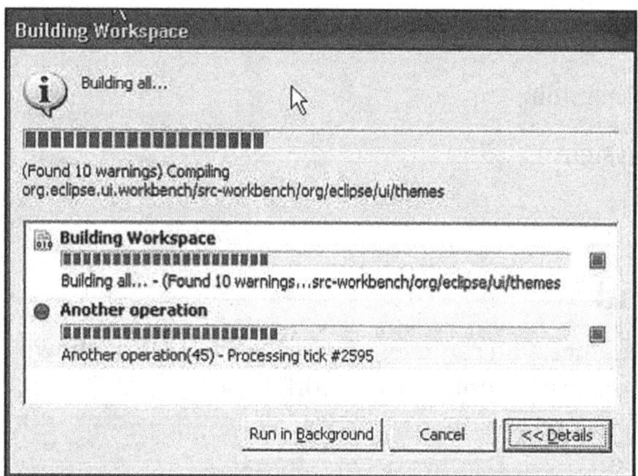


**Figure B-4.** *Viewing the details of all running operations*

# Setting Up a CVS Repository with Eclipse

A source control *repository* is a persistent store that coordinates multiuser access to the resources being developed by a team. Eclipse comes with built-in support of CVS and other source control tools.

## Creating a New Repository Location in Eclipse

Open the CVS Repositories view by selecting Window ➤ Show View ➤ Other on the main menu bar. Then select CVS ➤ CVS Repositories in the Show View dialog box, and click OK, as shown in Figure B-5. Another way to open a CVS repository is by using the Repository Exploring perspective.

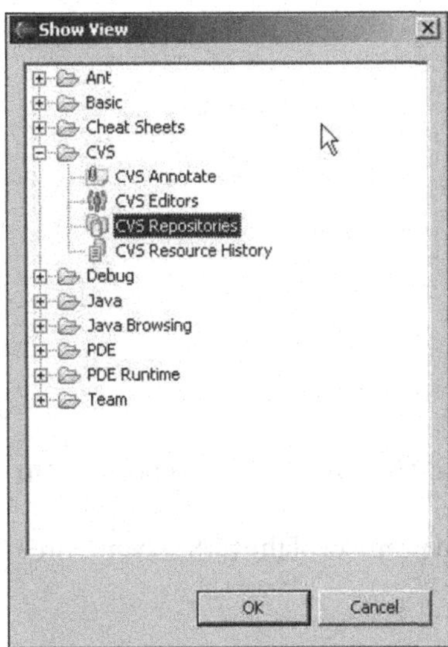


**Figure B-5.** *CVS views available in Eclipse*

Next, on the toolbar, click CVS Repository. Alternatively, from the context menu of the CVS Repositories view, select New ➤ Repository Location. The Add CVS Repository wizard will open, as shown in Figure B-6. Enter the information required to identify and connect to the repository location. In other words, in the Host field, type the address of the host (for example, enter **apress.com**). In the Repository Path field, type the path to the repository on the host (for example, enter **/home/rootd** or **d:/beehive**).

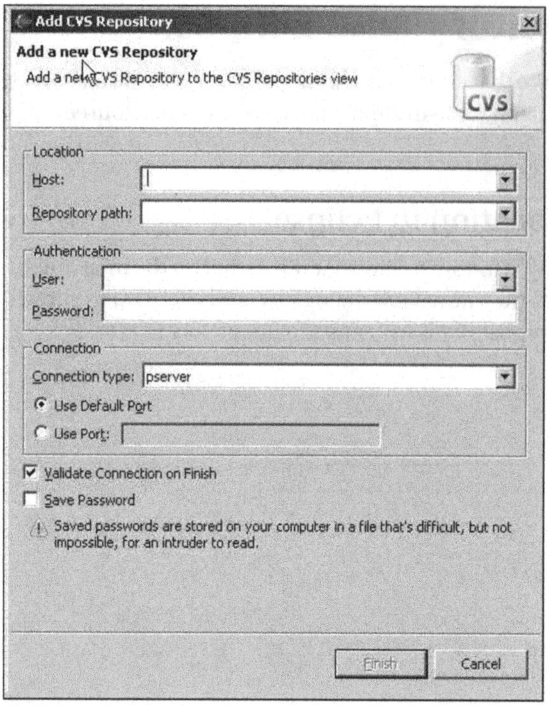

**Figure B-6.** *Adding a CVS repository*

In the User field, type the username under which you want to connect to the repository. In the Password field, type the password for your username.

From the Connection Type list, select the authentication protocol of the CVS server. Three connection methods come with the Eclipse CVS client:

- `pserver`: A CVS-specific connection method.
- `extssh`: An SSH 2.0 client included with Eclipse.
- `ext`: The CVS `ext` connection method that uses an external tool such as SSH to connect to the repository. The tool used by `ext` is configured in the Team ➤ CVS ➤ EXT Connection Method preferences page.

If the host uses a custom port, enable Use Port and enter the port number. You can optionally select Validate Connection on Finish if you want to authenticate the specified user to the specified host when you close this wizard. (If you don't select this option, the username will be authenticated later, when you try to access the contents of the repository.) You can optionally select Save Password if you want to save the password in the Eclipse keyring file so you don't have to enter the password again the next time you start Eclipse. The keyring file is stored on your local drive and doesn't use strong encryption, so don't enable this option for sensitive passwords. Click Finish to create the repository location.

## Using the CVS Checkout Wizard

The CVS Checkout wizard helps you check out one or more projects from a CVS repository. You can open the CVS Checkout wizard by choosing Checkout Projects from CVS in the Import wizard, as shown in Figure B-7. It's also available from the New ➤ Project menu, from the toolbar of the CVS Repository Exploring perspective, and when performing a Checkout As from the CVS Repositories view.

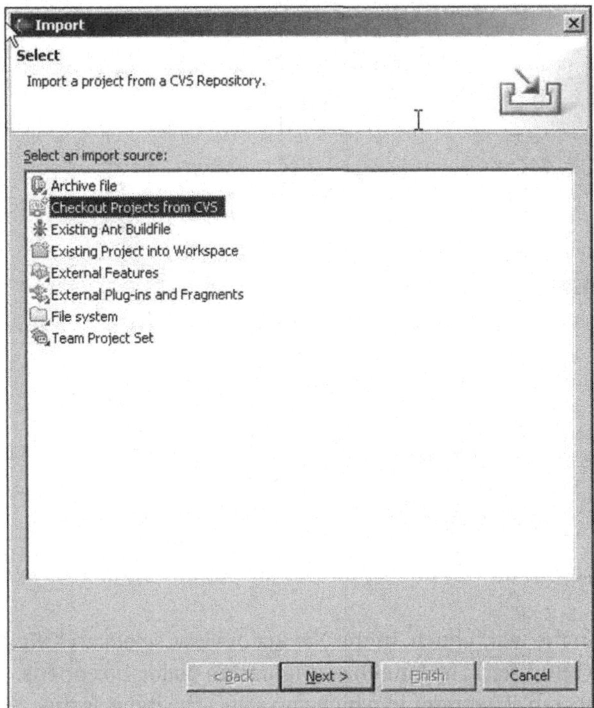


**Figure B-7.** *Choosing Checkout Projects from CVS in the Import wizard*

The first page of the wizard allows you to choose an existing repository location or create a new one. If you choose to create a new location, then the New Repository Location wizard will open.

## Taking Advantage of the Ant Support

Eclipse has Ant support that allows you to create and run Ant build files from the workbench. These Ant build files can operate on resources in the file system as well as on resources in the workspace.

Output from an Ant build file displays in the console view in the same hierarchical format you see when running Ant from the command line. Ant tasks (for example, `[mkdir]`) are hyperlinked to the associated Ant build file, and `javac` error reports are hyperlinked to the associated Java source file and line number.

You can add classes to the Ant classpath and add Ant tasks and types from the Ant runtime preferences page; select Window ➤ Preferences ➤ Ant ➤ Runtime, as shown in Figure B-8.

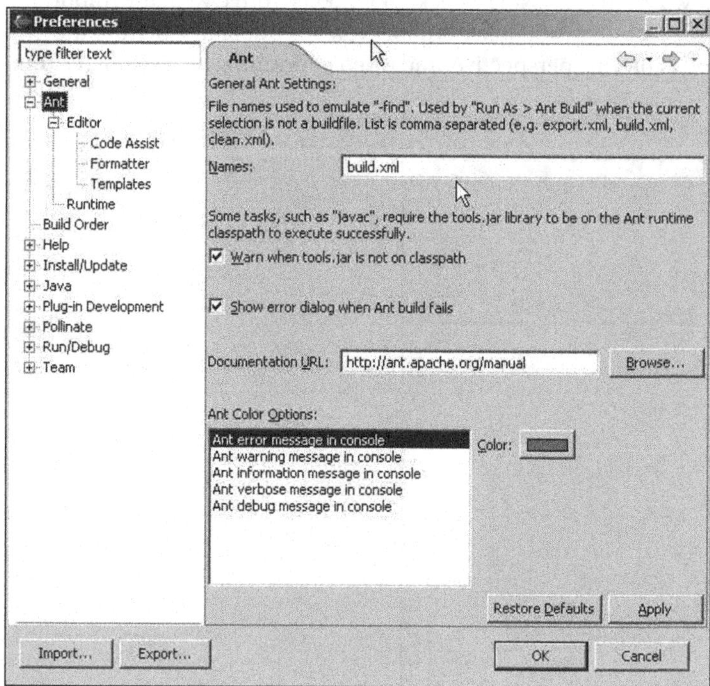


**Figure B-8.** *Setting up Ant in Eclipse*

You can also run an Ant build file in the workbench. In the Navigator view, select an XML file. From the file's pop-up menu, select Run Ant. The launch configuration dialog box opens.

Select some targets from the Targets tab. The order in which you select the items is the order in which they will run. The order is displayed in the Target Execution Order box at the bottom of the tab. You can change the order of the targets by clicking the Order button.

Furthermore, you can configure the options on the other tabs if you'd like. For example, on the Main tab, type any required arguments in the Arguments field. Click Run.

The Ant build file will run on the selected targets. Unless you disable the Capture Output option on the Main tab, the console will display any applicable execution results as the build file runs.

# Downloading and Installing Pollinate

Pollinate is an Eclipse technology project slated to build an Eclipse-based IDE and toolset that leverages the open-source Apache Beehive application framework. Basically, Pollinate is a plug-in to Eclipse that supports the Beehive framework. A combination of the Eclipse IDE and Pollinate, with some server such as Tomcat, makes a perfect environment for faster Beehive application development.

Pollinate relies on Sun's APT, so Eclipse needs access to APT during runtime using a command-line startup flag.

You can download and install the Pollinate plug-in in the Eclipse project in several ways:

- You can download Pollinate from the Update site.
- You can download the ZIP file from the Eclipse Web site.
- You can install Pollinate from the Eclipse CVS repository.

We'll cover the first two ways in the following sections. If you want, you can also download the source code and build Pollinate yourself. To use Pollinate, you'll need the following:

- JDK 1.5 Update 1 (also known as JDK 5.0 Update 1)
- Eclipse 3.1 M4
- WebTools 1.0 M2
- A local server such as Tomcat (see Appendix A)

## Installing Pollinate from the Update Site

To install Pollinate from the Update site, first launch the Eclipse IDE. It's important that you're running this with the JDK and not the JRE. Next, follow these steps:

1. Select Help ➤ Software Updates ➤ Find and Install.
2. In the Install/Update dialog box, select Search for New Features to Install.
3. On the next page, click the New Remote Site button.
4. Enter Pollinate, and go to `http://download.eclipse.org/technology/pollinate/update-site` in the New Update Site dialog box.
5. Expand Pollinate in the tree, and check Integration Builds.
6. On the next page, check Eclipse Pollinate Tools and complete the install.

The Pollinate install is more than 6MB, so be patient, as it will take a few minutes.

## Installing Pollinate from a ZIP File

Download the latest Pollinate integration build from `http://www.eclipse.org/pollinate/`, and unzip it into Eclipse. It gets unzipped into the plug-in folder that exists under the Eclipse home directory.

# Creating a New Beehive Project in Eclipse

After installing the Pollinate plug-in successfully, you can now create a new Beehive project by following these steps:

1. In Eclipse, select File ➤ New ➤ Other to open the New wizard, and then select Pollinate ➤ Web Application, as shown in Figure B-9.

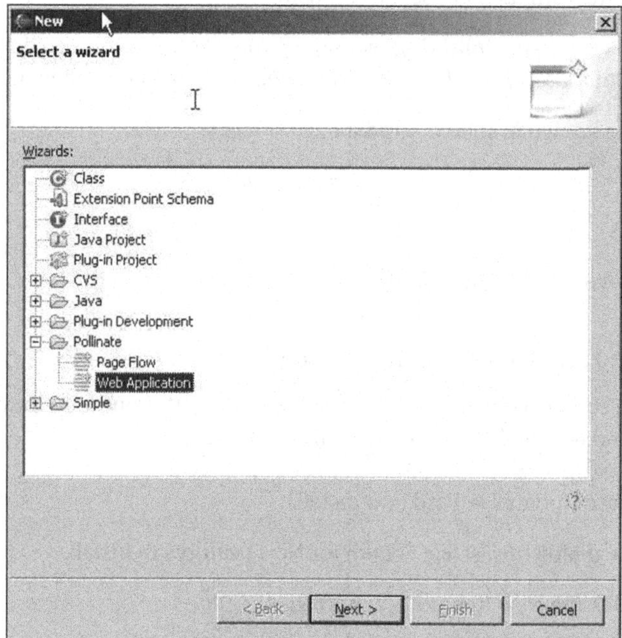


**Figure B-9.** *Creating a Beehive application in Eclipse Pollinate*

2. Click Next to move to the next page of the wizard, and enter the name of the new project, as shown in Figure B-10.

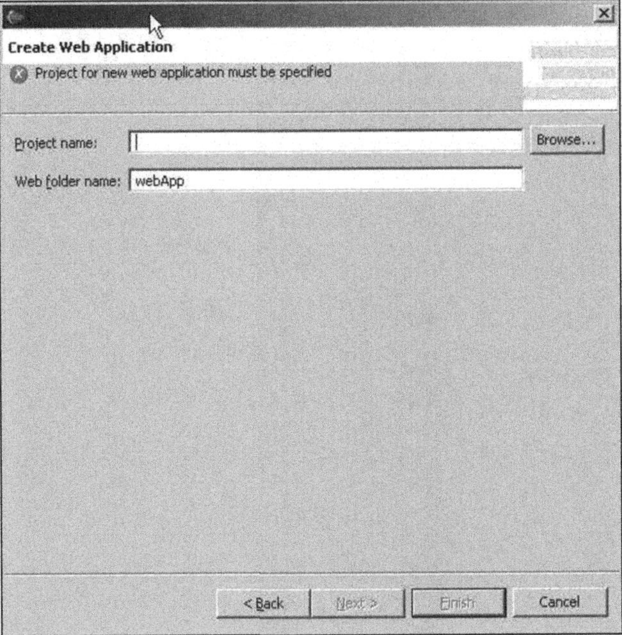


**Figure B-10.** *Naming your Beehive application in Eclipse Pollinate*

3. Enter the name of the project, and click Finish.
4. You can start or stop the runtime by selecting Pollinate ➤ Start Runtime or selecting Pollinate ➤ Stop Runtime.
5. To run the application, right-click the workspace directory in the Navigator view. Then select Run Web App.

The application code will be compiled, the Pollinate runtime will start, the application will deploy in Tomcat, and a new browser will open with the URL pointing to the application.

# So, What's Next?

Now you have all the tools to start working with Apache Beehive. You can jump right into Chapter 3 and begin writing some code.

APPENDIX C

■ ■ ■

# Contributing to Beehive and XMLBeans

If you've gotten this far in the book, you're probably a Beehive and XMLBeans expert. So, since you're now an expert, why not contribute to these projects and provide your input? This appendix covers the ways you can contribute.

Specifically, you can contribute to both Beehive and XMLBeans in these ways:

*Offer suggestions*: The simplest way to contribute is by reporting bugs and issues. Obviously, just like any other software, these projects are bound to have bugs. At the end of the day, the folks building these projects are human. We'll cover this in the "Subscribing to Lists" section.

*Submit code*: You can also submit code for bug fixes or enhancements. These are open-source projects, and they need community involvement to mature. The more people who contribute to the code base, the more value these projects will provide. We'll talk about this later in the "Contributing Code" section.

*Become a committer*: Once you've been recognized as a person who has submitted valuable code to these projects, you can be voted in as a committer. This means you'll actually be able to submit code to the source control system for this project. Visit `http://incubator.apache.org/beehive/contributors.html` to see the current list of committers for the Beehive project. Visit `http://xmlbeans.apache.org/community/index.html#Who+we+are` to see the current list of committers for the XMLBeans project.

## Subscribing to Lists

Before you can begin really contributing to the Apache Beehive project or XMLBeans, you should consider subscribing to some of the following lists and visiting the links mentioned. This will give you a feel for how things are progressing and potential areas where you think you can add value. We recommend exploring the archives for each list to understand the type and volume of communication that happens in each one.

## Beehive Lists

The following are the Beehive-related lists.

### Beehive User List

As the name suggests, this list is targeted to people like you who are using Beehive on a day-to-day basis. Post your bugs, issues, suggestions, or recommendations for enhancements to this list.

To subscribe to this list, send an e-mail to beehive-user-subscribe@incubator.apache.org.

To unsubscribe from this list, send an e-mail to beehive-user-unsubscribe@incubator.apache.org.

To see the archives for this list, visit http://nagoya.apache.org/eyebrowse/SummarizeList?listName=beehive-user@incubator.apache.org.

### Beehive Developer List

This is a mailing list for Beehive developers. Should you choose to submit code for this project, you'll need to subscribe to this list.

To subscribe to this list, send an e-mail to beehive-dev-subscribe@incubator.apache.org.

To unsubscribe from this list, send an e-mail to beehive-dev-unsubscribe@incubator.apache.org.

To see the archives for this list, visit http://nagoya.apache.org/eyebrowse/SummarizeList?listName=beehive-dev@incubator.apache.org.

### Beehive SVN/Wiki Change List

This is a mailing list where you can see every change to the Subversion (SVN) source control system for this project and to the Beehive wiki. This is a pretty high-volume list compared to the other two Beehive lists.

To subscribe to this list, send an e-mail to beehive-commits-subscribe@incubator.apache.org.

To unsubscribe from this list, send an e-mail to beehive-commits-unsubscribe@incubator.apache.org.

To see the archives for this list, visit http://nagoya.apache.org/eyebrowse/SummarizeList?listName=beehive-commits@incubator.apache.org.

---

■ **Note** Visit http://incubator.apache.org/beehive/mailinglists.html#Mailing+Lists for an up-to-date list of the Beehive mailing lists to which you can subscribe.

---

### Beehive Bug and Issue Tracking

The following is a site where you can see all the open issues, submit bugs, and get more information on the status on Beehive:

http://issues.apache.org/jira/secure/BrowseProject.jspa?id=10570

## XMLBeans Lists

The following are the XMLBeans-related lists.

### XMLBeans User List

As the name suggests, this list is targeted to people like you who are using XMLBeans on a day-to-day basis. Post your bugs, issues, suggestions, or recommendations for enhancements to this list.

To subscribe to this list, send an e-mail to `users-subscribe@xmlbeans.apache.org`.

To unsubscribe from this list, send an e-mail to `users-unsubscribe@xmlbeans.apache.org`.

To see the archives for this list, visit `http://nagoya.apache.org/eyebrowse/SummarizeList?listId=277`.

### XMLBeans Developer List

This is a mailing list for XMLBeans developers. Should you choose to submit code for this project, you'll need to subscribe to this list.

To subscribe to this list, send an e-mail to `dev-subscribe@xmlbeans.apache.org`.

To unsubscribe from this list, send an e-mail to `dev-unsubscribe@xmlbeans.apache.org`.

To see the archives for this list, visit `http://nagoya.apache.org/eyebrowse/SummarizeList?listId=278`.

### XMLBeans SVN/Wiki Change List

This is a mailing list where you can see every change to the Subversion (SVN) source control system for this project and to the Beehive wiki. This is a pretty high-volume list compared to the other two XMLBeans lists.

To subscribe to this list, send an e-mail to `commits-subscribe@xmlbeans.apache.org`.

To unsubscribe from this list, send an e-mail to `commits-unsubscribe@xmlbeans.apache.org`.

To see the archives for this list, visit `http://nagoya.apache.org/eyebrowse/SummarizeList?listId=276`.

---

■ **Note** Visit `http://xmlbeans.apache.org/community/index.html#Mailing+Lists` for an up-to-date list of the XMLBeans mailing lists to which you can subscribe.

---

# Contributing Code

The final goal is for you to contribute code to these projects. In the following sections, we'll talk about how you can do this.

## Contributing to Beehive

To contribute to the Beehive project, first you need to get the source code.

### Getting the Source to Beehive

Beehive uses the Subversion source control system. Subversion is a later incarnation of CVS. You can read about it and download a Subversion client at `http://subversion.tigris.org/`.

In whatever directory you want to download the source code (say, `beehive-src`), you need to run the following command:

```
svn checkout http://svn.apache.org/repos/asf/incubator/beehive/trunk
```

### Building the Code

Instead of repeating the material here and risking being out-of-date, we'll simply point you to the Beehive wiki where you can learn all you need to know about building and working with the source code that you've just downloaded:

```
http://wiki.apache.org/beehive/For_20Beehive_20Developers
```

### Understanding the Beehive Process

To understand the build and release process for Beehive, visit `http://wiki.apache.org/beehive/Release_20Process`.

### Understanding the Distribution Structure

To get a feel for the distribution structure for Beehive, visit `http://wiki.apache.org/beehive/Distribution_20Structure`.

## Contributing to XMLBeans

To contribute to the XMLBeans project, first you need to get the source code.

### Getting the Source to XMLBeans

Beehive uses the Subversion source control system. Subversion is a later incarnation of CVS. You can read about it and download a Subversion client at `http://subversion.tigris.org/`.

You can browse the XMLBeans source via ViewSVN/CVS at `http://svn.apache.org/viewcvs.cgi/xmlbeans/trunk/`.

In whatever directory you want to download the source code (say, `xmlbeans-src`), you need to run the following command:

```
svn co http://svn.apache.org/repos/asf/xmlbeans/trunk/
```

To get all the code, run this:

```
svn co http://svn.apache.org/repos/asf/xmlbeans/
```

### Building the Code

You can build the XMLBeans source using Ant. Under the source directory you used previously (`xmlbeans-src`), you should see a directory called `xml-xmlbeans\v1`. Change to this directory.

On Windows, run the following commands to build XMLBeans:

```
Xbeanenv
ant
```

On Unix, run the following commands to build XMLBeans:

```
xbeanenv.sh ant
```

### Visiting the Issue Log

Visit `http://issues.apache.org/jira/secure/BrowseProject.jspa?id=10436` to see the current issue log for XMLBeans.

## Grab Bag of Links

Here are some general links you might also find useful:

- Learn more about Beehive on the BEA dev2dev site at `http://dev2dev.bea.com/technologies/beehive/index.jsp`.
- Learn more about XMLBeans on the BEA dev2dev site at `http://dev2dev.bea.com/technologies/xmlbeans/index.jsp`.
- Learn more about Controls at `http://controlhaus.org/`.
- Learn more about the Eclipse Pollinate IDE at `http://www.eclipse.org/pollinate/`.

## So, What's Next?

We really hope you found this book productive and can use Beehive and XMLBeans on your projects. If you choose to contribute to these projects, all the better.

# Index

## A